I0792997

IMAGES
of America

NORTH TEXAS STATE FAIR AND RODEO

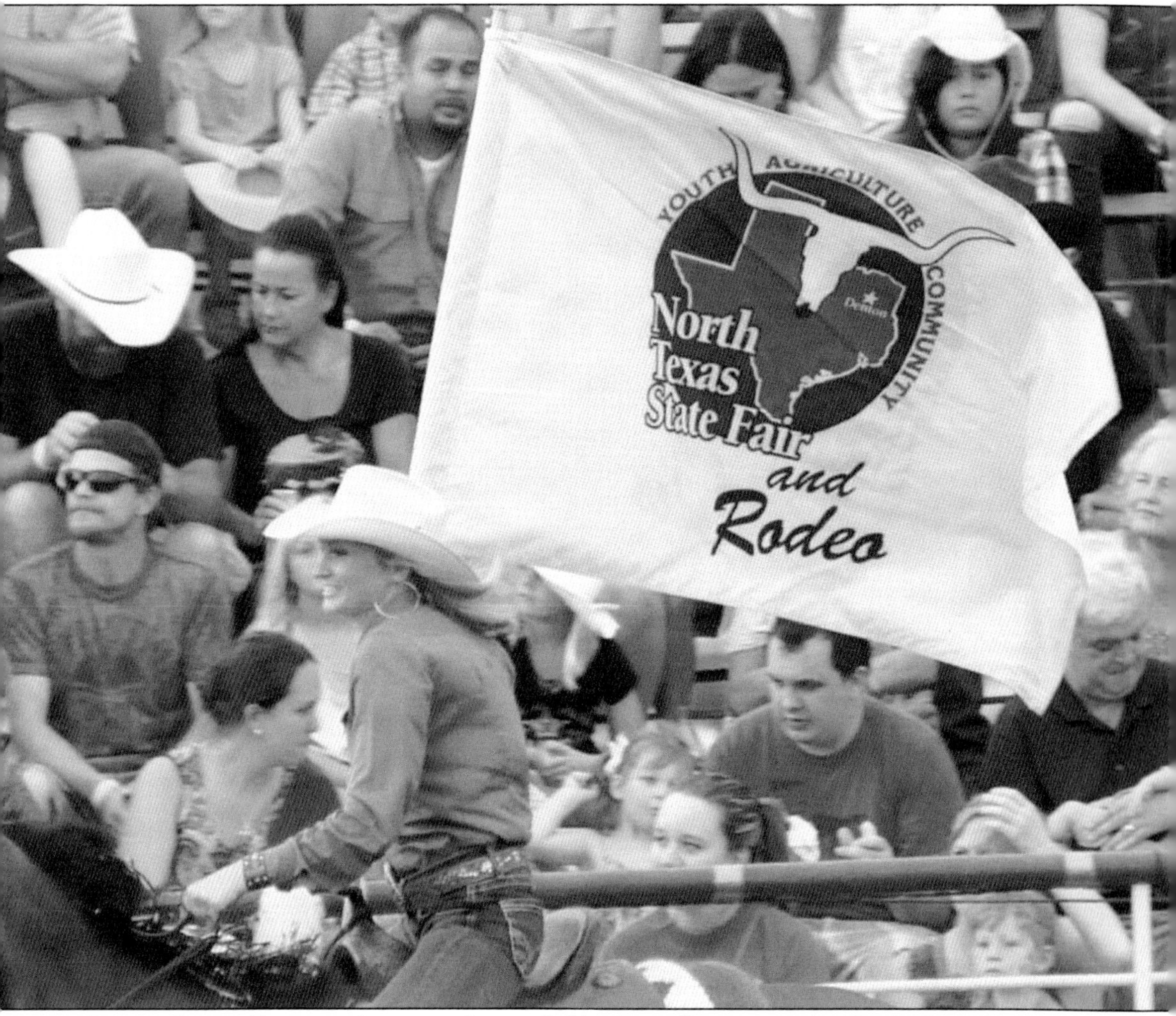

Rodeo Queen. Former rodeo queen Jessica Geldard proudly presents the North Texas State Fair and Rodeo flag to a packed arena. Geldard is now a member of the North Texas Fairgrounders, an all-female precision-mounted riding team. (Courtesy of Ronny Collins.)

On the Cover: Young Posse. The theme of the 2010 North Texas State Fair and Rodeo was "Don't Make Us Come Gitcha!" The young cowboys are ready to ride are, from left to right, Clay Akins, Ronnie Sellers, Tyler Akins, and Levi Nelson. (Photograph by Sara Barnes; courtesy of the North Texas Fair and Rodeo.)

IMAGES
of America

NORTH TEXAS STATE FAIR AND RODEO

Nanci Monroe Kimmey
and Georgia Kemp Caraway

ARCADIA
PUBLISHING

ISBN 978-1-4671-3493-4

Published by Arcadia Publishing
Charleston, South Carolina

Printed in the United States of America

Library of Congress Control Number: 2016935121

For all general information, please contact Arcadia Publishing:
Telephone 843-853-2070
Fax 843-853-0044
E-mail sales@arcadiapublishing.com
For customer service and orders:
Toll-Free 1-888-313-2665

Visit us on the Internet at www.arcadiapublishing.com

This book is dedicated to cowboys and cowgirls who have ridden, roped, and wrangled and especially to the volunteers, vendors, sponsors, and all the folks from Denton and beyond who have contributed to and honored the tradition of the North Texas State Fair and Rodeo.

Contents

ACKNOWLEDGMENTS

The authors extend their gratitude to Jim Bainbridge, of the Professional Rodeo Cowboys Association (PRCA); *Denton Record-Chronicle* (DRC); Denton Public Library (DPL); University of North Texas Portal to Texas History (UNT); the North Texas Fair and Rodeo archives (NTFR); newspapers.com; *Dallas Morning News* (DMN); James P. Owen, for the use of excerpts from his bestselling book, *Cowboy Ethics*; Denton Convention and Visitors Bureau (CVB); Sanger Historical Museum; the city of Ponder; and special kudos to Kim Cupit of the Denton County Office of History and Culture (DCOHC) for assistance in gathering research material and images.

Also, thanks to those who provided photographs from their personal collections, particularly Weldon Burgoon, the Earl Foreman family, Patsy Pitner Kelsoe, Will Williams, the Ken Burdick family, Jim and Tricia Bolz, and Sammy Andrews. We appreciate the professional photography of Terri Cage, James Hammer, Ronny Collins, Sara Barnes, Mindy Bruce, Al Key, Alex Lieban, Aaron Semas, Mickie Blagg, Jo Haigwood, Becky Alambar, Earl Armstrong, Roger Caldwell, Bruce Davis, Thomas Judd, Arthur Baker, Don Shugart, Carl Oberman, and Todd Brewer (the official fair photographer).

We had indispensable access to research materials, books, and articles by those in whose footsteps we followed, and they cannot go without gratitude. Kim Wendt Collinsworth wrote her bachelor's degree paper on the fair, and her research was integral in the fair receiving a Texas State Historical Marker. Historians E. Dale Odom, Ed F. Bates, C.A. Bridges, Hollace Hervey, Nita Seals, and the creators of the Texas State Historical Association's *Handbook of Texas Online* deserve recognition for their important contributions to previous works.

Many thanks to Bob Montgomery, whose encyclopedic knowledge of and engaging lectures about Texas history have delighted people for decades. Barbara Harpool Hall deserves praise for her contributions as employee, friend, and volunteer. Heartfelt gratitude to Weldon Burgoon, whose memory astounds and amazes.

Special credit goes to Dorcas Monroe, my mother, who introduced me to the love and excitement of this vocation through her employment at the State Fair of Texas; to my daughter Ryan and son-in-law Ryan, who became second-generation volunteers; and to my husband, Ralph Kimmey, who understands my passion for making memories. Thanks also go to Georgia's partner, Oscar Blankemeyer, who believes she can do anything she sets her mind to do. Very special thanks to Glenn Carlton and the North Texas State Fair Association Board of Directors for their support.

INTRODUCTION

Denton, established in 1857, is the seat of Denton County. It was named for John B. Denton, a pioneer and itinerant Methodist preacher and lawyer who was mortally wounded in a Keechi Indian ambush in 1841. Denton is located 39 miles north of Dallas and Fort Worth, both of which are noted for their fair and rodeo activities.

In 1881, the Texas & Pacific Railway and Missouri Pacific Railroad began to offer passenger and freight service in Denton. These services changed the lives of early Denton residents who, until that time, had been engaged in ranching and subsistence farming. The railroads offered them freight service for money crops and cattle—exporting both to other parts of the state and the nation—as well as the prospect of passenger travel.

John S. Chisum, who became one of the most famous cattlemen in the West, operated his first ranch in Denton County. Numerous Denton County ranchers—including William Crow Wright, Joe M. Waide, Edward W. Forester, Burk Burnett, and J.W. Medlin—raised and bred cattle and horses for sale.

The North Texas State Fair and Rodeo took more than 130 years to develop into what it is today. The evolution of the fair is a tale of trials, tribulation, and triumph.

The predecessor of the North Texas State Fair and Rodeo was reported in the October 15, 1885, *Denton Doings* as consisting of two days of running and trotting horse races, which were sponsored by the Denton County Fair and Blooded Stock Association (DCFBSA). Blooded stock are animals that are entirely or largely purebred. The Denton venue was a 40-acre tract bordered by Avenue A and Welch, West Hickory, and Mill Streets that was used by stock owners to qualify their horses to enter races at the Dallas State Fair and Exposition.

The DCFBSA was organized on May 16, 1895, to host an annual fair and a half-mile horse race. The next race was held in September 1896 and featured three rabbit races, three horse races (running, trotting, and pacing), and a stock show. In October 1896, the association was reorganized and incorporated with capital stock of $10,000 held by J.W. Medlin, W.H. Pierce, W.A. Miller, W.P. Parker, M.S. Stout, J.C. Coit, J.P. Blount, and others.

The 1897 event featured livestock and horse shows, plus exhibits in the floral hall that featured ladies' handwork, preserves, artworks, culinary skills, and expertise in horticulture. The event also included shows featuring many breeds of cattle, swine, mules, and horses, as well as merchants' displays. Also popular were events highlighting the expertise of female drivers and matched teams; the horse and mule races were always the high point of the day. Crowds gathered for the three-eighths-mile free-for-all dash that paid $75 to the winner and the four-and-a-half-furlong race that paid $100. The fastest mule in the half-mile race won $5, but the crowd-pleaser involved a bet on second place because that prize was five gallons of S.A. Bayless's fine elderberry wine. Many jockeys pulled up on their steeds to ensure a second-place finish.

According to the *Dallas Morning News*, in 1898, a machinery hall was added to the fairgrounds. The newspaper also reported that a "negro cakewalk [took] place at the grounds each night." J.W. Medlin touted the fair of 1899 as the "greatest county Fair, not only in Texas, but in the entire south." From 1900 until 1903, the fair continued hosting horse races and featuring exhibit spaces. However, a Texas law against gambling was enacted in late 1903 and resulted in a shutdown of the fair until the 1920s.

Several temporary locations in Denton hosted the fair during the 1920s and 1930s until a suitable permanent location could be acquired. World War II, however, disrupted any possibility of holding another fair until the men and women serving the country returned home and available livestock could be replenished. In 1949, W.C. Kimbrough donated a permanent site that would serve as the setting for the fair for the next 70 years. The fair and the North Texas

State Fair Association fell under the helm of two men, James Roden and Ken Burdick, from the 1960s through the 1990s. Their leadership brought innovation and professionalism to the fair and increased fundraising activities, recognition, and attendance. More importantly, they placed an emphasis on the participation of children and upgrading the rodeo.

The new century brought with it new leadership in the form of Glenn Carlson, Nanci Kimmey, and a strong and progressive board of directors. Under their guidance, the fair has become one of the largest and most recognized among its peers, winning many state awards for excellence. The popularity of the headlining performers draws large crowds, and the high quality of the rodeo attracts the best rodeo men and women in the business. These achievements have grown the fair to annual attendance of more than 175,000 and millions of dollars in revenues.

Many names have been used for the association and the fair throughout the years, each reflecting the progression of the growth and stature of the fair. Association names included Denton County Fair and Blooded Stock Association (DCFBSA); Denton County Agricultural Fair Association (DCAFA); and, currently, North Texas State Fair Association (NTSFA). The event operated under the names Denton County Fair (DCF); Denton County Agricultural and Livestock Fair (DCALF); Denton County Agricultural Fair and Rodeo (DCAFR); North Texas State Fair and Rodeo (NTSFR); and, most recently, North Texas Fair and Rodeo (NTFR).

Let us now begin a journey through the history of the North Texas State Fair and Rodeo from its humble beginnings to its current activities, achievements, and accomplishments.

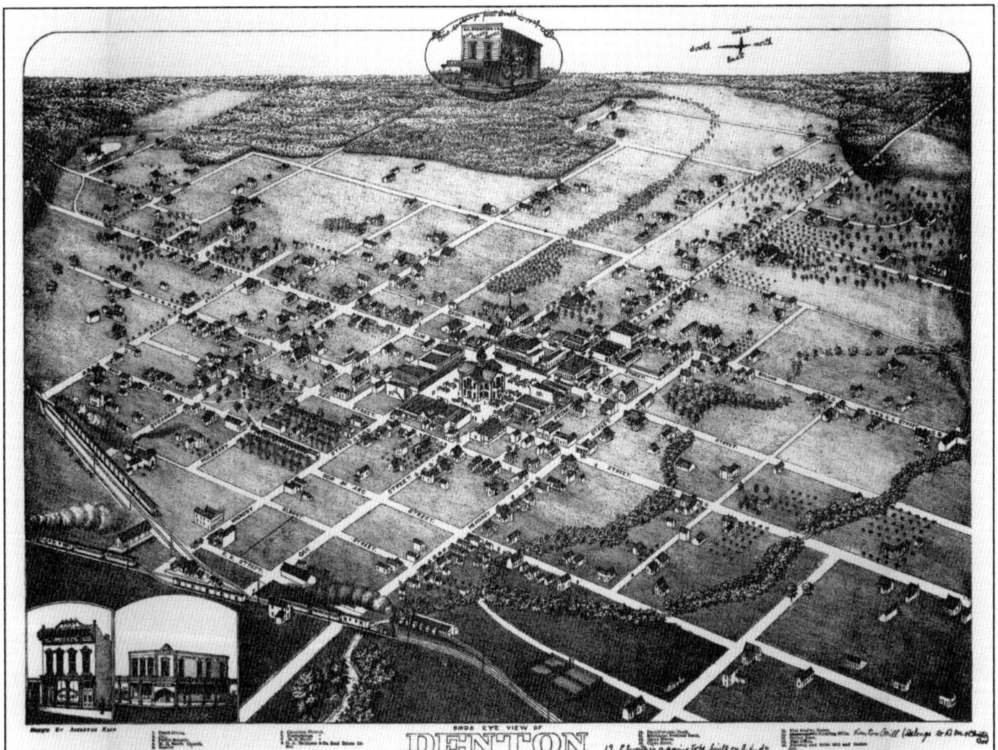

Bird's-Eye View of Denton, Texas, 1883. During the earliest days of the formation of the DCFBSA, the fairgrounds were located in the undeveloped northwest part of the city. This area was heavily wooded yet had cleared acreage that was suitable for a racetrack and fairgrounds. (Courtesy of DCOHC.)

One

The Roundup Years

Beginnings (1885–1930s)

The earliest years of what would become the North Texas State Fair and Rodeo were not well documented in photographs. However, several newspaper articles published in the *Dallas Morning News* give a glimpse of the activities that occurred between 1885 and 1903 that led to the creation of the Denton County Fair. The newspaper reported that in 1890, association stockholders had the opportunity to purchase shares of the fairgrounds that were being divided into lots. That action halted the Denton County Fair and Blooded Stock Association (DCFBSA) show, which was first held in 1885, until 1895. A DCFBSA program of the 1899 horse races is shown in this chapter and is a rare and invaluable archival document.

In 1900, the fair was organized into various departments, including the Negro Department, which was intended to attract colored attendees. The second day of the fair was designated as "Negro Day," during which programs resulted in attendance of "about 500 of their own race, and a good-sized crowd of white people," according to the *Dallas Morning News*.

The installation of more than 1,000 32-candlepower incandescent lights allowed the first night horse race to be run at the fair in 1901. In 1903, the Texas Legislature outlawed gambling, which included horse racing. As a consequence, legalized horse racing in Denton County came to an end. When this happened, the DCFBSA board sold the fairgrounds at public auction as 40 residential lots, including improvements, thus ending eight years of fair activity in Denton County.

The years between 1904 and 1915 were dormant fair years until the Denton County Fair was moved to Sanger, where it remained until 1917. In 1920, the fair started up again in Denton. For two years, the Denton County Fair was held on an airfield in Carroll Park. For the next two years, exhibits were displayed in temporary buildings, and tents were erected in the new city park. The fair moved to the athletic grounds of the North Texas State Teachers College for one year (1924), then moved back to the city park for five more years. Finally, in 1930, the fair was held in what organizers hoped would be a permanent location on Exposition Street. Throughout the 1930s, the fair expanded its buildings, entertainment venues, and stature as the county's foremost fair; however, when World War II started at the end of the decade, it took its toll as most available livestock and eligible men were shipped off to aid in the war effort.

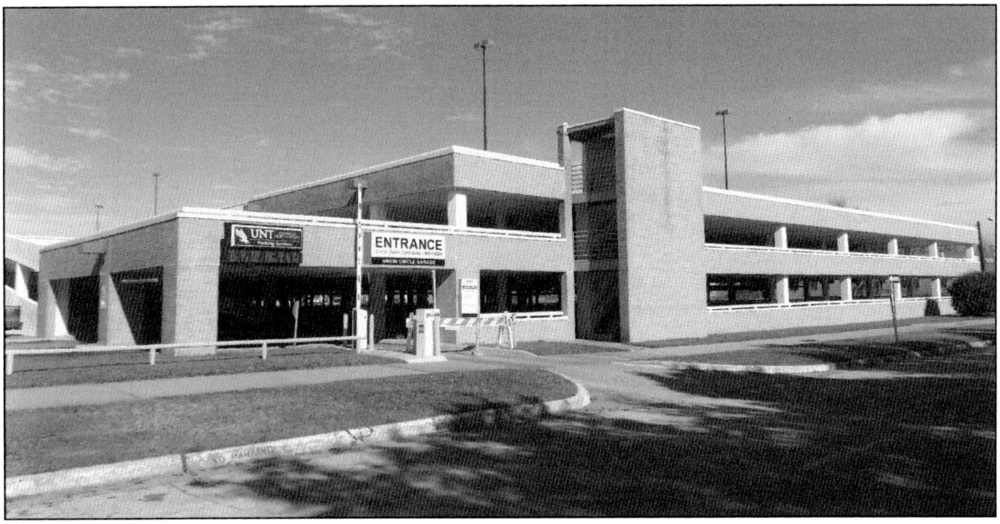

Racetrack Location. In 1885, the racetrack and fairgrounds were located on a 40-acre tract bordered by Avenue A and Welch, West Hickory, and Mill (currently Eagle) Streets near what became the North Texas Normal College. The racetrack was located at 1105 West Chestnut Street, where the West Ward School stood for many years and where a University of North Texas (UNT) parking garage (pictured) now stands. A long line of stables was built across the north end of the fairgrounds. (Courtesy of NTFR.)

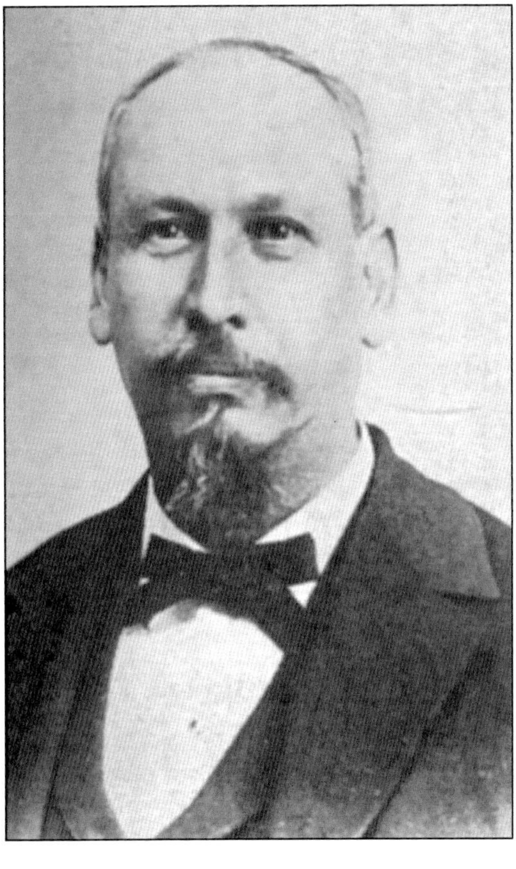

City Leader and First President of the DCFBSA. William Henry (W.H.) Pierce (1842–1927) promoted better livestock in Denton County and did much for the livestock industry as the first president of the Denton County Fair and Blooded Stock Association (DCFBSA). Pierce also served as president of the Texas Swine Breeders Association. He was elected county surveyor in 1886 and served in that capacity for 26 years. (Courtesy of DCOHC.)

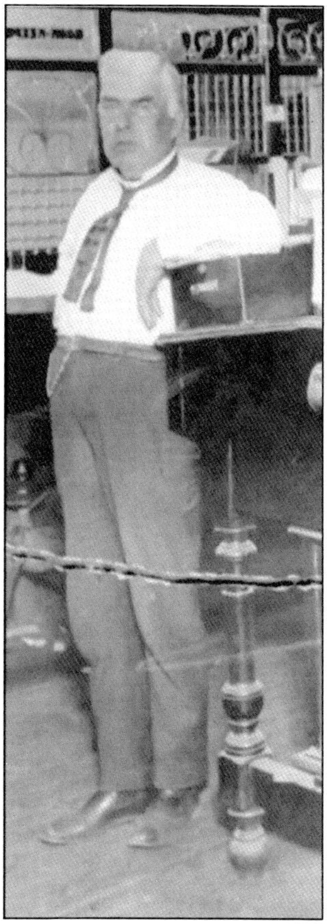

Earliest Denton County Fair and Blooded Stock Association (DCFBSA) Officers and Directors. In 1895, the DCFBSA officers were W.H. Pierce, president; A.H. Gee, vice president (right); W.P. Parker, secretary; and J.C. Coit, treasurer. The board of directors included J.W. Medlin (below), John Payne, J.E. Koonce, A.J. Nance, J.M. Weeks, Dr. William Whitten, J.F. Day, Dr. C. Lipscomb, and S.F. Reynolds. (Both, courtesy of DCOHC.)

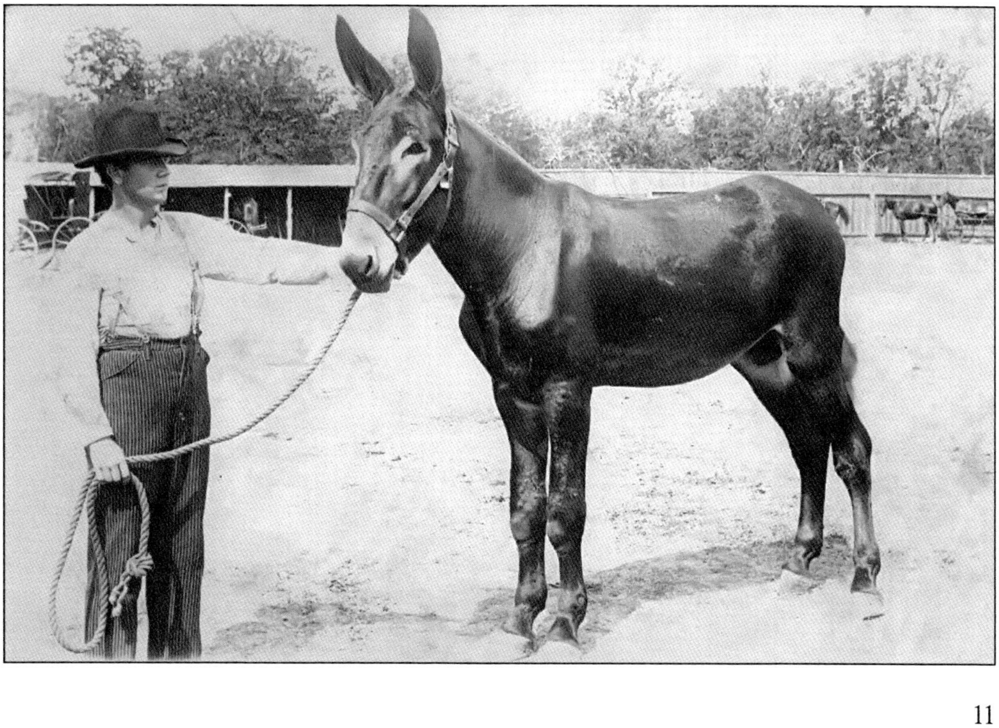

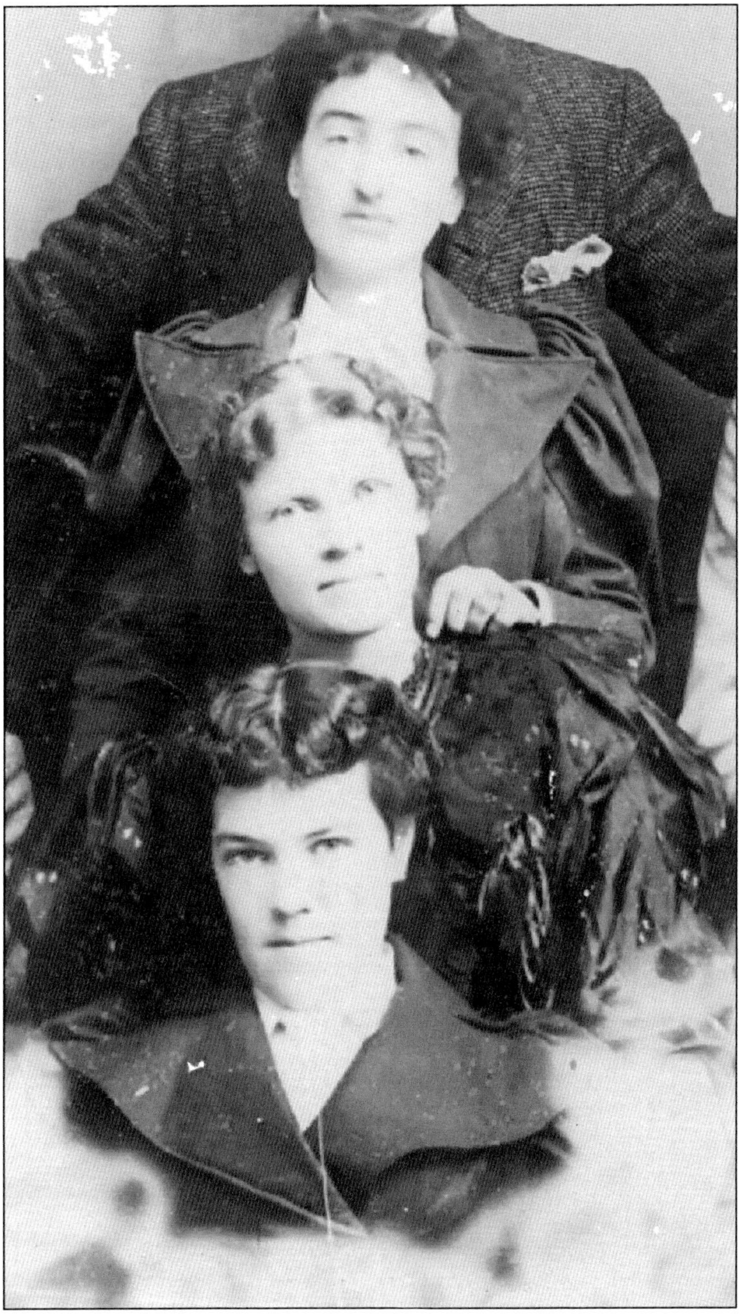

EARLY FAIR PARTICIPANTS. Prominent women of the community presented their domestic wares for judging in numerous categories. Participants in the 1897 contests included, from top to bottom, Myrtle Wright Magee (oil paintings); Lee Williams, Ladies Department superintendent (Battenburg and Princess lace); and Effie Wright Williams (embroidered linens). It also included Mrs. J.W. Medlin (sweet pickles and peach preserves), Mrs. W.H. Pierce (fruit preserves, pickles), Mrs. A.J. Nance (tea cakes, apple jelly, and knitted purse), Lily Stroud (crochet collar), Anna Brown (worsted quilt), Mattie Merrill (hand sewing), Jennie Collier (paper flowers), Mrs. C.L. Herbert (crazy quilt), and Lizzie Smoot (jelly cake). (Courtesy of DCOHC.)

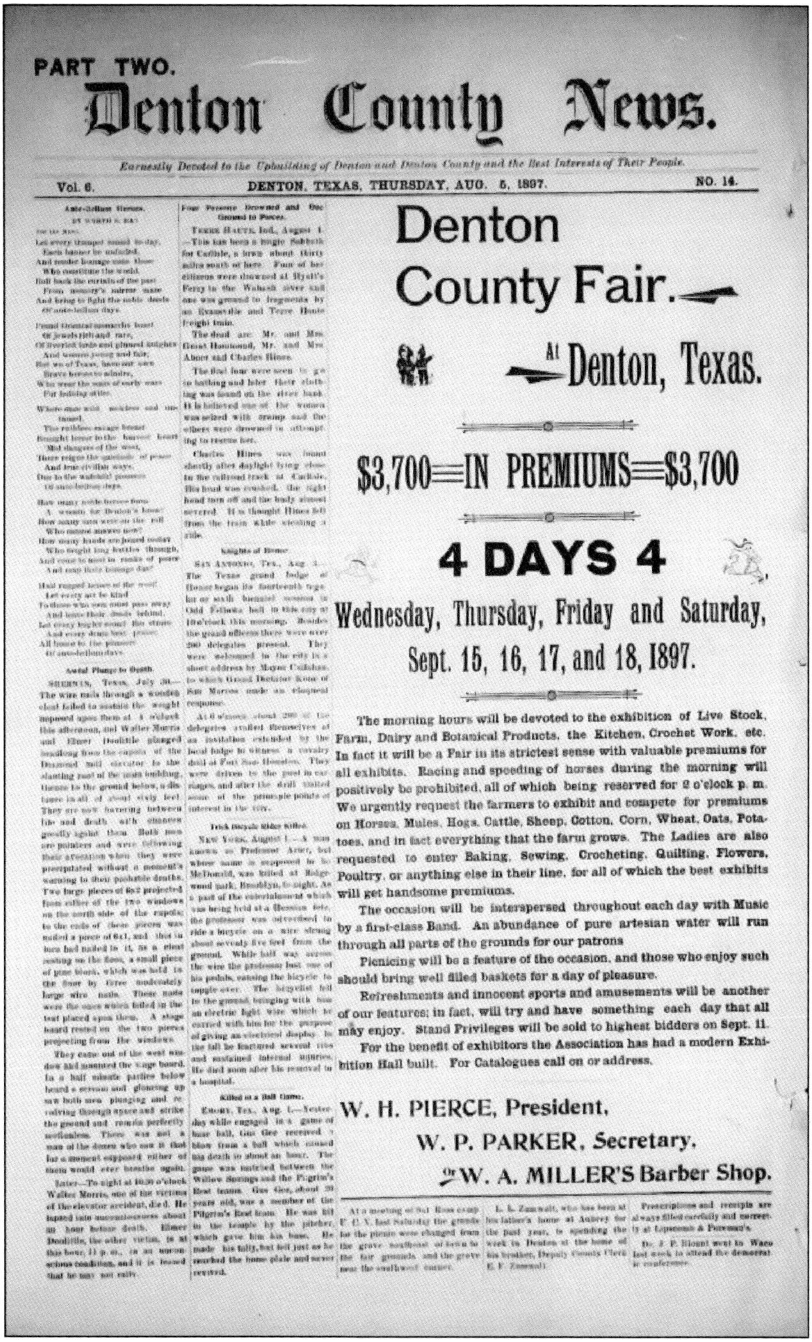
PART TWO.

Denton County News.

Earnestly Devoted to the Upbuilding of Denton and Denton County and the Best Interests of Their People.

Vol. 6. DENTON, TEXAS, THURSDAY, AUG. 5, 1897. NO. 14.

Denton County Fair.

At Denton, Texas.

$3,700=IN PREMIUMS=$3,700

4 DAYS 4

Wednesday, Thursday, Friday and Saturday,

Sept. 15, 16, 17, and 18, 1897.

The morning hours will be devoted to the exhibition of Live Stock, Farm, Dairy and Botanical Products, the Kitchen, Crochet Work, etc. In fact it will be a Fair in its strictest sense with valuable premiums for all exhibits. Racing and speeding of horses during the morning will positively be prohibited, all of which being reserved for 2 o'clock p. m. We urgently request the farmers to exhibit and compete for premiums on Horses, Mules, Hogs, Cattle, Sheep, Cotton, Corn, Wheat, Oats, Potatoes, and in fact everything that the farm grows. The Ladies are also requested to enter Baking, Sewing, Crocheting, Quilting, Flowers, Poultry, or anything else in their line, for all of which the best exhibits will get handsome premiums.

The occasion will be interspersed throughout each day with Music by a first-class Band. An abundance of pure artesian water will run through all parts of the grounds for our patrons.

Picnicing will be a feature of the occasion, and those who enjoy such should bring well filled baskets for a day of pleasure.

Refreshments and innocent sports and amusements will be another of our features; in fact, will try and have something each day that all may enjoy. Stand Privileges will be sold to highest bidders on Sept. 11.

For the benefit of exhibitors the Association has had a modern Exhibition Hall built. For Catalogues call on or address.

W. H. PIERCE, President,

W. P. PARKER, Secretary,

@ W. A. MILLER'S Barber Shop.

DENTON COUNTY NEWS, 1897. The 1897 fair was held for four days in September. The morning events included exhibitions of livestock; farm, dairy, and botanical products; food products; crochet work; and other items vying for "handsome premiums." Prominent nurseryman Sam A. Bayless showed his prize-winning nursery stock. The afternoon was reserved for horse racing. According to the article shown here, "the occasion will be interspersed throughout each day with Music by a first-class Band. An abundance of pure artesian water will run through all parts of the grounds for our patrons." (Courtesy of DRC at DCOHC.)

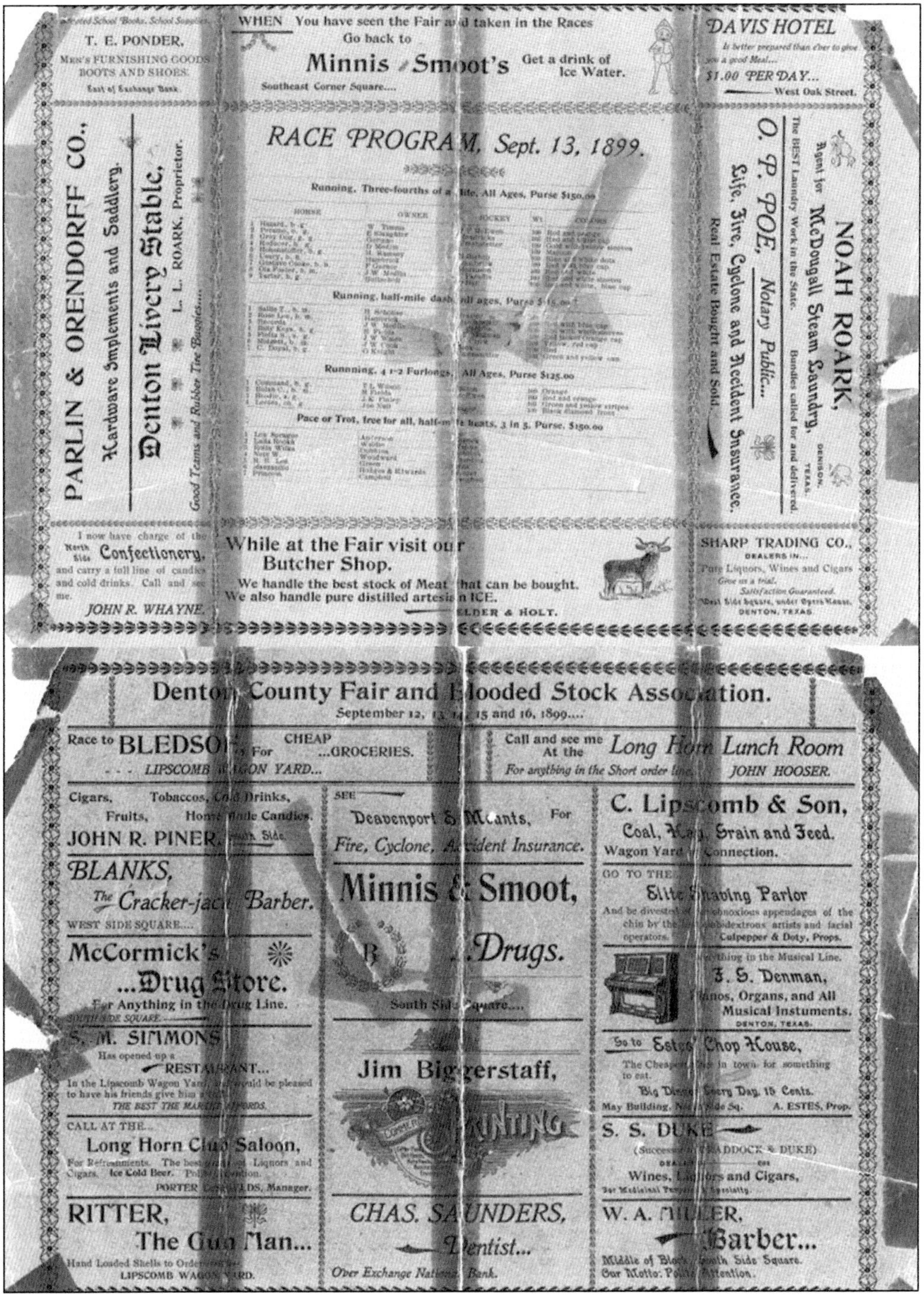

T. E. PONDER,
MEN'S FURNISHING GOODS
BOOTS AND SHOES
East of Exchange Bank

WHEN You have seen the Fair and taken in the Races
Go back to
Minnis & Smoot's Get a drink of Ice Water.
Southeast Corner Square....

DAVIS HOTEL
$1.00 PER DAY...
West Oak Street.

PARLIN & ORENDORFF CO.,
Hardware Implements and Saddlery.

Denton Livery Stable,
L. L. ROARK, Proprietor.
Good Teams and Rubber Tire Buggies....

RACE PROGRAM, Sept. 13, 1899.

Running, Three-fourths of a Mile, All Ages, Purse $150.00

Running, half-mile dash, all ages, Purse

Running, 4 1-2 Furlongs, All Ages, Purse $125.00

Pace or Trot, free for all, half-mile heats, 3 in 5. Purse, $150.00

NOAH ROARK,
Agent for McDougall Steam Laundry,
DENISON, TEXAS.
The BEST Laundry Work in the State. Bundles called for and delivered.

O. P. POE, Notary Public...
Life, Fire, Cyclone and Accident Insurance.
Real Estate Bought and Sold.

I now have charge of the North Side Confectionery, and carry a full line of candies and cold drinks. Call and see me.
JOHN R. WHAYNE.

While at the Fair visit our Butcher Shop.
We handle the best stock of Meat that can be bought.
We also handle pure distilled artesian ICE.
ELDER & HOLT.

SHARP TRADING CO.,
DEALERS IN...
Pure Liquors, Wines and Cigars
Satisfaction Guaranteed.
DENTON, TEXAS.

Denton County Fair and Blooded Stock Association.
September 12, 13, 14, 15 and 16, 1899....

Race to BLEDSOE's For CHEAP ...GROCERIES.
LIPSCOMB WAGON YARD...

Call and see me At the Long Horn Lunch Room
For anything in the Short order line. JOHN HOOSER.

Cigars, Tobaccos, Cold Drinks, Fruits, Home Made Candies.
JOHN R. PINER, South Side.

BLANKS, The Cracker-jack Barber.
WEST SIDE SQUARE....

McCormick's ...Drug Store.
For Anything in the Drug Line.
SOUTH SIDE SQUARE.

S. M. SIMMONS
Has opened up a RESTAURANT...
In the Lipscomb Wagon Yard, and would be pleased to have his friends give him a trial.
THE BEST THE MARKET AFFORDS.

CALL AT THE...
Long Horn Club Saloon,
For Refreshments. The best of Liquors and Cigars. Ice Cold Beer.
PORTER REYNOLDS, Manager.

RITTER, The Gun Man...
Hand Loaded Shells to Order.
LIPSCOMB WAGON YARD.

SEE Deavenport & McCants, For Fire, Cyclone, Accident Insurance.

Minnis & Smoot, ...Drugs.
South Side Square....

Jim Biggerstaff,
PRINTING

CHAS. SAUNDERS, Dentist...
Over Exchange National Bank.

C. Lipscomb & Son,
Coal, Hay, Grain and Feed.
Wagon Yard in Connection.

GO TO THE Elite Shaving Parlor
And be divested of obnoxious appendages of the chin by the ambidextrous artists and facial operators.
Culpepper & Doty, Props.

Everything in the Musical Line.
J. S. Denman,
Pianos, Organs, and All Musical Instuments.
DENTON, TEXAS.

Go to Estes' Chop House,
The Cheapest place in town for something to eat.
Big Dinner Every Day, 15 Cents.
May Building, North Side Sq. A. ESTES, Prop.

S. S. DUKE
(Successor to MADDOCK & DUKE)
DEALER IN
Wines, Liquors and Cigars,
For Medicinal Purposes a Specialty.

W. A. MILLER, Barber...
Middle of Block, South Side Square.
Our Motto: Polite Attention.

DENTON COUNTY FAIR AND BLOODED STOCK ASSOCIATION (DCFBSA) RACE PROGRAM. This program includes a schedule of events and races held during the week of September 12–16, 1899. The program also contains advertisements for various attractions and businesses in Denton, including launderers, gun shops, shoe stores, barbers, grocers, furniture stores, confectioners, butcher shops, hotels, restaurants, and drugstores. (Courtesy of DPL.)

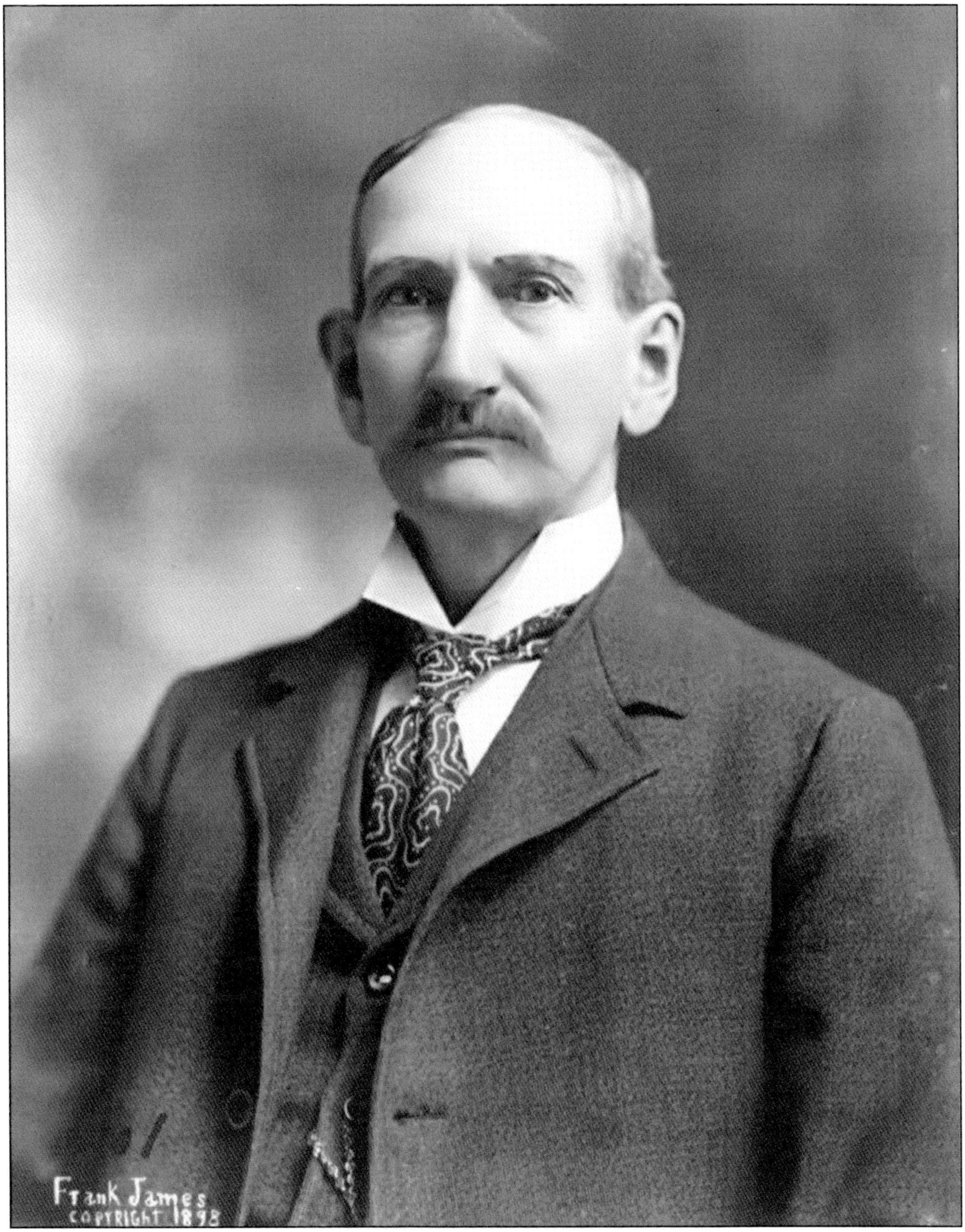

Outlaw Frank James. On March 11, 1900, the *Dallas Morning News* reported that Frank James, older brother of famed outlaw and thief Jesse James, wrote a letter to fair secretary W.E. Smoot, of the Denton County Fair and Blooded Stock Association, for a consideration that he (James) come to Denton the next September and act as the starter for the races. His offer was refused, but he served as the starter for the races at the 1900 Texas State Fair and Dallas Exposition. He paid his own way and donated his salary to those in Galveston who suffered after the "Great Galveston Storm" hurricane of 1900. (Courtesy of D.J. Taylor.)

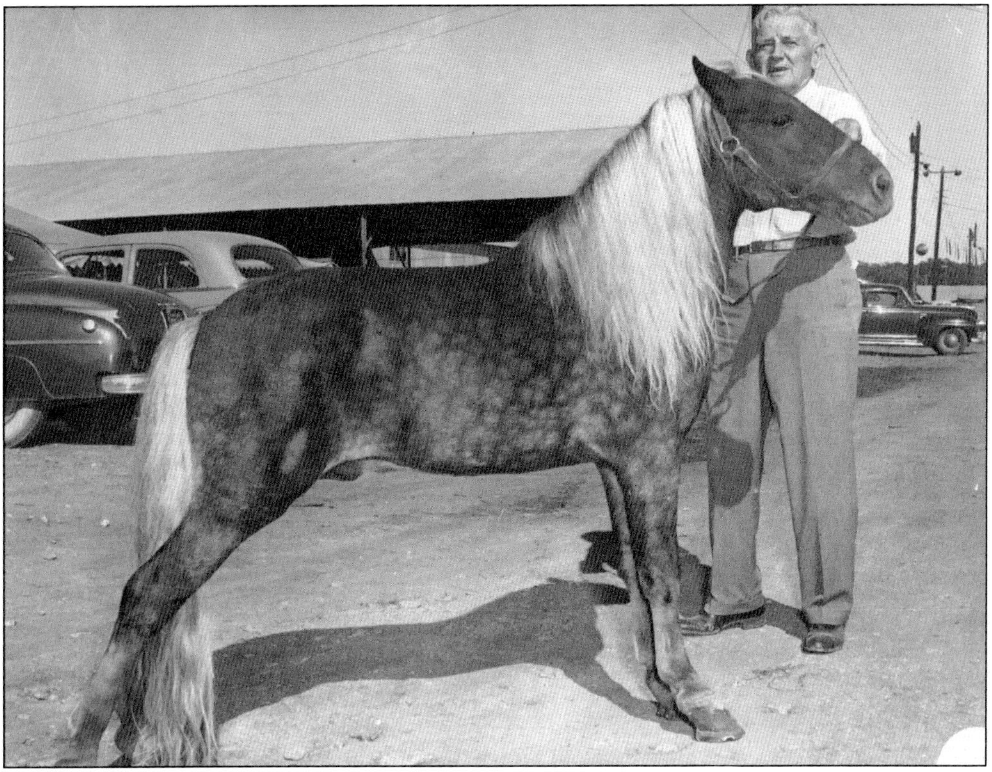

Will Williams' Shetland Pony Farm. Williams started his Shetland pony farm in 1905 with a foundation herd of four imported mares and 20 of the best American stallions and mares. By 1951, Williams had registered more Shetland ponies with the American Shetland Pony Club than any other breeder in the United States. He served as president of the fair association in 1952. The above photograph shows Williams and his silver-dapple stallion, Reveille Patton, in front of a shed on the fairgrounds. His daughter Branche Williams is shown in the below photograph with one of her Shetland mares and a foal. (Both, courtesy of the Williams Collection at DCOHC.)

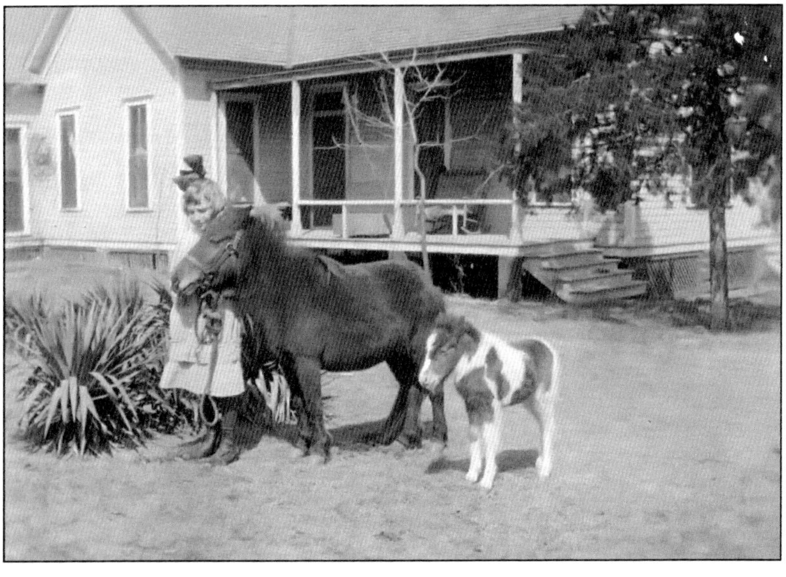

Branche Williams. Branche Williams, daughter of Will Williams, became a renowned figure in the American Shetland pony business. She developed an interest in ponies as a very young girl. She is shown at right with Sensation, one of her father's major herd stallions. Will Williams lived by the creed that "we've always been firm in the belief that blood will tell and have always bought the best breeding stock from the best pony farms in this country," as stated in a Williams Pony Sale brochure. Branche, shown below with Gangster, dedicated her life to breeding and selling prize ponies. (Both, courtesy of the Williams Collection at DCOHC.)

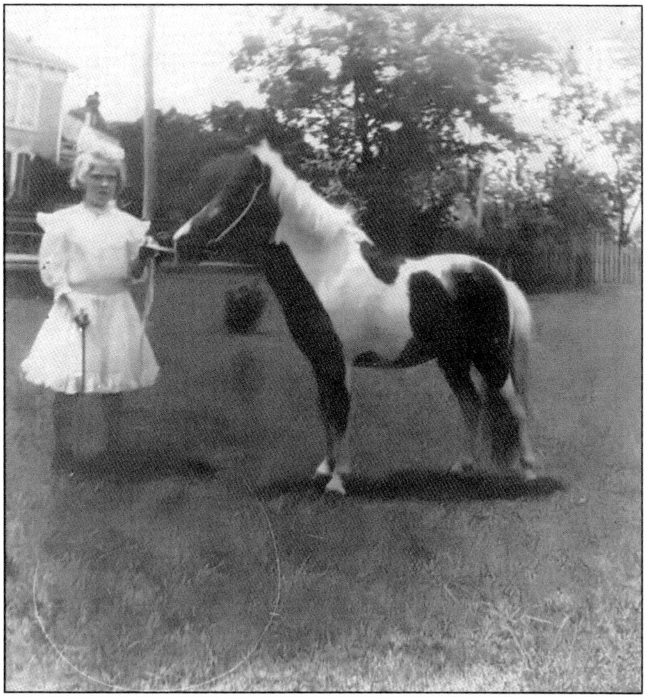

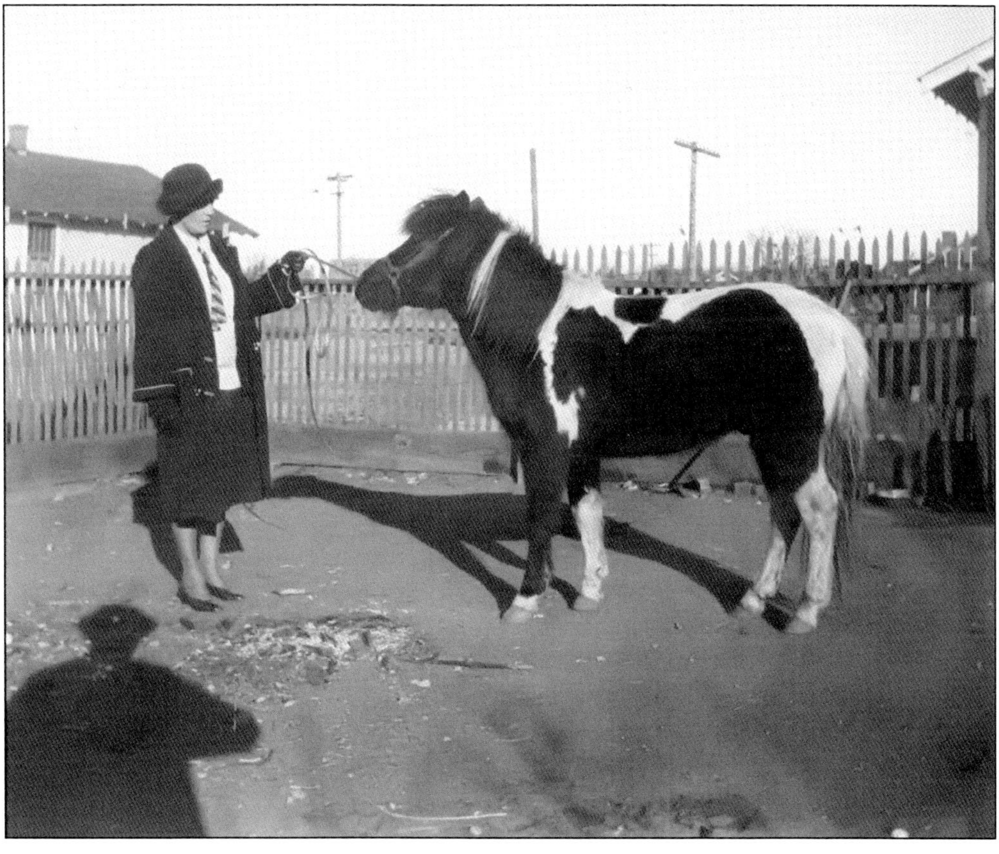

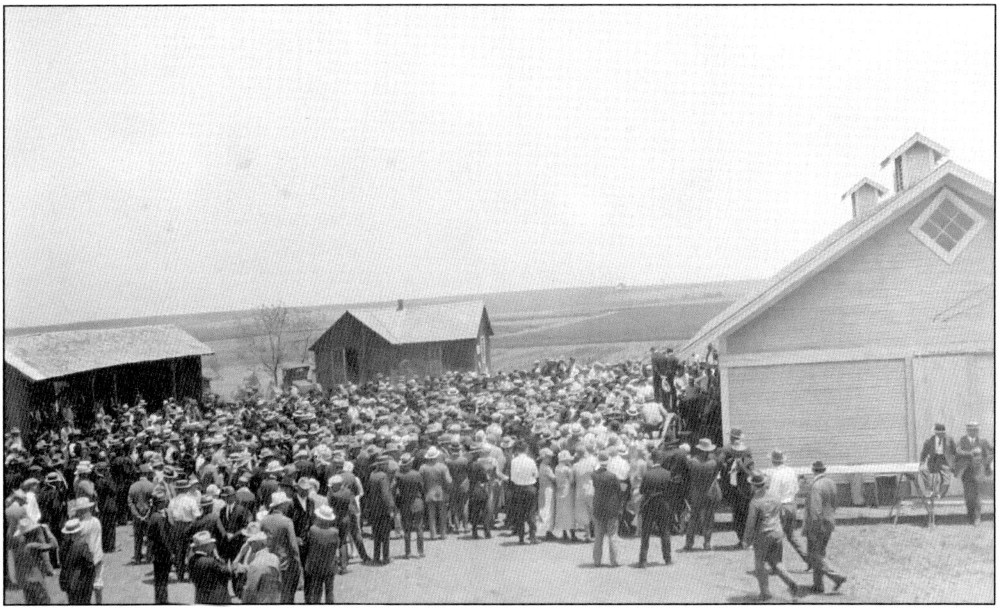

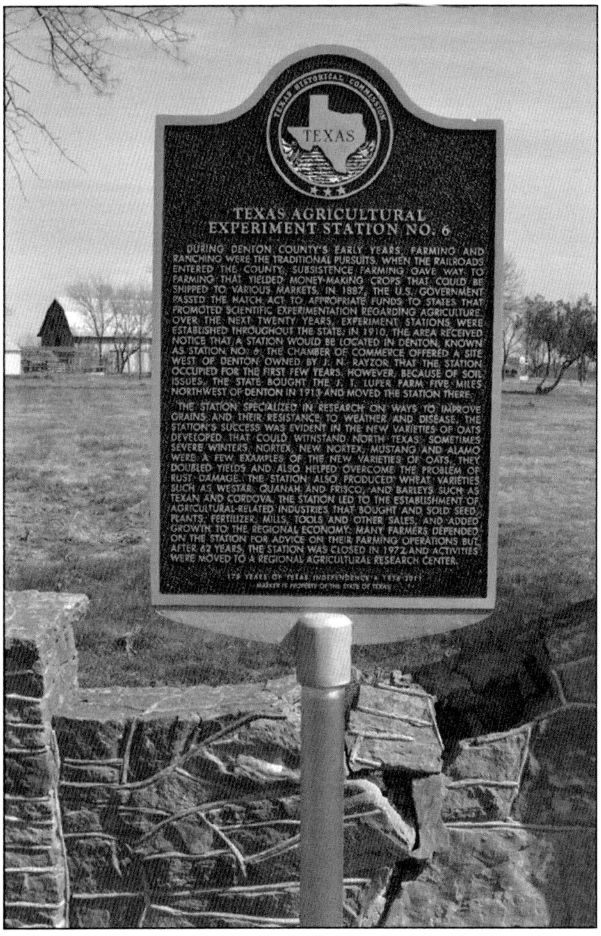

TEXAS AGRICULTURAL EXPERIMENT STATION NO. 6. The first Texas Agricultural Experiment Station in Denton County, Station No. 6, was established in 1910 west of Denton on J.N. Rayzor's land. The State of Texas established experiment stations to conduct research about crop and livestock management. According to the historical marker pictured at left, "because of soil issues, the state bought the J.T. Luper farm five miles northwest of Denton in 1913 and moved the station there," where "many farmers depended on the station for advice on their farming operations but after 62 years, the station was closed in 1972 and activities were moved to a regional agricultural research center." Farming, ranching, and agriculture formed the basis of the North Texas State Fair and Rodeo. (Both, courtesy of DCOHC.)

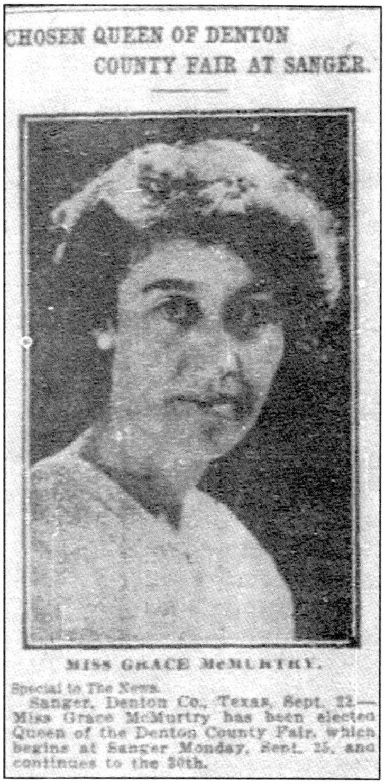
CHOSEN QUEEN OF DENTON COUNTY FAIR AT SANGER.

MISS GRACE McMURTRY.

Special to The News.

Sanger, Denton Co., Texas, Sept. 22—Miss Grace McMurtry has been elected Queen of the Denton County Fair, which begins at Sanger Monday, Sept. 25, and continues to the 30th.

Denton County Fair in Sanger. The Denton County Fair moved to Sanger in 1915 and remained there until 1917. The aerial photograph shown below is the only known image from the time when the Denton County Fair was held in Sanger. Although little is known about this three-year span of the Denton County Fair's history, the *Dallas Morning News* reported that 28-year-old Grace McMurtry was chosen as Queen of the Denton County Fair in 1916. That year, about $2,000 in prizes and premiums were given away, and the event spanned six days. There is no recorded evidence that the fair was held in Sanger for more than those three years. (Right, courtesy of DMN; below, courtesy of Sanger Historical Museum.)

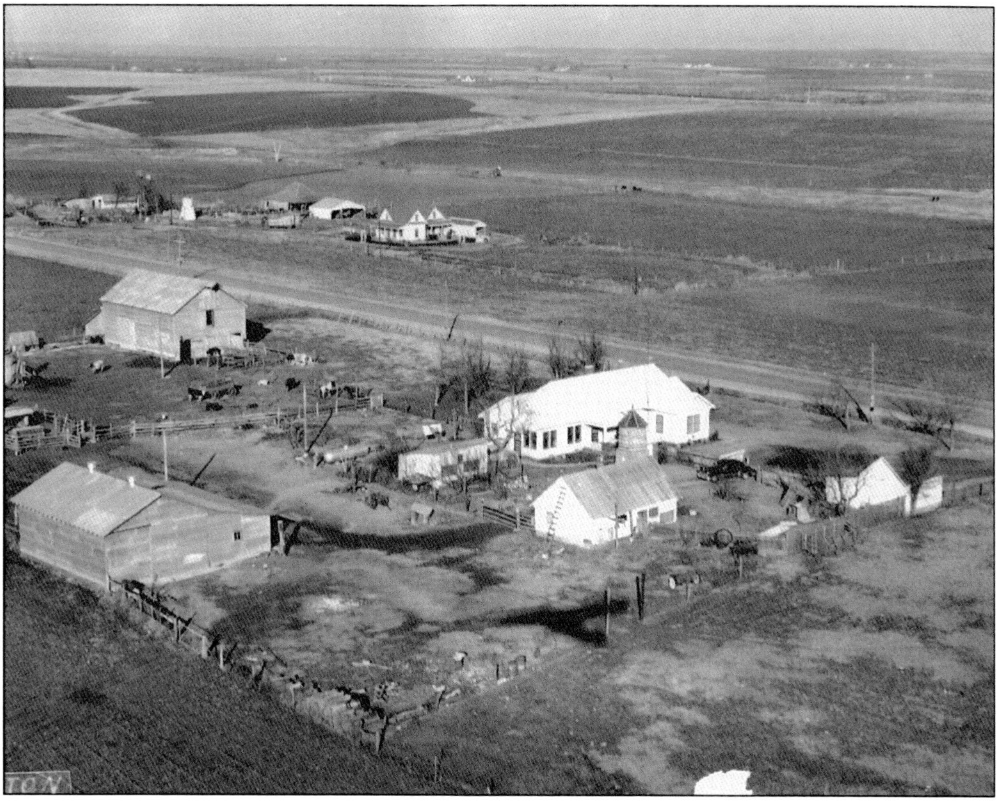

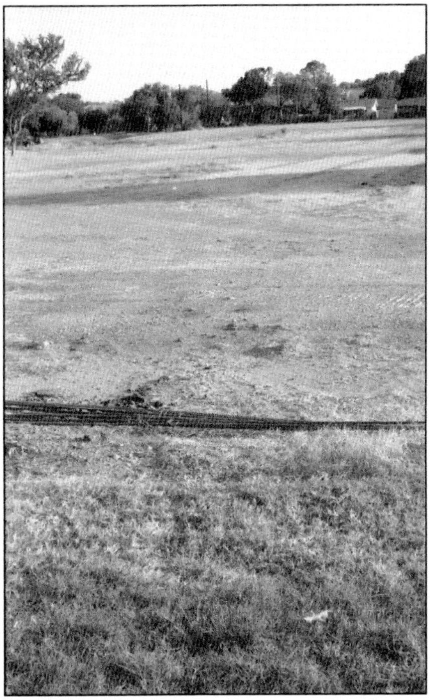

Back to Denton: Carroll Park. Since the former fairgrounds had been sold for residential lots in 1903, Denton did not have a location for the fair until 1920. In 1920, the Denton County Fair and Livestock Show was most likely held at Carroll Park. This park was an airfield located near the present-day Denton Independent School District Administration Building on University Drive. The first carnivals of the Denton County Fair and Livestock Show, featuring an assortment of rides, sideshows, and games of chance, were held in conjunction with the showing of livestock. (Courtesy of NTFR.)

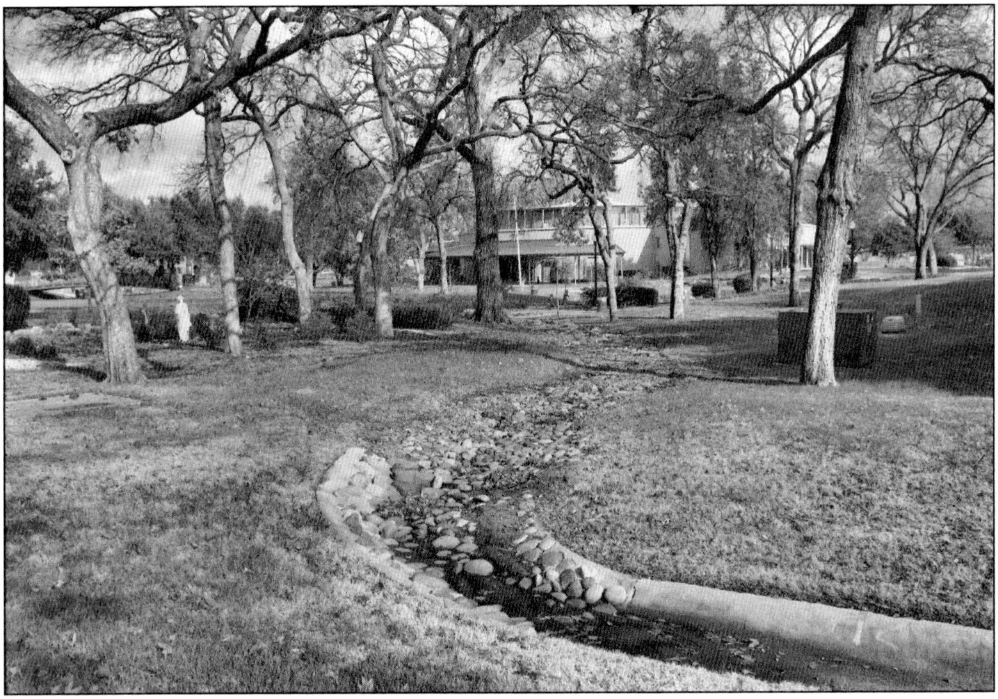

Agricultural and Livestock Fair in City Park. In November 1921, the Denton County Fair was held in the new City Park, where the African American community of Quakertown had formerly been located. In 1922, the name of the fair was changed to the Denton County Agricultural and Livestock Fair, with exhibits held in temporary buildings and tents erected in the park. The fair was held in City Park until 1924. (Courtesy of DCOHC.)

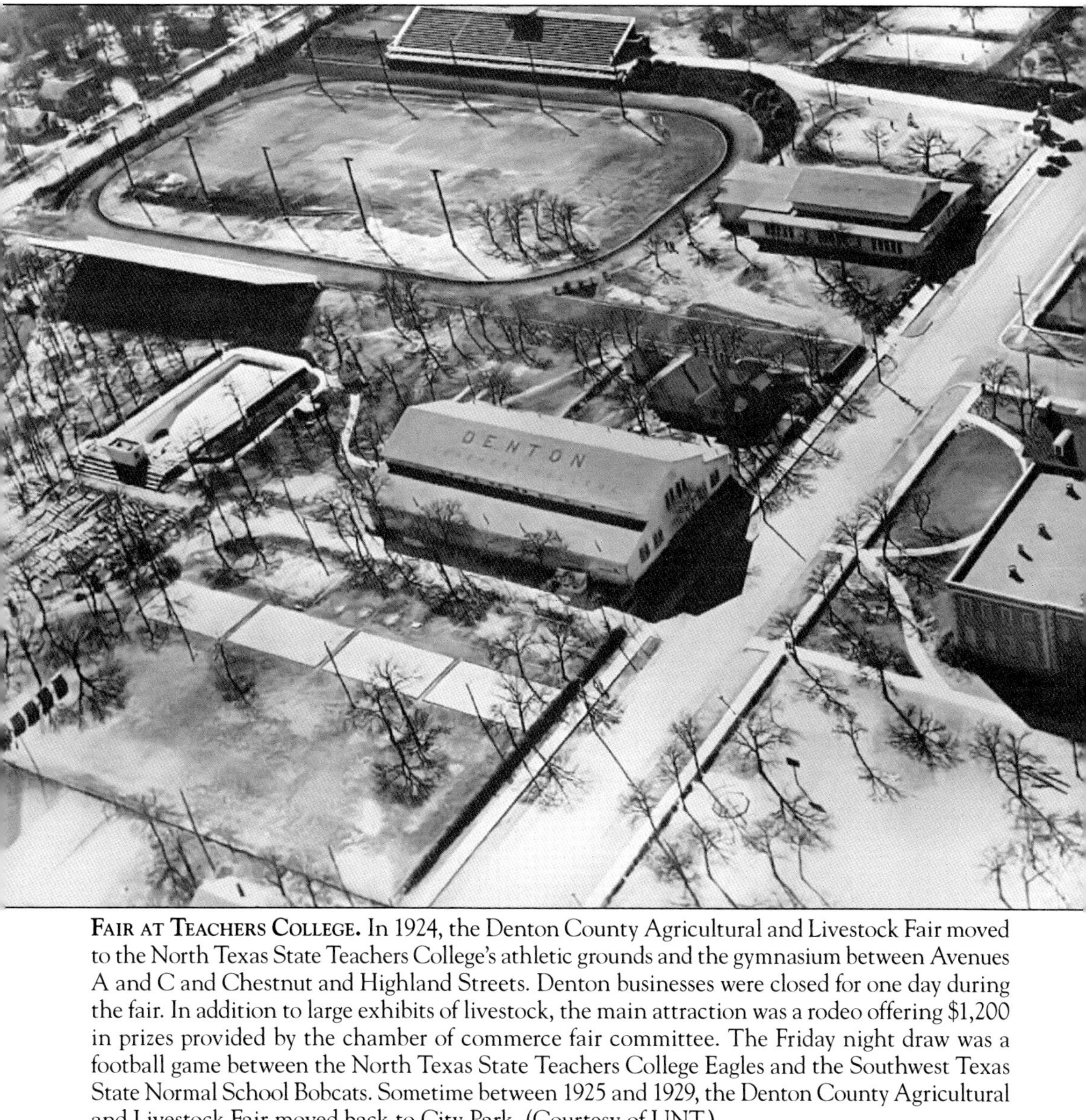

Fair at Teachers College. In 1924, the Denton County Agricultural and Livestock Fair moved to the North Texas State Teachers College's athletic grounds and the gymnasium between Avenues A and C and Chestnut and Highland Streets. Denton businesses were closed for one day during the fair. In addition to large exhibits of livestock, the main attraction was a rodeo offering $1,200 in prizes provided by the chamber of commerce fair committee. The Friday night draw was a football game between the North Texas State Teachers College Eagles and the Southwest Texas State Normal School Bobcats. Sometime between 1925 and 1929, the Denton County Agricultural and Livestock Fair moved back to City Park. (Courtesy of UNT.)

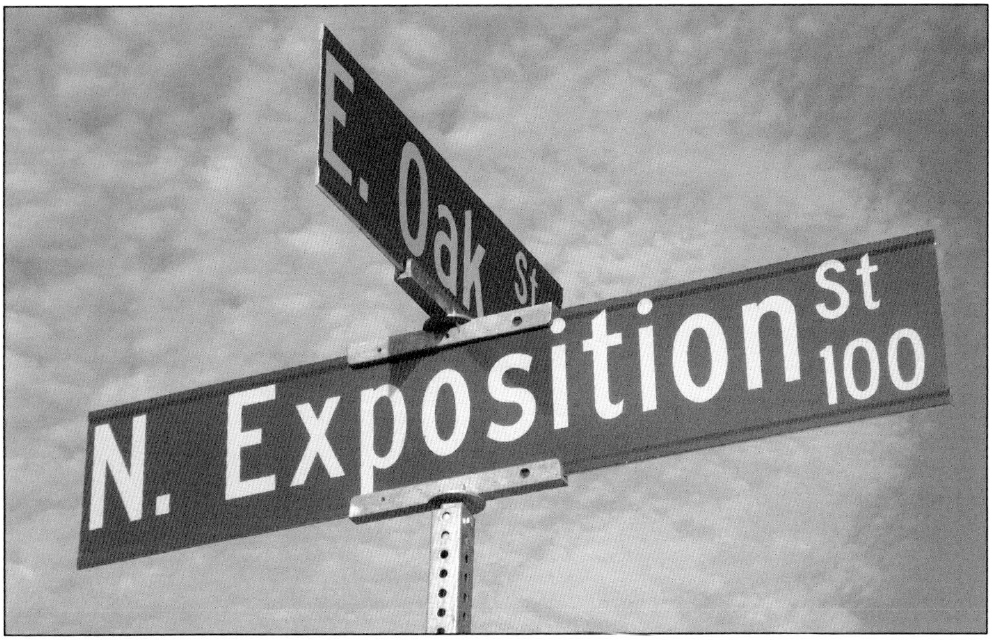

FAIR AT EXPOSITION STREET. Although the Denton County Agricultural Fair Association (DCAFA) was inaugurated in 1928, the Denton County Agricultural and Livestock Fair was officially incorporated and chartered in 1930 and relocated to 13 acres bordered by East Hickory and East Oak Streets at Exposition Street. (Courtesy of NTFR.)

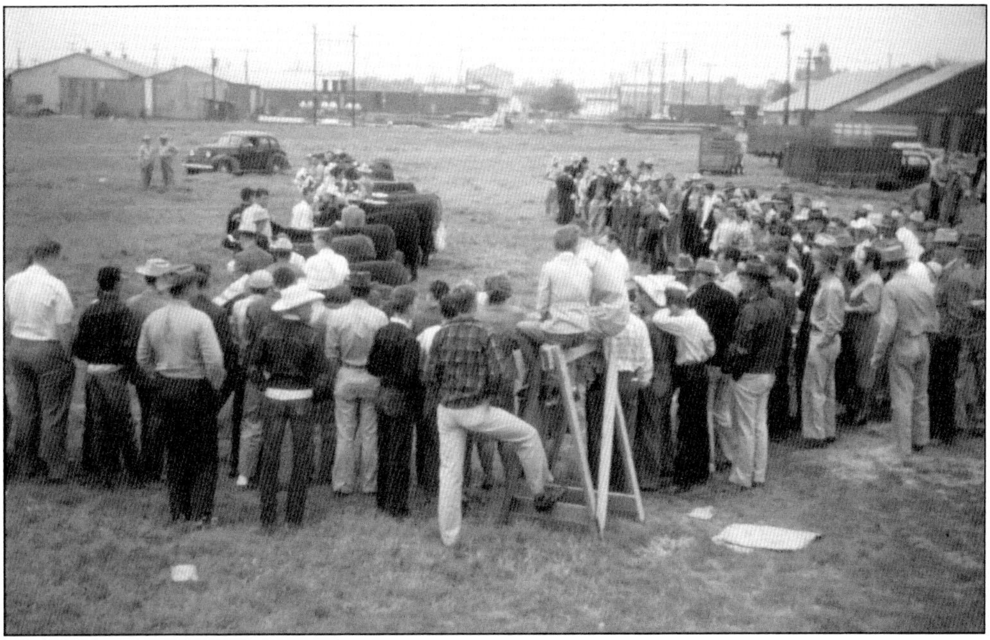

BEEF COWS TO DAIRY CATTLE. Dairy cows replaced trail-driven beef cattle as the predominant area industry after the 1881 arrival of the Texas & Pacific Railroad in Denton. Denton County's 1930 Census reflected a total of 34,000 cows. Cattle-raisers throughout the county brought their stock to Denton for sale and trade, as shown in this 1950s photograph of a field near Exposition Street. (Courtesy of DCOHC.)

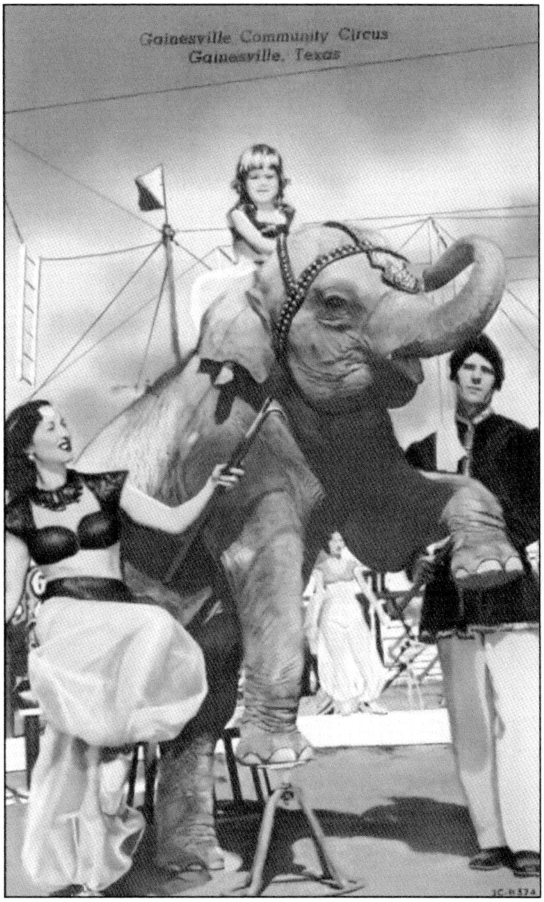

Ramping up the Entertainment. Fair entertainment took on a more important role in the early 1930s. Denton played host to acts like the Gainesville Community Circus (right) and the Light Crust Doughboys (below), a group sponsored by Burrus Mill owner (and future governor of Texas) W. Lee "Pappy" O'Daniel. Denton celebrated its diamond anniversary in 1932 with 'Fessor Graham's North Texas State Teachers College stage band treating crowds to performances equally as entertaining as those of the more well known groups. (Right, courtesy of Jim and Tricia Bolz; below, courtesy of lightcrustdoughboys.org.)

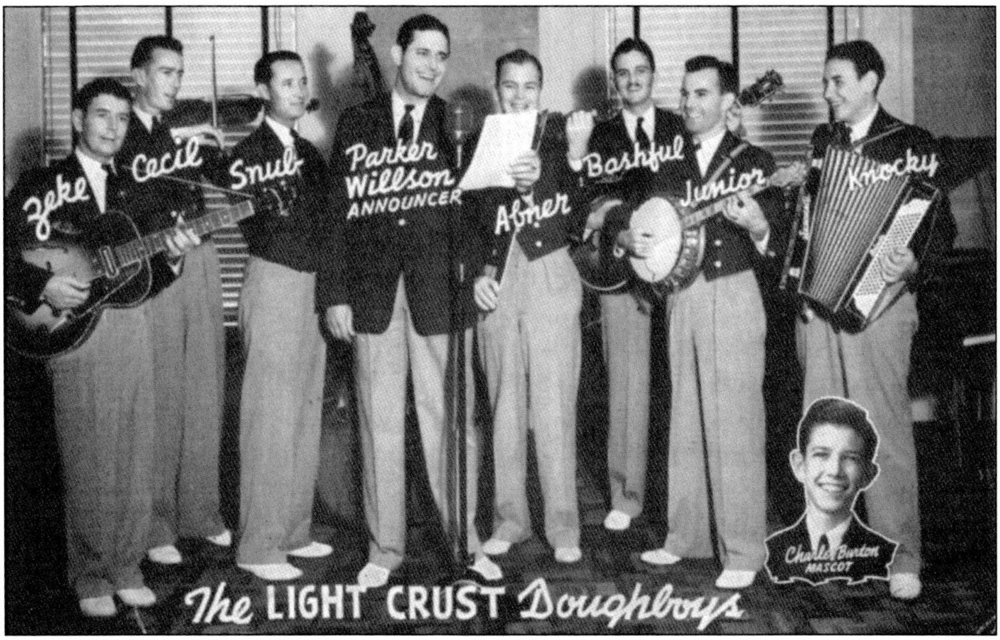

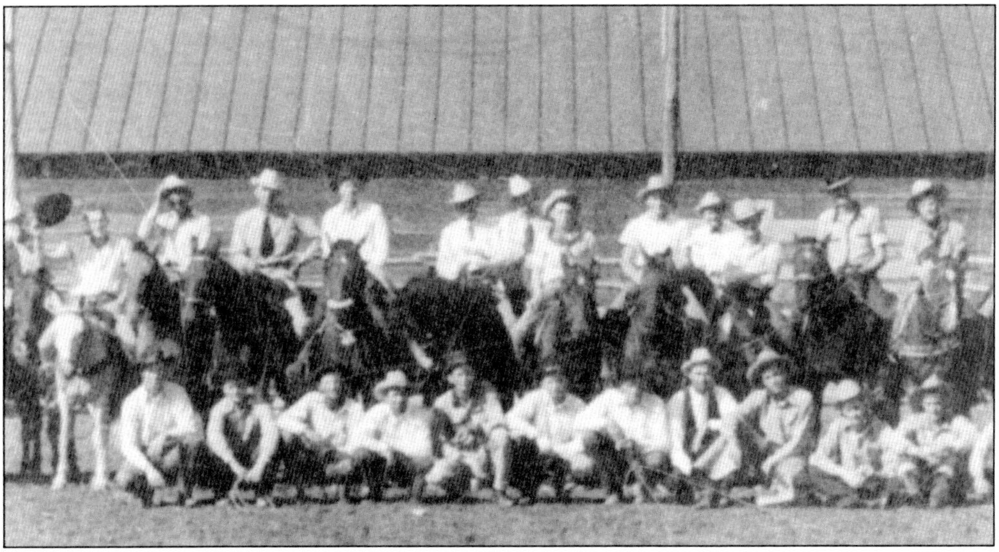

Line up to Rodeo up. In the above photograph, rodeo contestants at the 1934 Denton County Agricultural and Livestock Fair line up before competing. Some of these cowboys would become members of the Cowboys' Turtle Association—so named because they were slow to form but unafraid to stick their necks out to get what they wanted. The association, a result of a 1936 cowboy strike in Boston (below), was the forerunner to the Rodeo Cowboys Association (RCA) and the current Professional Rodeo Cowboys Association (PRCA). (Above, courtesy of Weldon Burgoon; below, courtesy of *Western Horseman*.)

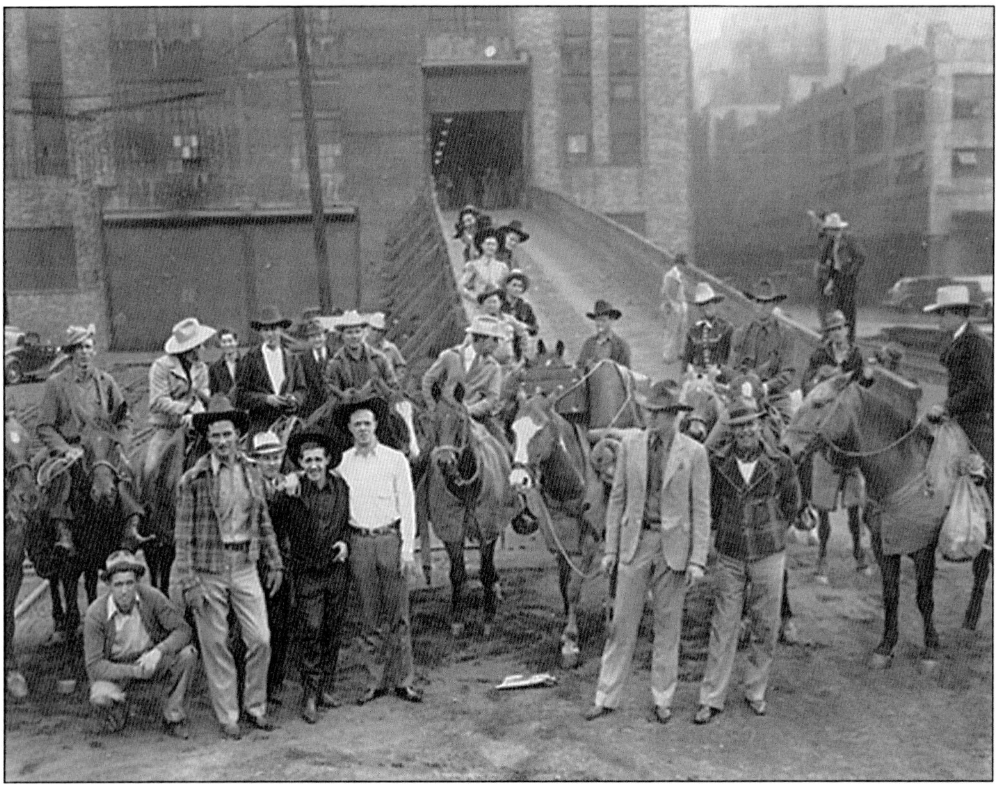

Tickets to the Fun. One of Denton's prominent merchants, the Boston Store, sponsored the printing of these 1936 raffle tickets. Many of Denton's businesses supported the fair and ran special sales to attract fair attendees. Some businesses closed their doors for a short time during the fair to allow their employees to take part in the festivities. (Courtesy of Jim and Tricia Bolz.)

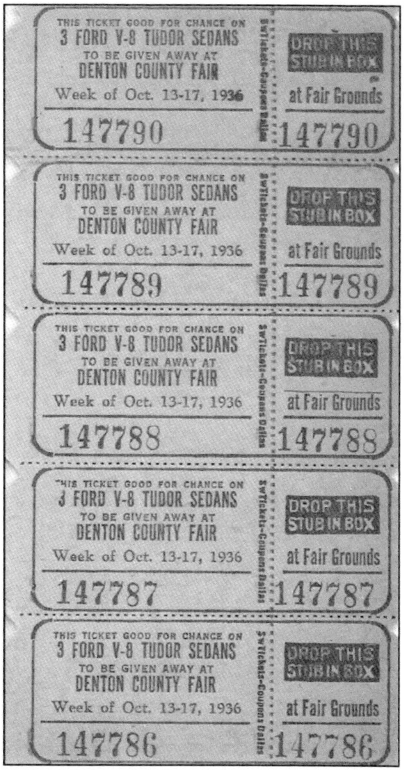

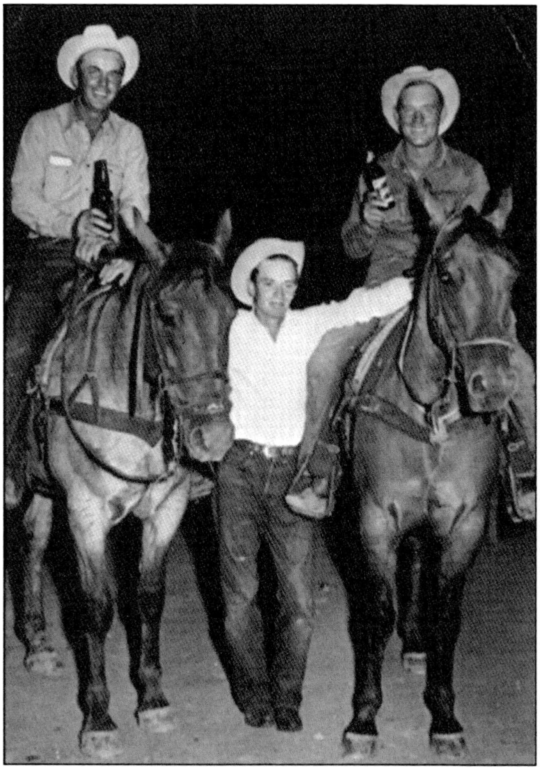

Ponder Rodeo. According to the Town of Ponder website (www.pondertx.com), the Ponder Rodeo began in 1939, "with everyone pitching in to help build the arena and local women's groups selling refreshments. Admission was twenty-five cents. The rodeo remained in Ponder until 1942, when it was moved to Denton because of gas and rubber rationing during World War II." In 1946, the rodeo moved back to Ponder and into a new 3,500-seat arena. These three unidentified cowboys participated in the Ponder rodeo before it moved to Denton, which started its own rodeo in 1950. (Courtesy of DCOHC.)

Confer on Denton County Fair

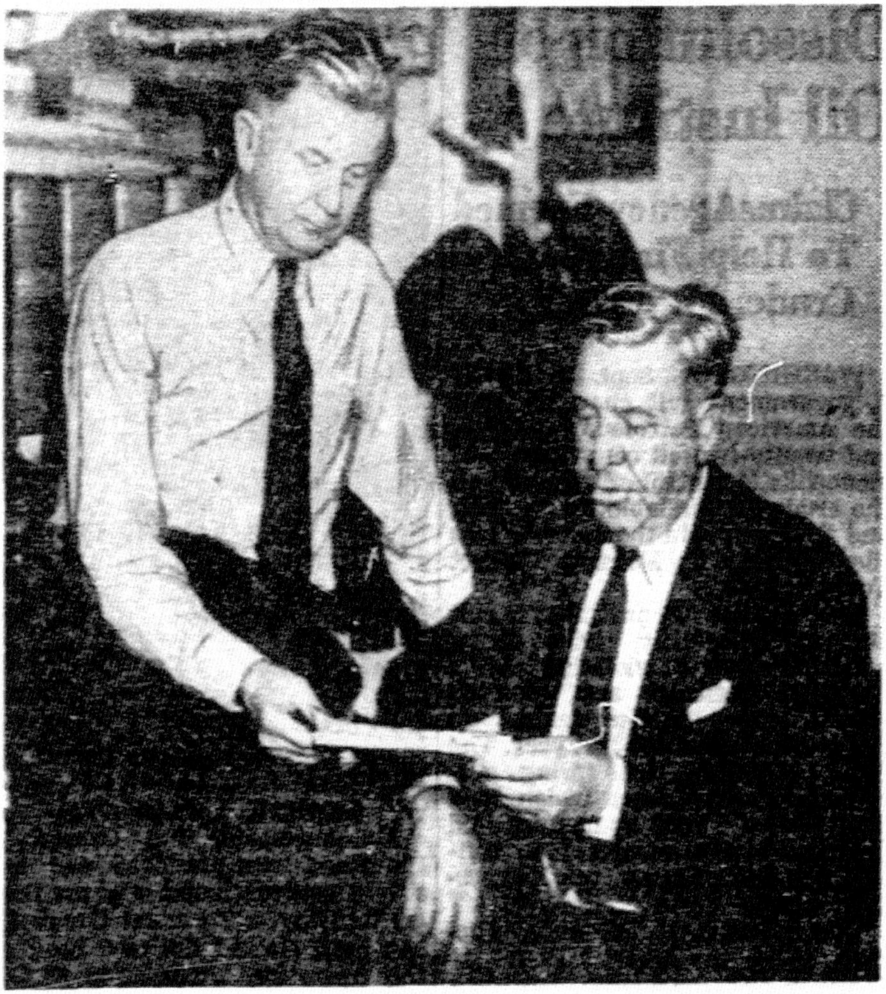

DENTON, Texas, Sept. 30.—Officials of the 1940 Denton County Fair checked last-minute arrangements here Monday on the eve of the five-day show, Oct. 1-5. Standing, left, is Manager O. L. Fowler of the Denton Chamber of Commerce, secretary of the fair association, conferring with R. J. Edwards, publisher of the Denton Record-Chronicle, association president for the second successive year.

A NEW ERA. An October 1, 1940, *Dallas Morning News* article announced that R.J. Edwards (right), publisher of the *Denton Record-Chronicle*, was elected president of the Denton County Agricultural Fair Association. That year, several buildings and a temporary amphitheater were constructed on the fairgrounds. A mile-long parade circled the downtown square—in front of 20,000 spectators lining the streets—and ended at the fairgrounds. Fair activities included a pioneer pageant depicting the history of Denton, with pioneers over 70 years of age receiving free season tickets to the fair. The first swine show was held since the Depression, contributing to a successful way to end the decade. Edwards and Otis Fowler, manager of the Denton Chamber of Commerce and secretary of the fair association, served into the 1940s. (Courtesy of DMN.)

Two

Going through the Mill

Wartime and Postwar (1940–1950s)

The advent of World War II created some of the most trying years that the fair would face. The *Dallas Morning News* reported in 1940 that a gala parade opened the Denton County Agricultural Fair with a "battalion of Texas Defense Guard and a State College for Women float featuring the Goddess of Freedom as the key motif of the parade." All of Denton marched in "picturesque procession" to the delight of "thousands of spectators lining the sidewalk. Freedom was depicted by Miss Joy Miller, a graduate student at TSCW, made up to represent the figure which tops the dome of the Washington Capitol."

From 1941 to 1945, World War II had a devastating effect on the United States. Denton held war drives for scrap metal and kept busy wrapping bandages. Cattle, poultry, hogs and pigs, and grain were shipped off to feed the troops. The town sent many of its young men to war. The Ponder Rodeo moved to Denton in 1942, even though the Denton fair was cancelled during the World War II years. The Ponder Rodeo moved back to Ponder in 1946 and remained there until 1950, when it permanently closed.

In 1946, the Denton County Agricultural Fair Association reopened with a two-mile-long pioneer parade. The fair was cancelled again in 1948 when the expansion of the eastern part of the city created a lack of adequate parking at the Exposition Street site.

The fair was back on track in 1949 after a gift of land from Dr. W.C. Kimbrough to the Denton County Agricultural Fair Association. This gift introduced a new era for the fair, as it provided it with the permanent home where it remained for the next 67 years and is still held today.

Men such as Weldon Burgoon, R.J. Edwards, Otis Fowler, Earl Foreman, and H.M. Pitner took leadership roles on the fair association board, striving to keep the fair afloat.

In 1956, the association's name was changed to the Denton County Fair Association, and in 1958, fair stockholders voted to change the name to the North Texas State Fair Association. This change allowed the event to accept funding from and showcase the Shetland Pony Association.

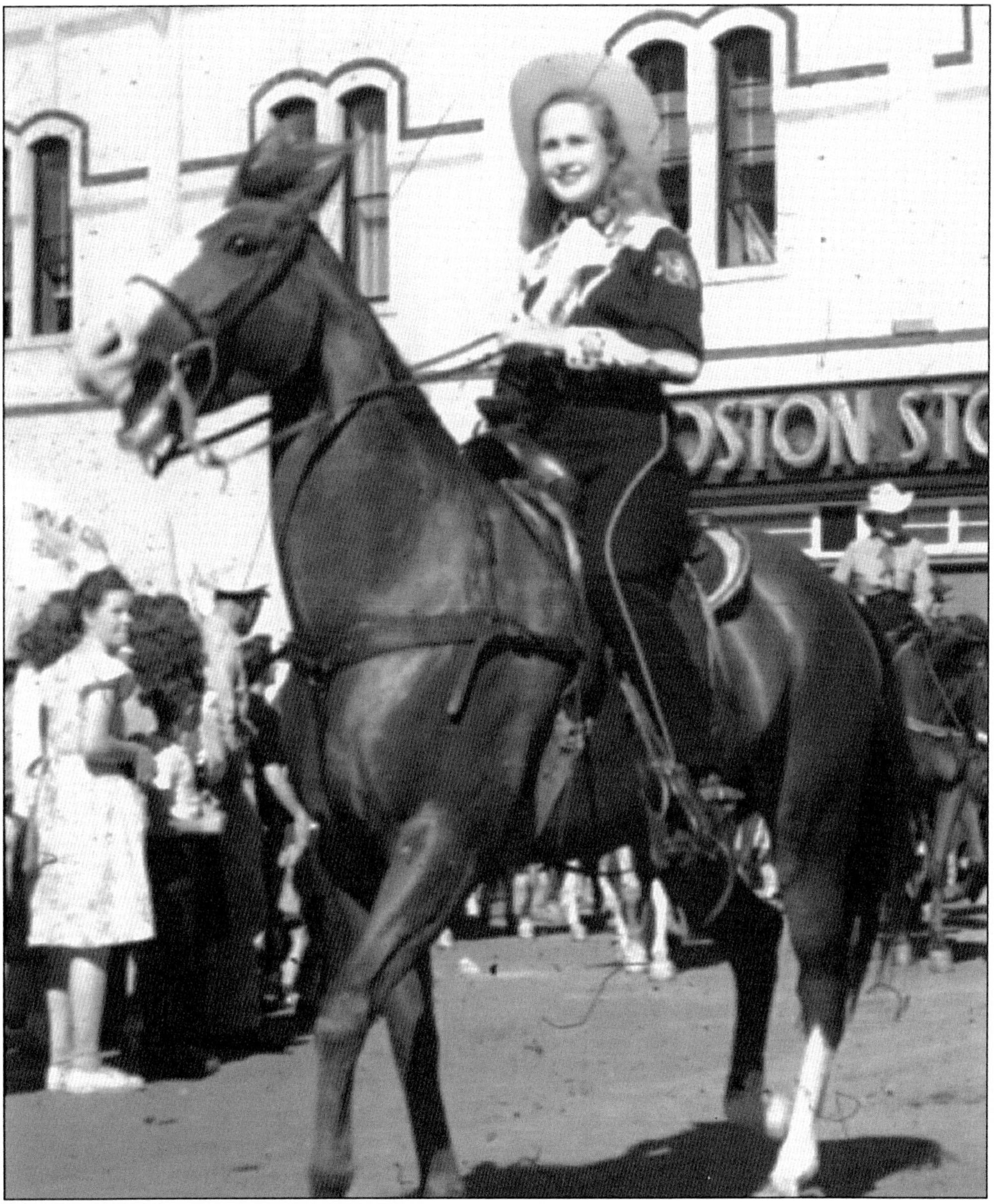

Madeline Murphree, Cowgirl Beauty. Madeline Murphree was selected by the junior chamber of commerce to represent Denton in the Arlington Downs Western Beauty Revue in August 1946. In September 1946, Murphree represented the Town and Country Roundup Club in the Pioneer Parade that opened the Denton County Centennial Fair. She is pictured here leading the Town and Country Roundup Club around the downtown square. (Courtesy of DCOHC.)

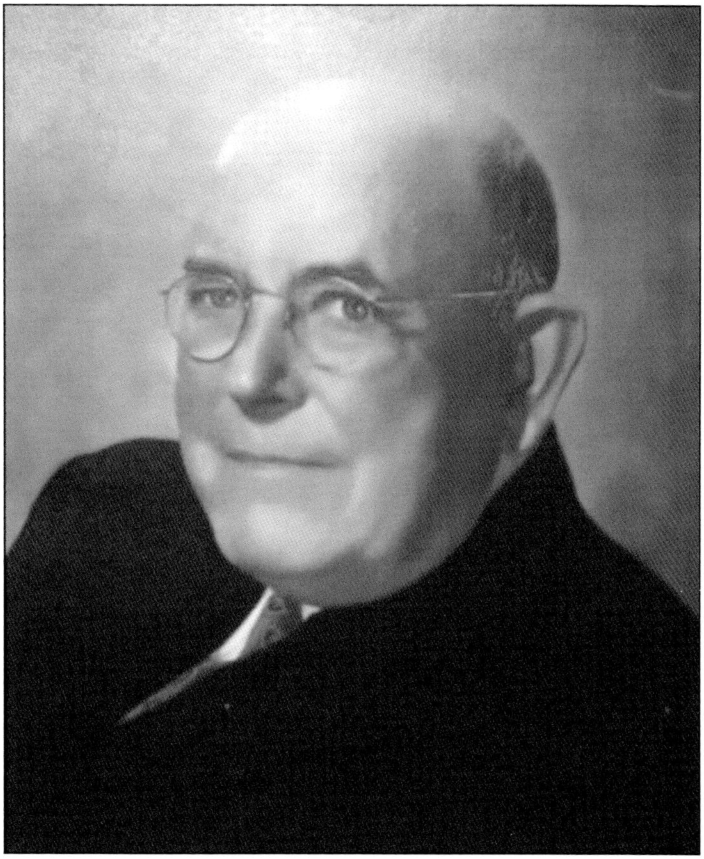

Wallace Calvin (W.C.) Kimbrough, Philanthropist. Dr. Kimbrough (1875–1952), a pioneering Denton physician, sold 22 acres of land to the Denton County Agricultural Fair Association for $5 in April 1948. This parcel of land is located in Denton on Highway 24 (now University Drive) at Beaumont Street (now Carroll Boulevard). On opening day in 1949, the fairgrounds were named in honor of Kimbrough. Kimbrough remained active on the fair association board for many years. The fair has remained at this site for the last 67 years and is currently still held here. (Both, courtesy of NTFR.)

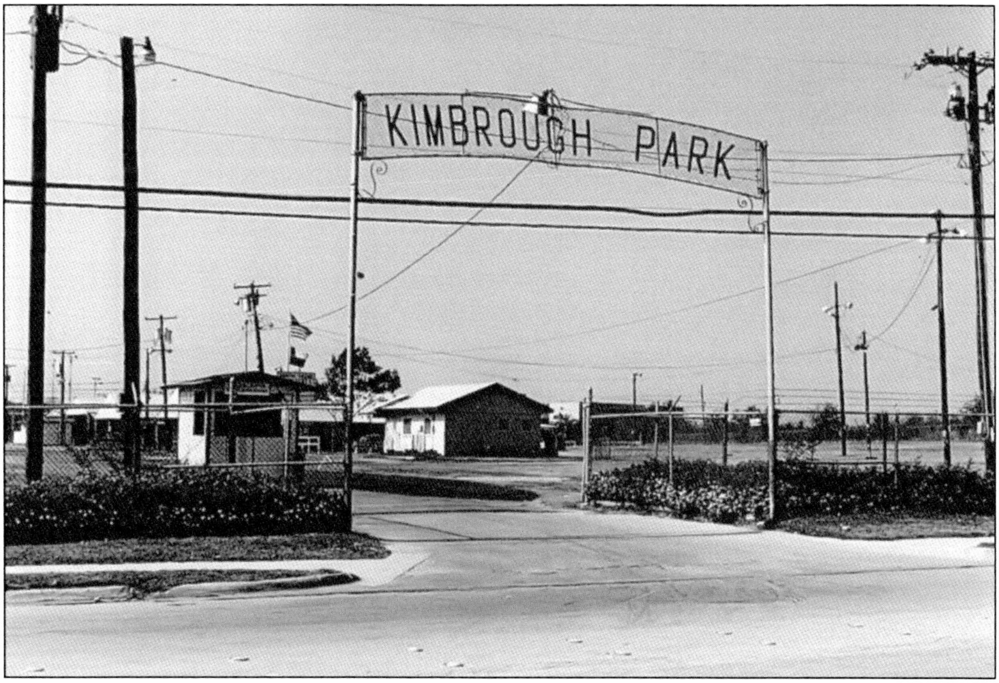

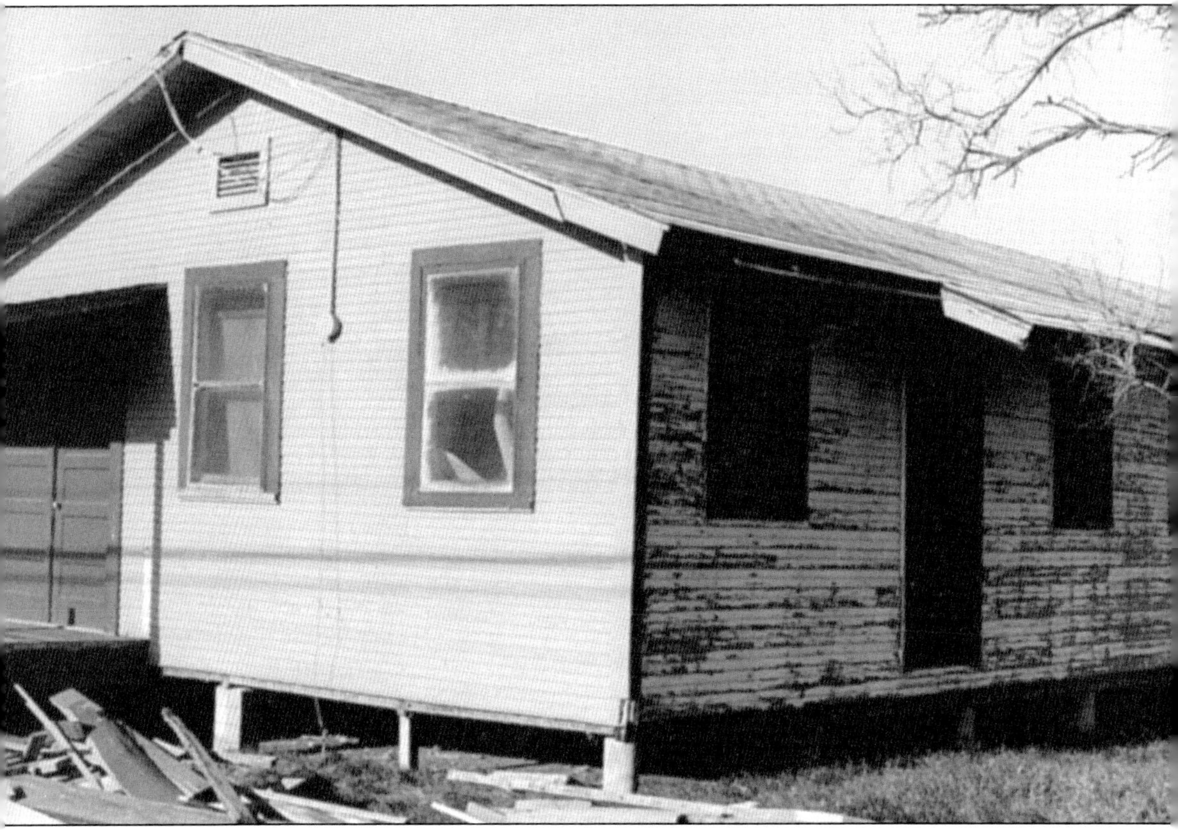

FAIR HALL, 1940s. Fair Hall was on the fairgrounds property at the time that Dr. W.C. Kimbrough sold the land to the fair association. The building was originally used at Camp Howze, an infantry replacement training center and World War II–era German prisoner-of-war camp adjacent to Gainesville in Cooke County. When the camp was dismantled in 1942, Denton County acquired the building and located it on the Kimbrough tract of land to use for a GI school. Denton County donated the building, a desk, a wooden file cabinet, and four chairs to the fair association at the time of the Kimbrough sale (in 1948). (Courtesy of NTFR.)

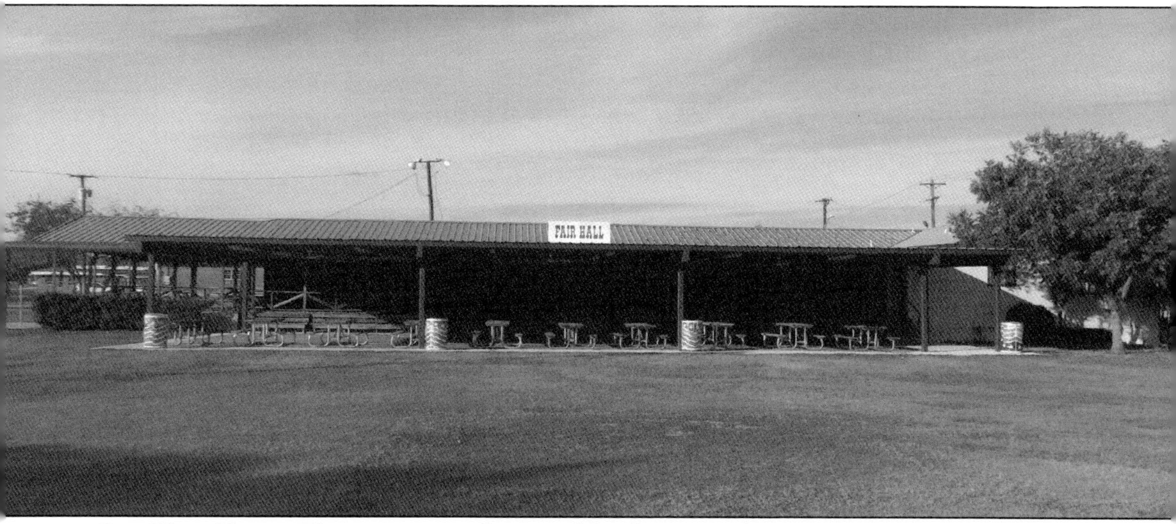

FAIR HALL TODAY. The renovation of Fair Hall has been a work in progress since the 1940s. Two new porches, carpet, paneling, and a refinished floor made the facility a more attractive income-producing space where people could hold reunions, birthdays, wedding receptions, and corporate functions. Due to tornadic activity, Fair Hall was strengthened with a steel frame and received a new roof. During the fair, the building is partitioned into spaces for the photography exhibit and the VIP/green room for dignitaries and musical artists. (Courtesy of NTFR.)

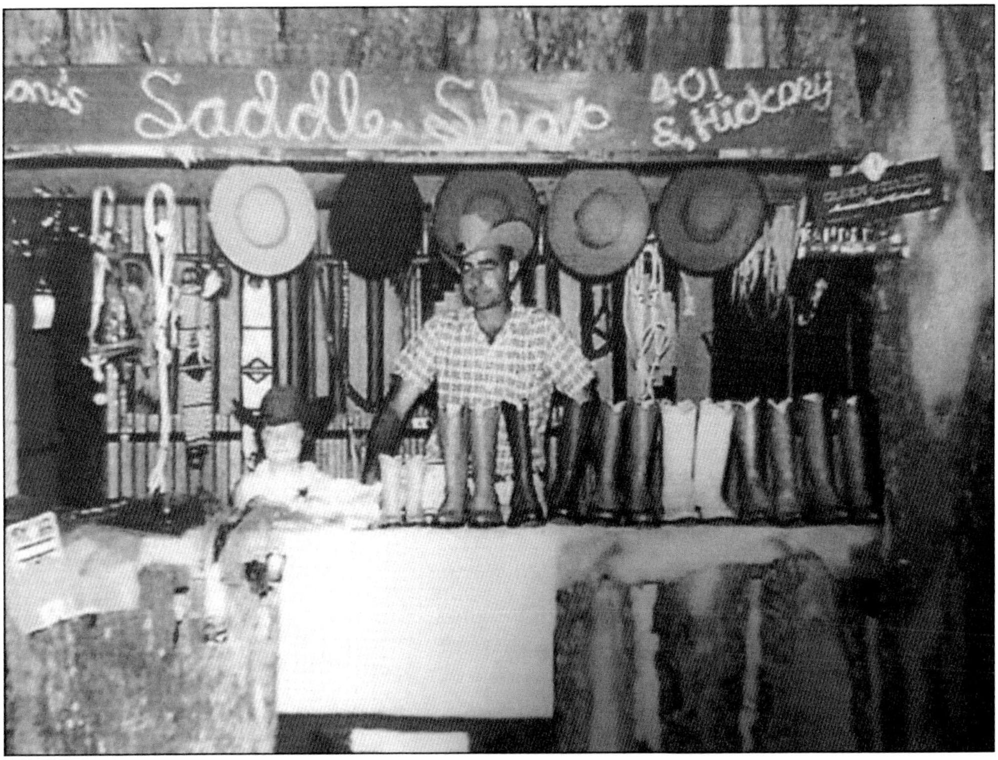

Weldon Burgoon, A Cowboy's Cowboy. Weldon Burgoon got his start at age 11 competing against senior ropers. In 1946, at age 16, he won $64 and the tie-down roping title. Burgoon earned his living on the rodeo circuit for several years before opening Weldon's Saddle Shop. From 1957 to about 1987, he operated a commercial booth, which had a sawmill lumber facade, in the fair exhibit building. It was the last permanent structure that remained in the commercial exhibit building at the fairgrounds. (Both, courtesy of Weldon Burgoon.)

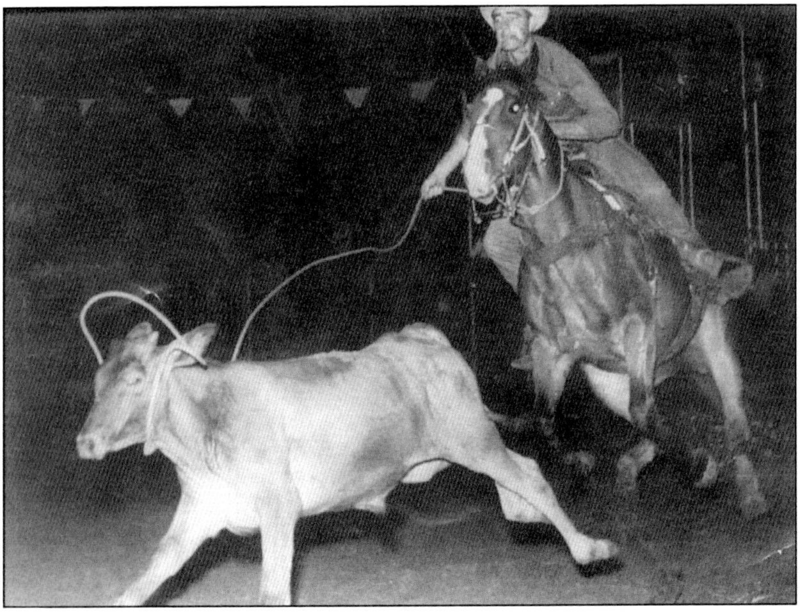

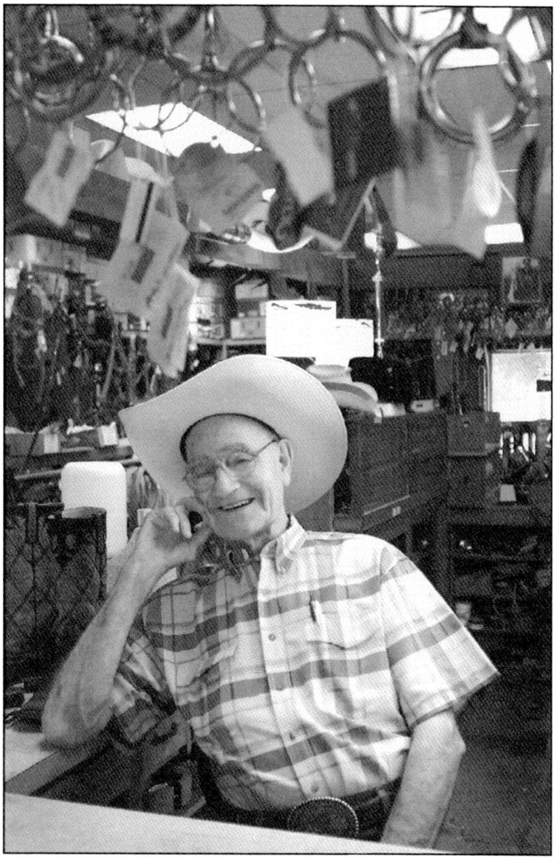

Weldon Burgoon, Hall of Famer. Burgoon has served as rodeo and fair chairman, still sponsors the Mutton Bustin' event, and helped spur the chamber of commerce farm and ranch tour. He started the Denton Junior Stampede and the Denton County Youth Fair, Rodeo, and Horse Show. Burgoon—a legendary cowboy, businessman, youth sponsor, and ambassador—was inducted into the Texas Rodeo Cowboy Hall of Fame in 2010. (Right, courtesy of CVB; below, courtesy of NTFR.)

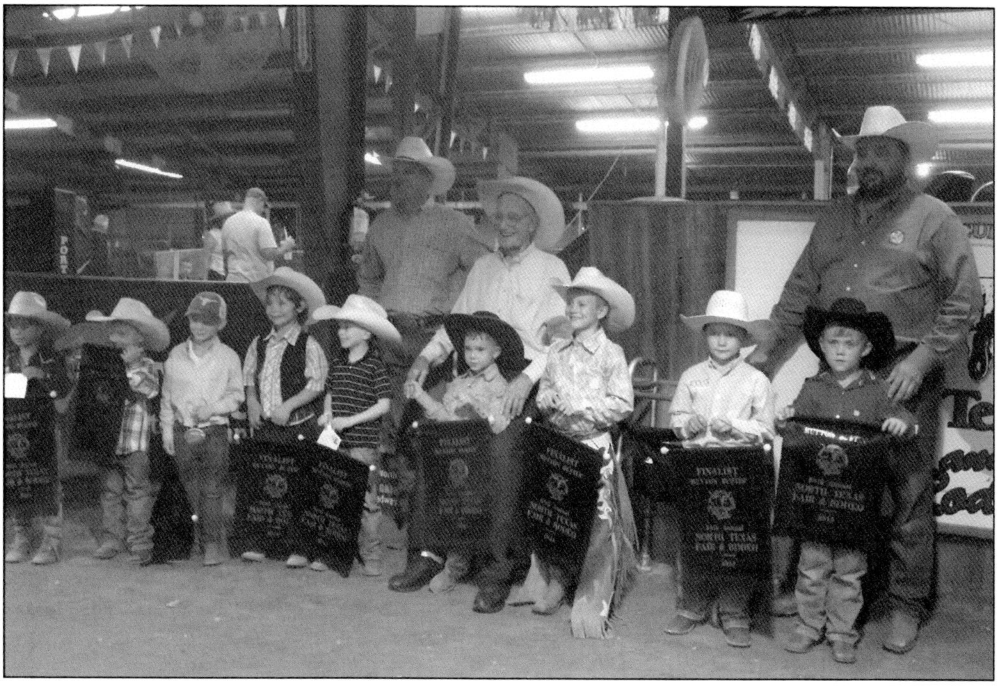

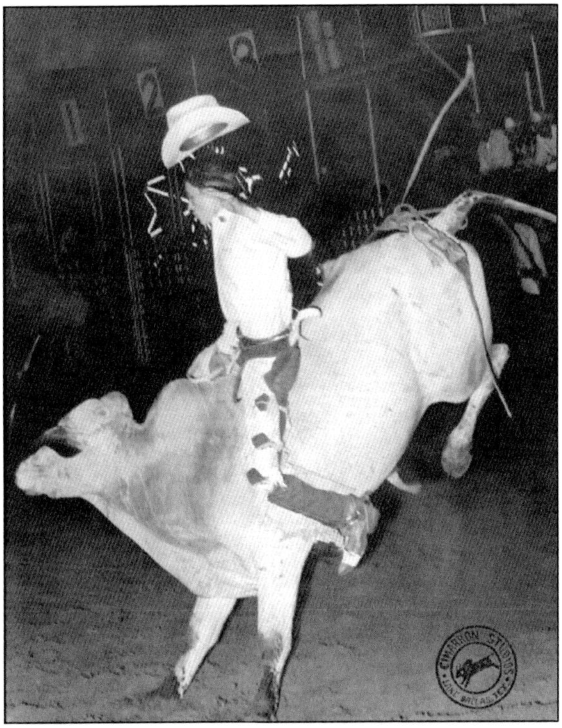

Denton County Rodeo Association (DCRA). The DCRA sponsored its first rodeo in June 1950 at the Denton County Fairgrounds. DCRA owned all its own livestock and produced between 18 and 20 Saturday night rodeos each year, also producing outside rodeos under RCA sanction. Earl Foreman, Doc Pitner, Claude Castleberry, Mark Hannah Sr., Jack Skiles, and Lyle Montgomery served on the board of the rodeo association, and Marjorie Pitner served as secretary. Events included bareback bronc riding, steer wrestling, calf roping, saddle bronc, barrel racing, and bull riding. Seventeen-year-old Tommy Calvert Sr. (left) scored 68 on Bull 101 and took third place in this junior rodeo. Buster McNatt is riding a rank bronc in the 1950 photograph below. (Left, courtesy of the Calvert family; below, courtesy of DCOHC.)

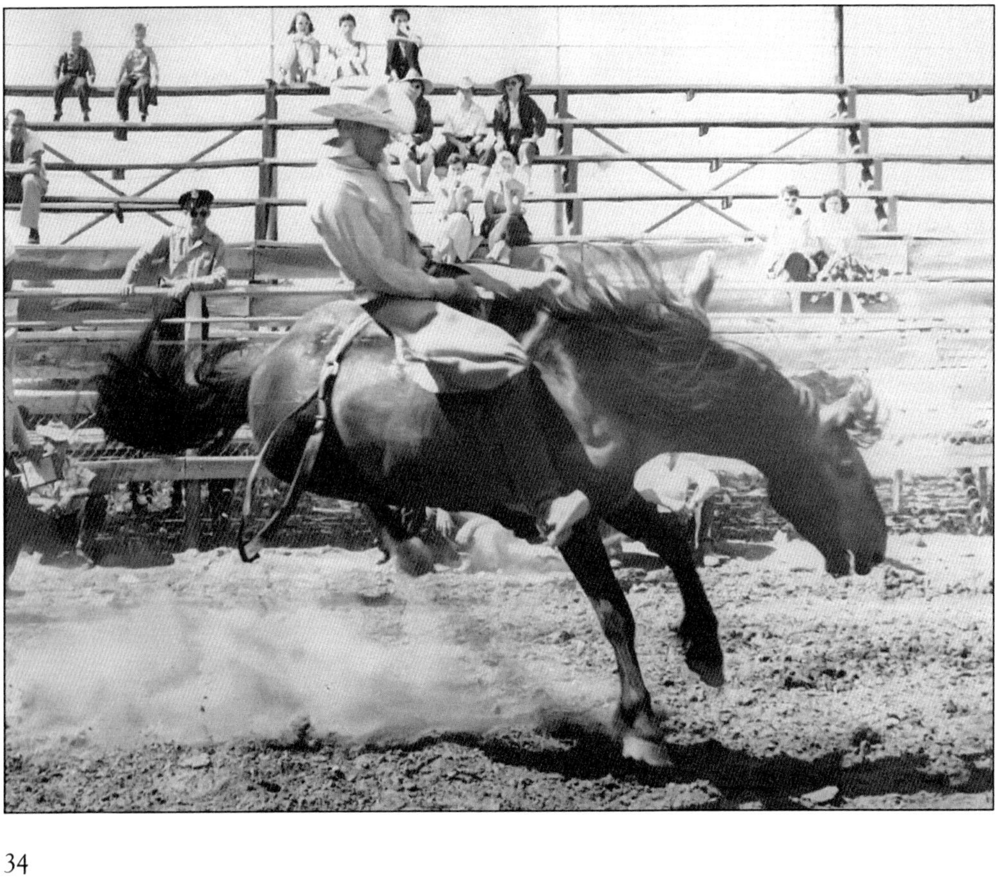

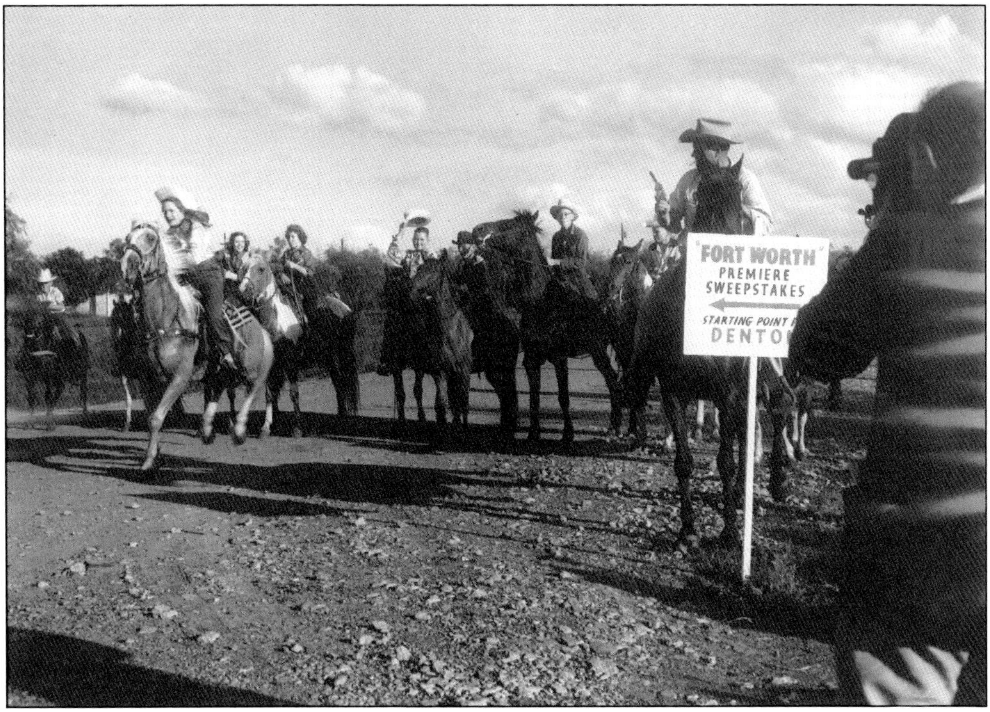

FORT WORTH STAMPEDE. Denton, Weatherford, Cleburne, and Dallas sponsored a four-city horse race to celebrate the 1951 world premiere of the movie *Fort Worth*. Each city selected a horse and rider who would travel 10 miles on their respective highways to the Worth Theatre. Madeline Murphree Sullivan represented Denton. The first rider to arrive at the theater won a $250 prize and a custom-made saddle from Leddy's of Fort Worth. An event held beforehand at the Denton County Fairgrounds was filmed as a newsreel to be broadcast in all theaters showing the movie. Anyone who showed up at the Campus Theatre premiere opening in Western garb and on horseback received a free pass to the movie. (Both, courtesy of DCOHC.)

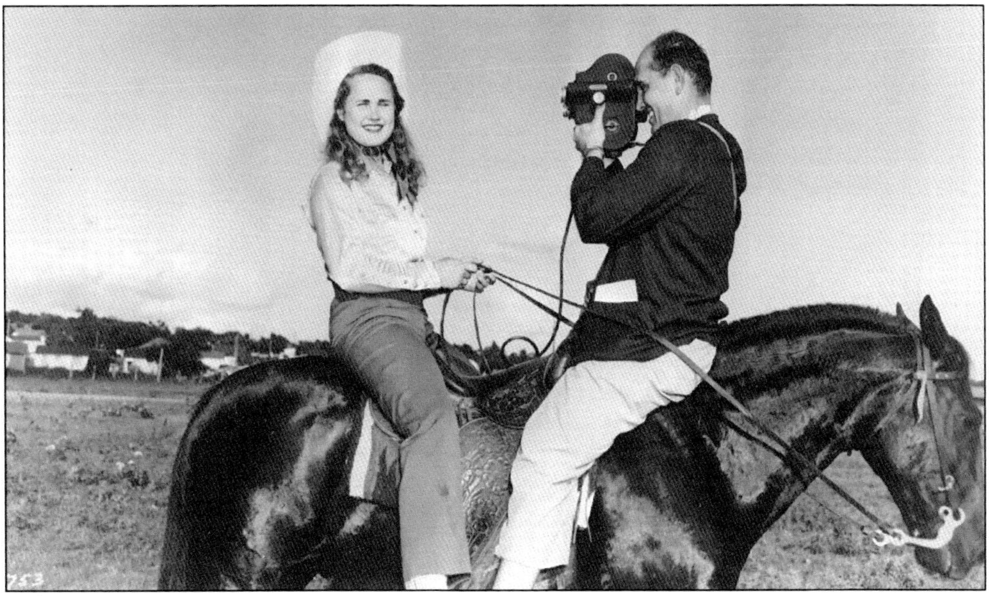

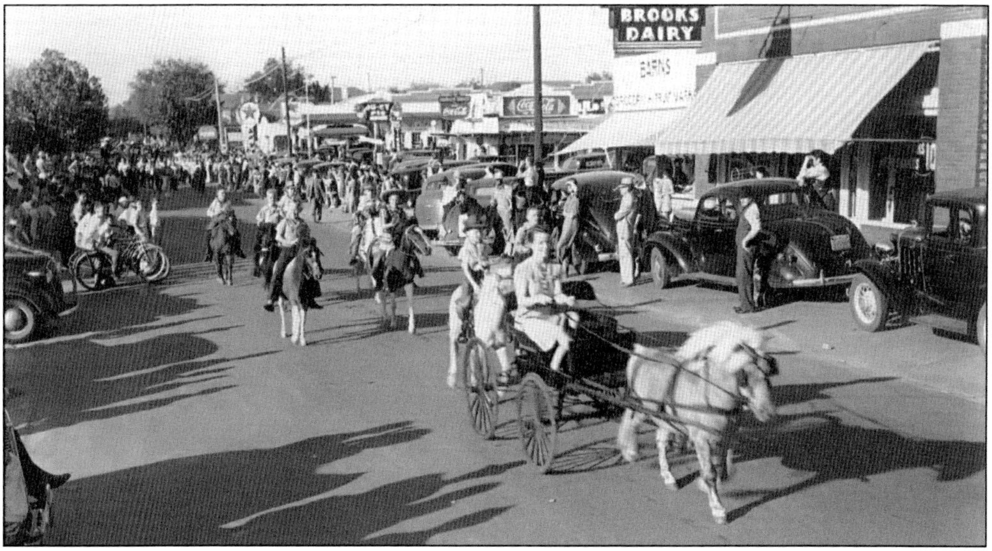

Fair Parade. The fair parade has been a tradition in Denton since the first documented one, which was held in 1956. Under the leadership of Joe Evans, the 1956 parade committee consisted of H.M. "Doc" Pitner, Jack Vanderhoff, and the Sheriff's Posse. Kathryn Davis Williams is shown driving the lead Shetland pony wagon past the original Brooks Dairy location on Locust Street near downtown Denton. (Courtesy of DPL.)

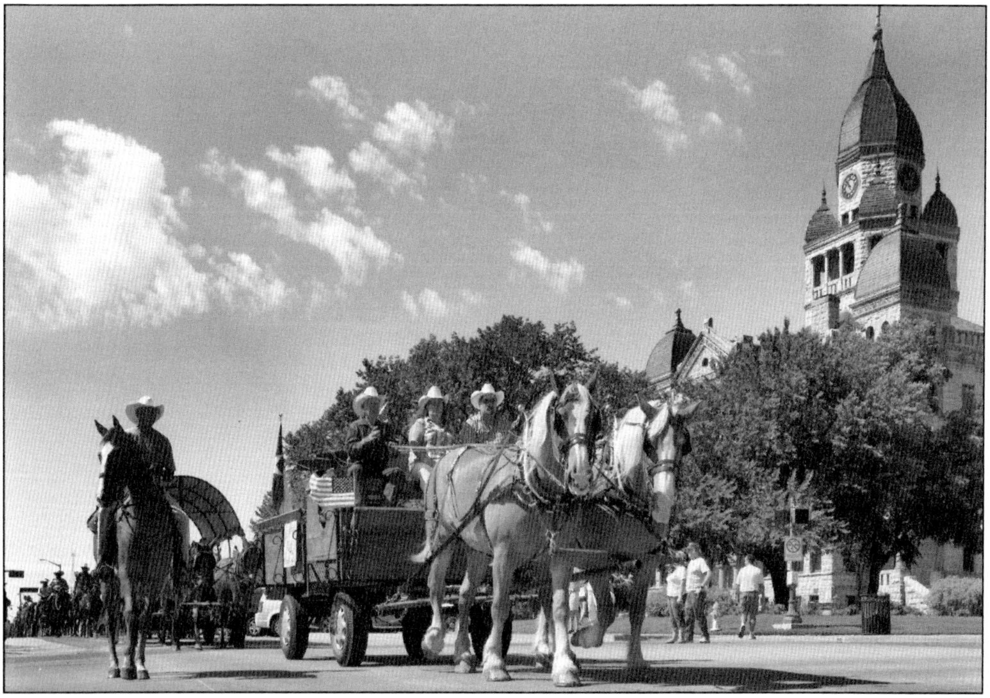

Centennial Parade. Denton began celebrating the 100th anniversary of the founding of the city on April 22, 1957, with a parade around the downtown square. The tradition remains in place today with the fanfare of the North Texas State Fair Association parade held each August. Horses and wagons have always played an important role in the parade through this growing North Texas town. (Courtesy of DPL.)

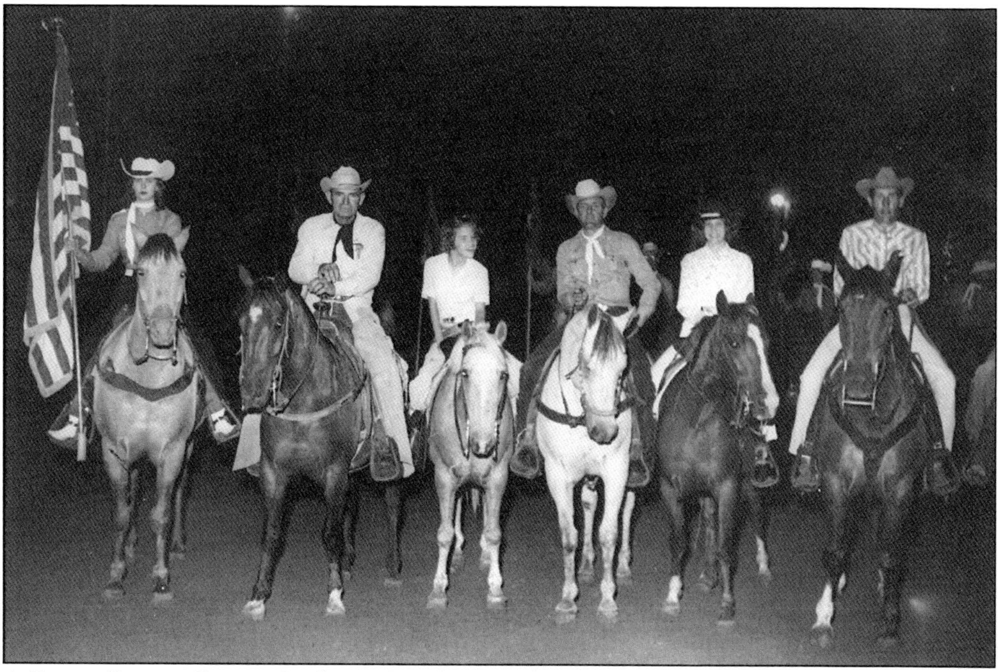

A Brave Barrel Racer. In this 1950s photograph, an unidentified young woman (third from left in the above image) participated in the grand entry prior to the rodeo performance. Despite her handicap, she heroically competed in the barrel racing competition. Protective safety belts attached to the saddle enabled her to ride a cloverleaf pattern around the barrels. She was a true representative of the brave and resilient spirit of cowgirls. (Both, courtesy of NTFR.)

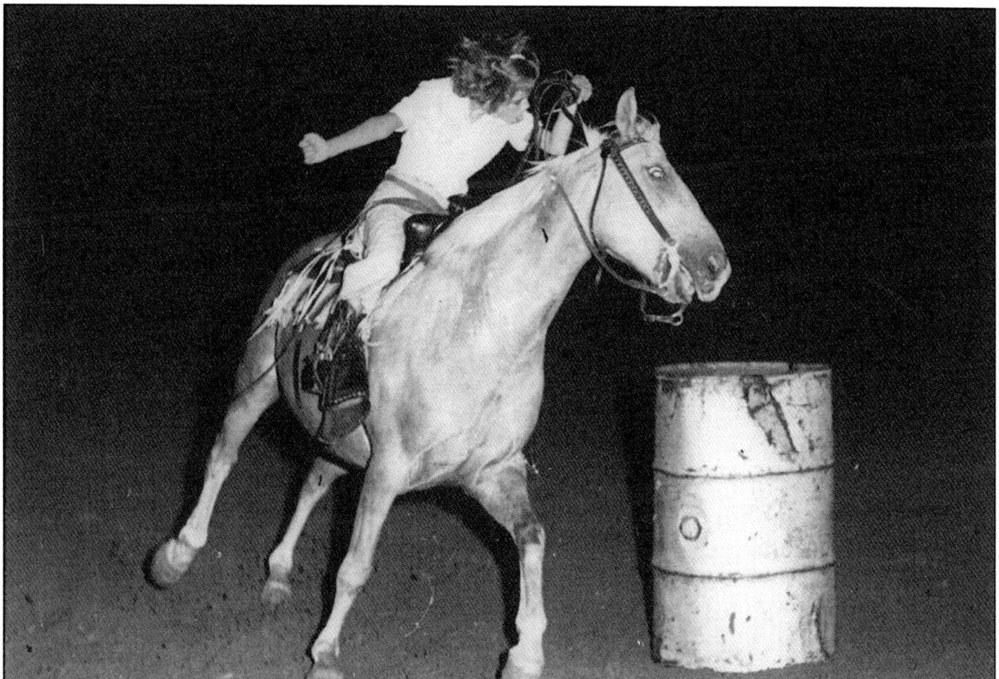

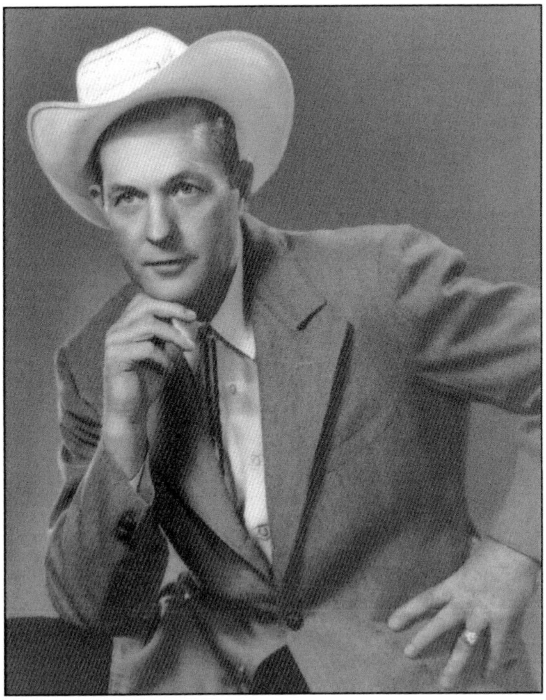

H.M. "Doc" Pitner. Homer Melton "Doc" Pitner was among a group of Denton businesspeople who helped create and organize the Denton County Rodeo Association and served as a longtime member of the North Texas State Fair Association board. Pitner raised champion Pony of the Americas (POA), medium-sized ponies with the coloration of the Appaloosa, the muscle and bone of the American Quarter Horse, and the refinement of the Arabian. In addition to being a board member, Pitner served as a rodeo announcer at the fair. (Both, courtesy of Pitner Collection at DCOHC.)

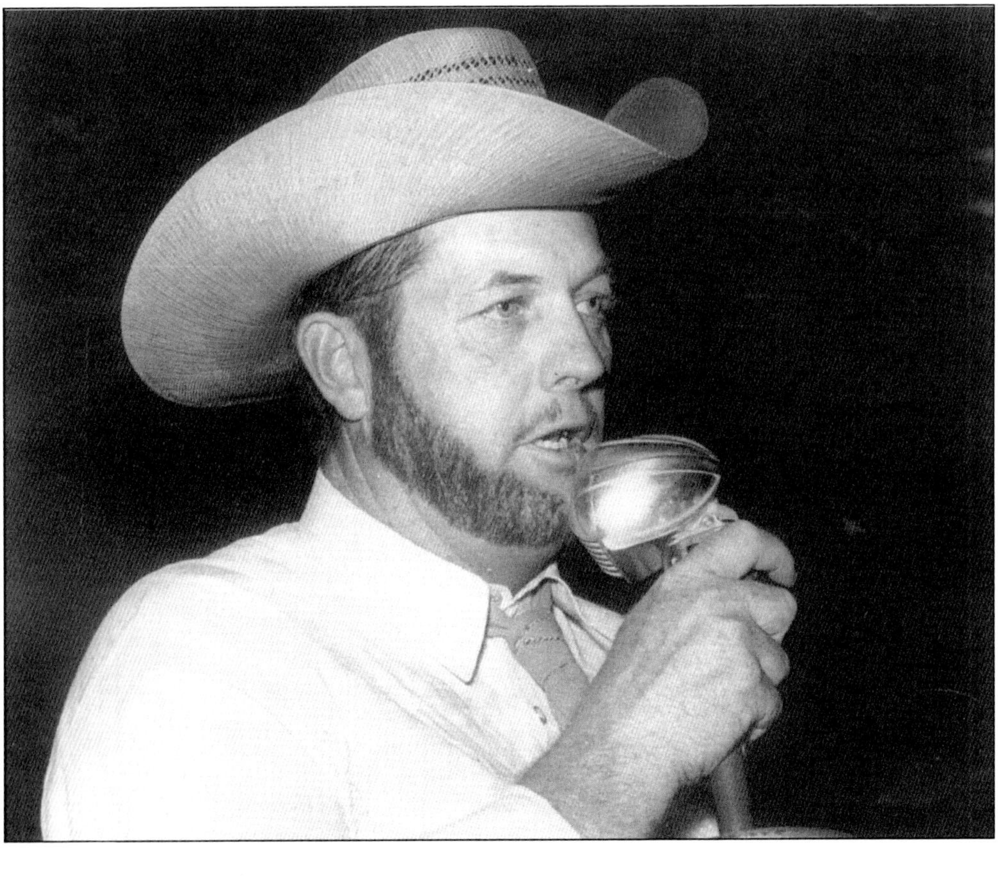

The Legacy of Marjorie and Doc Pitner. Marjorie Pitner, wife of H.M. "Doc" Pitner, was equally involved with the DCRA, serving as its secretary. She shared her husband's passion for raising and training POAs and Shetland ponies and is shown at right with her three-time championship Shetland pony, Gray Cloud Superior. Doc and Marjorie instilled their love of raising ponies and the rodeo in their daughters, Patsy Pitner Kelsoe (at left in the below image) and Linda Pitner Riley (at right in the below image). Both daughters were selected as North Texas rodeo queens in the 1950s. The work ethic handed down to the girls from their parents served them well as they took over the family business, Roselawn Memorial Park. (Both, courtesy of the Pitner Collection at DCOHC.)

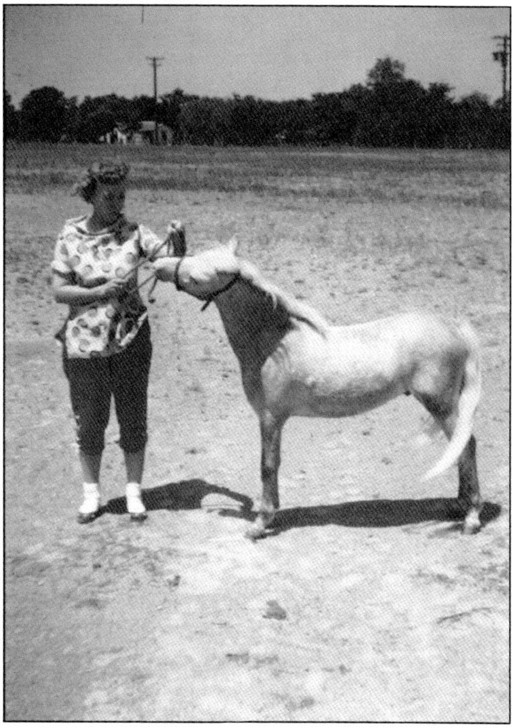

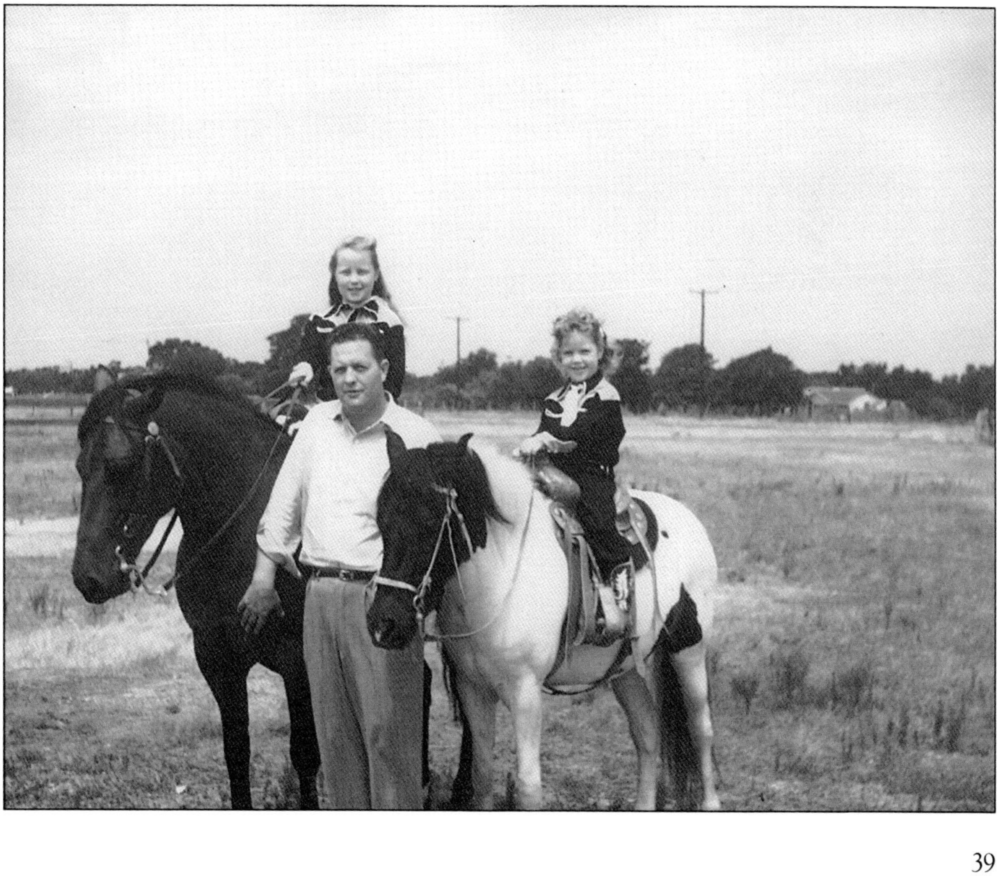

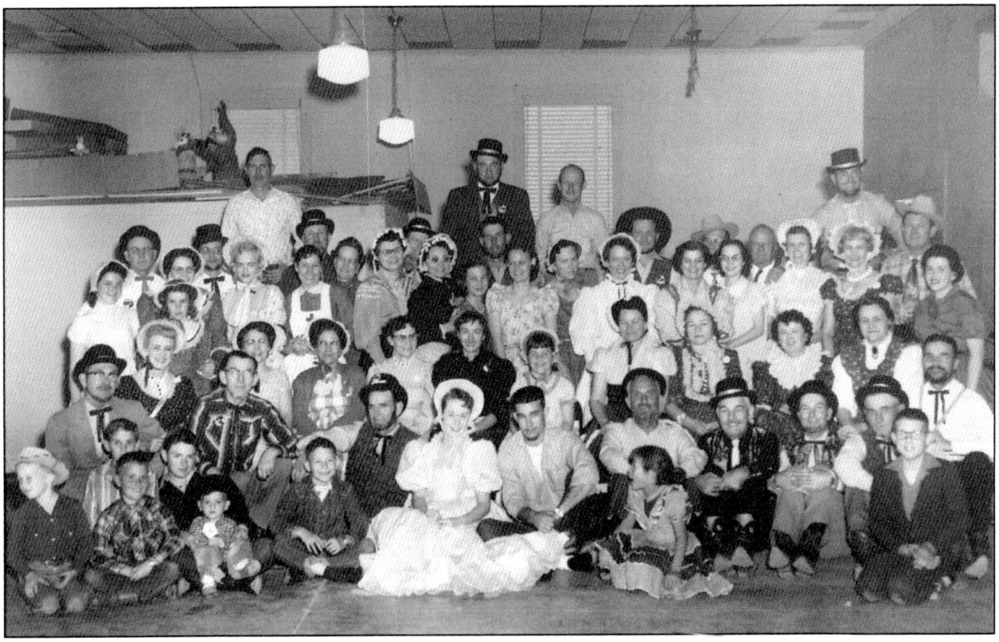

Centennial Queen at the Fairgrounds. Patsy Pitner earned the title of Centennial Queen in 1957 during the city of Denton's 100th birthday celebration. She is shown above (first row, center) among Denton Roundup Club members. Her sister Linda is also pictured (at far left in the third row). The members of the club are dressed in traditional garb, and the men are sporting bow ties and Brothers of the Brush beards. In the below photograph, members of the fair board and their wives are gathered for the fair's centennial celebration picture. Pictured are, from left to right, (first row) Earl Foreman, Lynn Mallow, Francis Mallow, Laura Wilson, Alice Pockrus, J.T. Wilson's daughter, Vita Hamilton, and Clarence Phillips; (second row) two unidentified men, H.M. "Doc" Pitner, Lane Grissom, Dutch Lor[r]ance, Bud Watson, Pete Pockrus, Paul Hamilton, and two unidentified men. (Both, courtesy of Pitner Collection at DCOHC.)

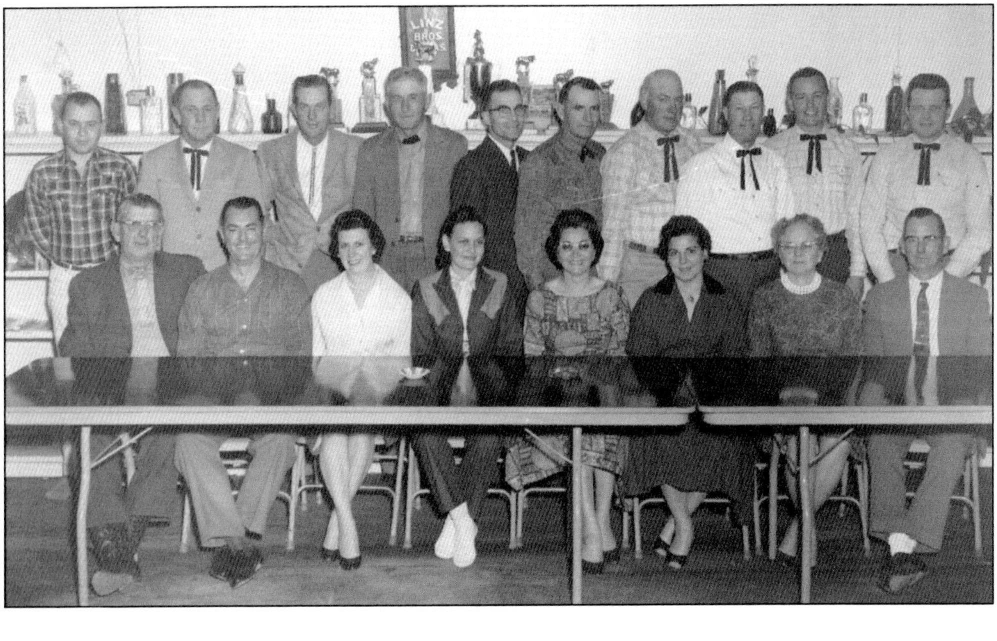

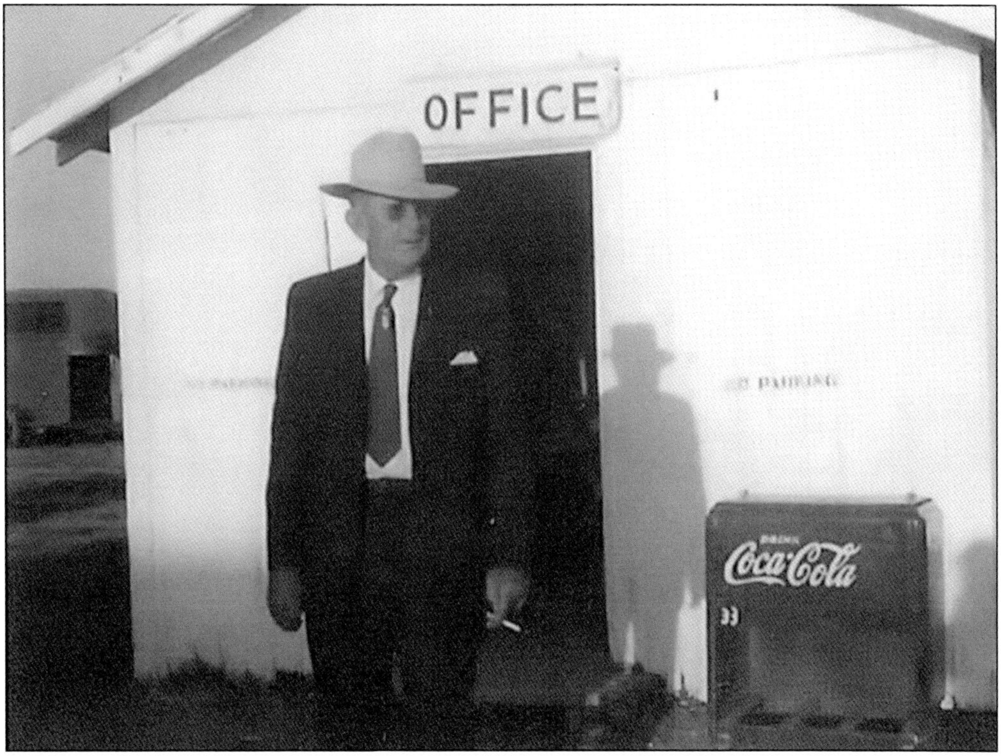

EARL FOREMAN. Earl Foreman (1900–1963), a county commissioner and president of the Denton County Agricultural Fair Association from 1958 to 1963, was one of the more influential members of the fair board of directors after serving as a board member on the Denton County Rodeo Association. Foreman, a stock contractor for the rodeos, is pictured above in front of the fair office building. In the below photograph, Paul Gallo (left) and Foreman are holding the poster for the official opening of Denton's rodeo in the early 1950s. Gallo owned Paul's Western Shop, which was located on West Hickory Street and was noted for its landmark large red horse, Levi; the shop specialized in "saddles, tack, western wear, and boots for the entire family." (Both, courtesy of the Foreman family.)

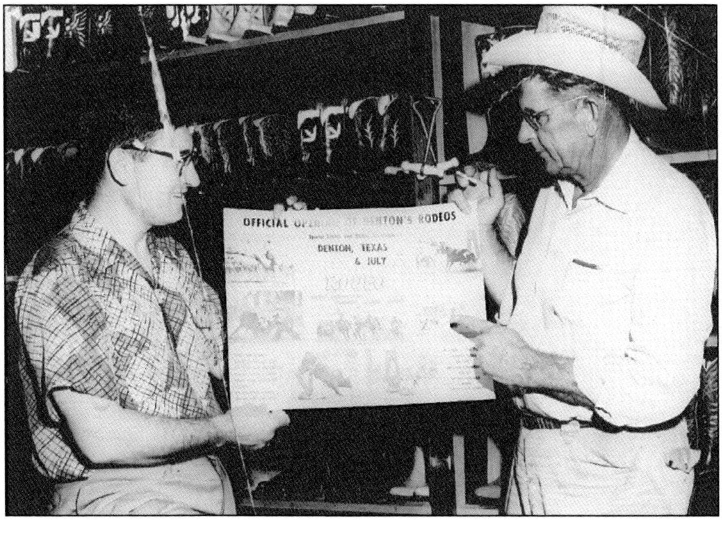

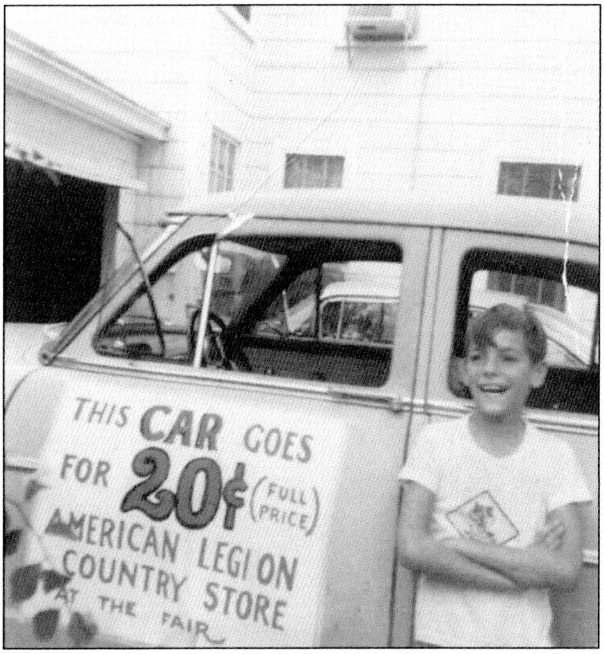

RAFFLING OFF CARS. The earliest car raffle at the fair occurred in 1936, when three lucky fair attendees won Ford V8 Tudor sedans. In 1957, the Frank Wallace family, from Justin, Texas, won a new 1957 Chevrolet. Seven-year-old Laurence McClendon (right) won a 1954 Packard Clipper Deluxe in 1961 with ticket No. 1,000, which his father purchased for him at a country store. Although McClendon never drove the car, it was stored in his family's barn until recently. Bill Allen, president of the fair association, is shown in the 1970s photograph below spinning the raffle barrel, about to make someone the lucky winner of a new car or truck. (Left, courtesy of Donna and Laurence McClendon; below, courtesy of DRC.)

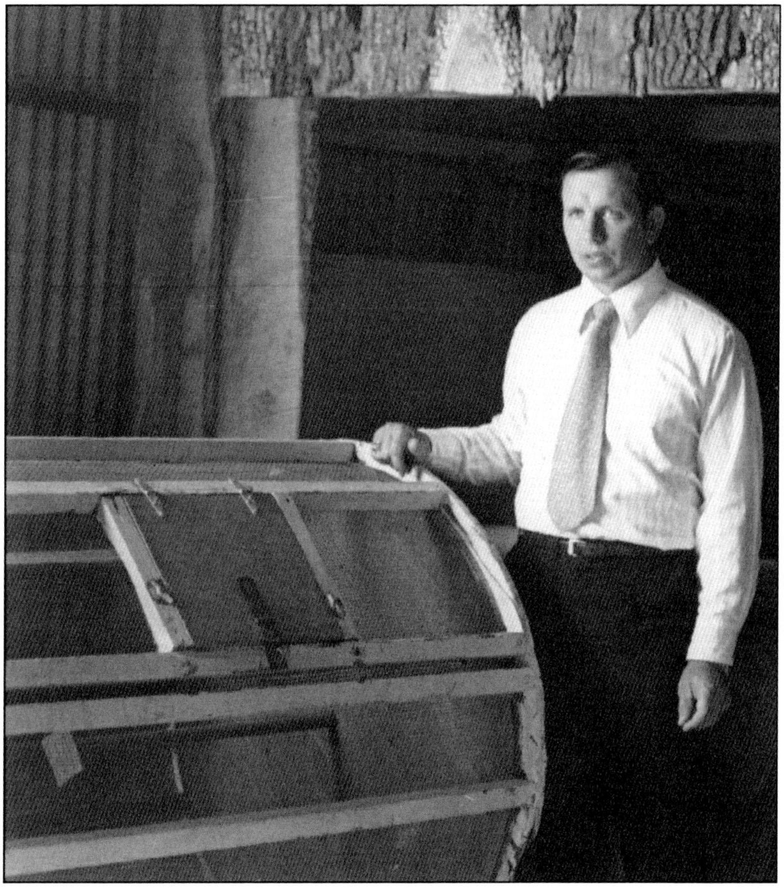

Three

It's Gatherin' Time

Driving On (1960s–1990s)

This chapter begins with the 1960s, a turbulent decade for a nation that found itself at war overseas amidst protests against that war. The fair association continued to struggle to maintain interest in county fairs during these times.

From the 1960s until August 1984, the North Texas State Fair and Rodeo operated under the Denton County Agricultural Fair Association. This agreement remained in place for almost 25 years. In August 1984, the fair began to be led by the North Texas State Fair Association (NTSFA). This change allowed the group to have more universal recognition among other fair associations. In the 1960s, the Denton County Rodeo Association sold their equipment and facilities to the NTSFA.

When Bob Powers joined the fair association in 1971, he provided his professional skills as an accountant and his enthusiasm as a community leader to promote the fair's activities. Powers' dedication and service inspired many others to devote themselves to making the North Texas State Fair and Rodeo (NTSFR) one of the best events in the region.

James Roden took over the helm in 1973 as president of the association, a position he held for 10 years. When Wally Reed, former board president, passed the gavel to Roden, they ushered in a new era of leadership under a paid employee. Over the next 17 years, Roden faced several difficult decisions about how to keep the fair an economically viable venue during a time when many fairs and rodeos experienced waning interest. Roden dealt with these concerns and managed to keep the NTSFR moving forward.

On August 16, 1982, fair stock certificates were converted to membership certificates, and in 1986, the association became a 501(c)(3).

In June 1986, as part of the Texas Sesquicentennial Wagon Train, 87 covered wagons camped overnight at the Denton County Fairgrounds.

Also in 1986, the fair association dreamed of moving to a 125-acre plot off South Locust Street, near Denia, and building a $10 million complex with a 7,000-seat coliseum. Those hopes crumbled when fair officials failed to sell the current 21-acre fairgrounds.

In 1987, the fair was expanded to a nine-day event—to include two weekends—and continued to grow at a steady rate over the next 10 years. In 1996, the fair association purchased an additional 11.5 acres to accommodate the need for additional parking.

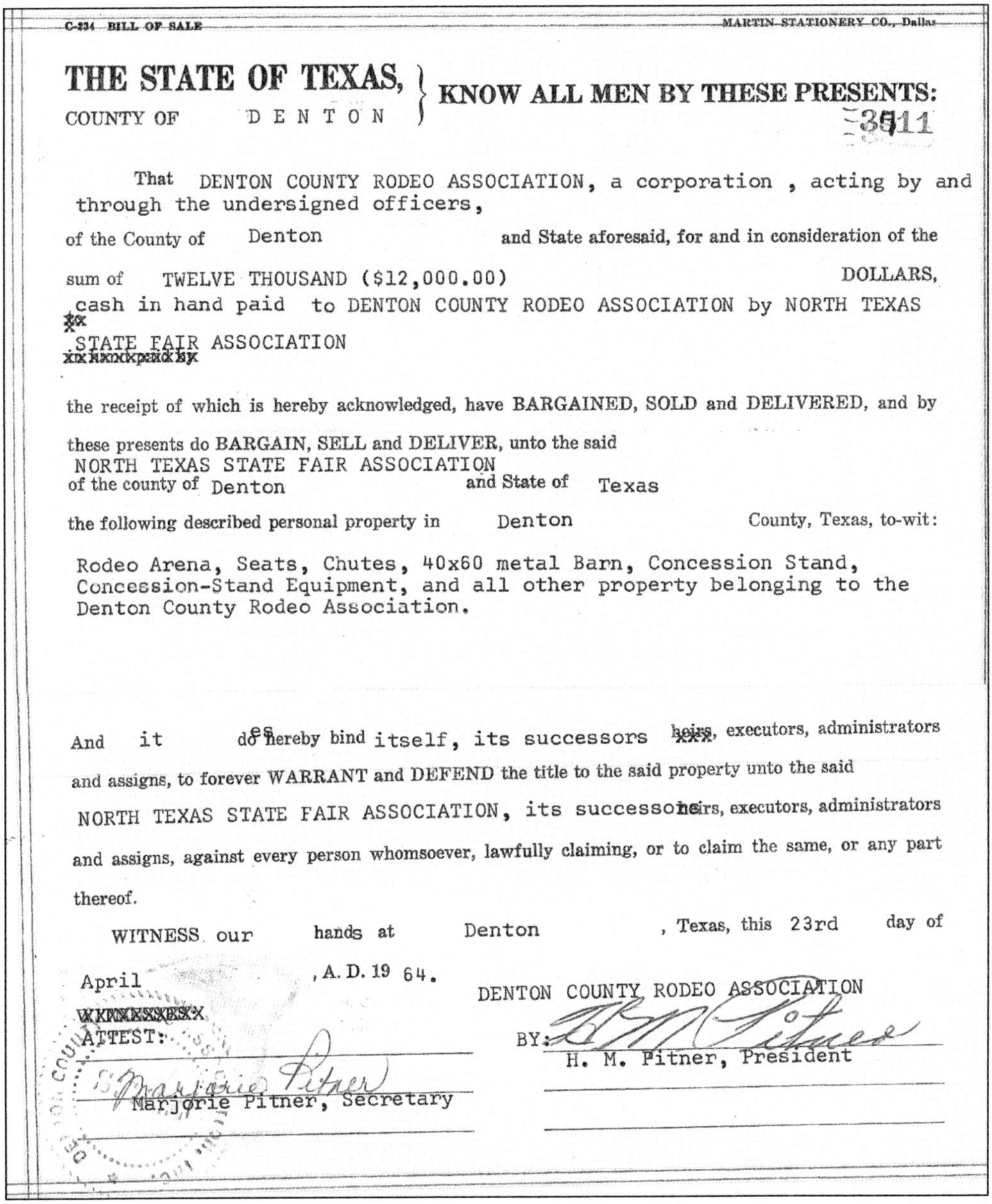

C-234 BILL OF SALE — MARTIN STATIONERY CO., Dallas

THE STATE OF TEXAS, } KNOW ALL MEN BY THESE PRESENTS:
COUNTY OF DENTON }

3511

That DENTON COUNTY RODEO ASSOCIATION, a corporation , acting by and through the undersigned officers,

of the County of Denton and State aforesaid, for and in consideration of the

sum of TWELVE THOUSAND ($12,000.00) DOLLARS,

cash in hand paid to DENTON COUNTY RODEO ASSOCIATION by NORTH TEXAS STATE FAIR ASSOCIATION

the receipt of which is hereby acknowledged, have BARGAINED, SOLD and DELIVERED, and by these presents do BARGAIN, SELL and DELIVER, unto the said NORTH TEXAS STATE FAIR ASSOCIATION

of the county of Denton and State of Texas

the following described personal property in Denton County, Texas, to-wit:

Rodeo Arena, Seats, Chutes, 40x60 metal Barn, Concession Stand, Concession-Stand Equipment, and all other property belonging to the Denton County Rodeo Association.

And it does hereby bind itself, its successors heirs, executors, administrators and assigns, to forever WARRANT and DEFEND the title to the said property unto the said NORTH TEXAS STATE FAIR ASSOCIATION, its successors heirs, executors, administrators and assigns, against every person whomsoever, lawfully claiming, or to claim the same, or any part thereof.

WITNESS our hands at Denton , Texas, this 23rd day of April , A. D. 19 64.

DENTON COUNTY RODEO ASSOCIATION

ATTEST:

Marjorie Pitner
Marjorie Pitner, Secretary

BY: H M Pitner
H. M. Pitner, President

SELLING THE DENTON COUNTY RODEO ASSOCIATION. H.M. and Marjorie Pitner, as founders and board members of the DCRA, which built the rodeo arena at the fairgrounds, were instrumental in selling the contents of the fairgrounds—including the rodeo arena, seats, chutes, metal barn, concession stand, and equipment—to the North Texas State Fair Association NTSFA for $12,000 in 1964. This money provided for many needed improvements to the fairground facilities. (Courtesy of NTFR.)

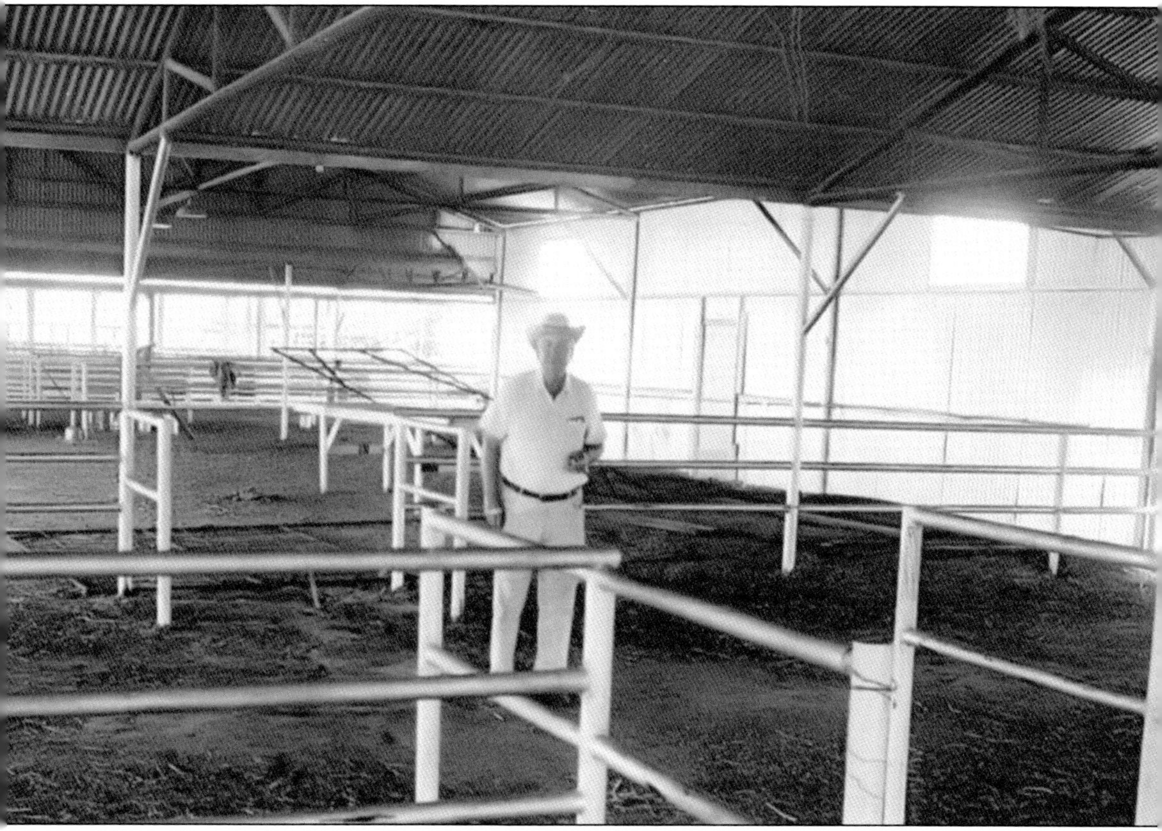

WITH A LITTLE HELP FROM OUR FRIENDS. During the 1960s, the Lions Club of Denton partnered with the fair. Members of the club took tickets at the carnival and at the gates. Lions Club member Harry Owens, pictured here in the livestock barns, later formulated a plan with rodeo chairman Weldon Burgoon to add a youth rodeo event, "21 and Under," to the program to increase attendance. (Courtesy of DCOHC.)

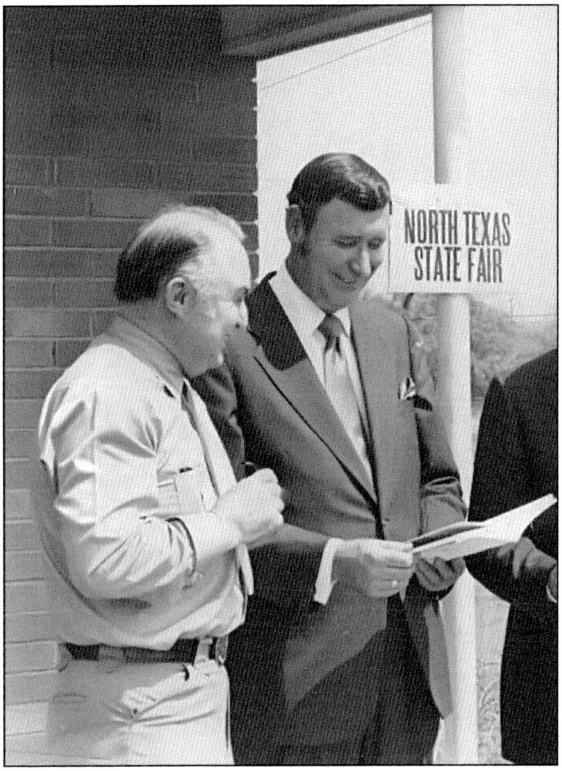

PARADE PREPARATIONS. In the 1971 photograph at left, Rex Cauble (left) and Carnie Marsh, North Texas State Fair and Rodeo parade chairman, are standing in front of the fair office making final preparations for the parade. Cauble owned two upscale Western wear retail stores called Cutter Bill's Western World, named after his famous cutting horse, Cutter Bill. Lt. Gov. Ben Barnes was the 1971 grand marshal and rode Cutter Bill in the parade. The photograph below reflects the immense efforts of the parade committee and community. The North Texas Fairgrounders led the parade around the square displaying the six flags that have flown over Texas. (Left, courtesy of DRC; below, courtesy of NTFR.)

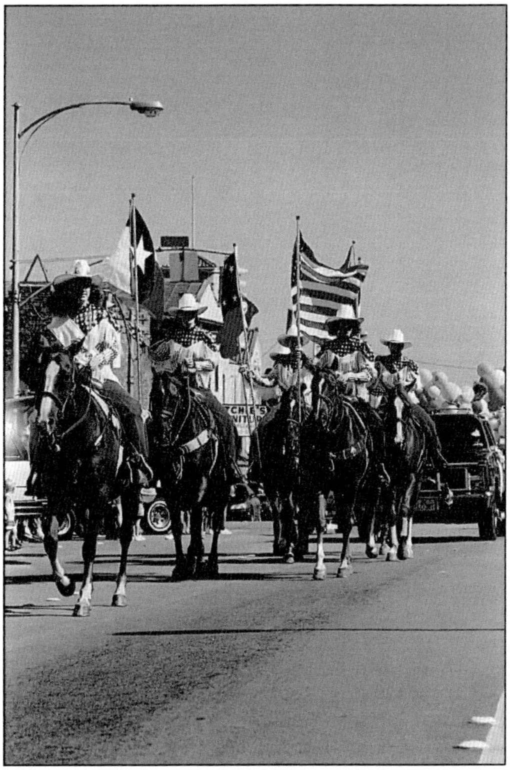

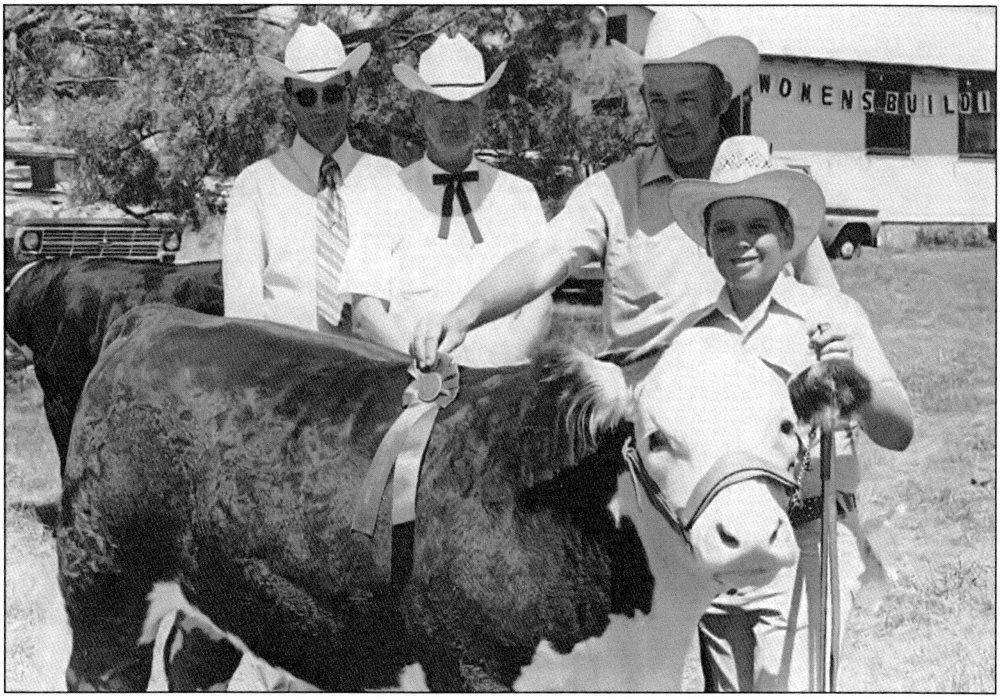

Best of the Rest. In the above photograph, the 1971 Youth Stock Grand Champion Hereford winner, John South, is shown with, from left to right, Odis Lowe, Perry Burns, and Tim Reeves. South went on to become the Denton County assistant extension agent from 1971 to 1973 before moving to Decatur to serve 14 years in Wise County. He retired in 2001 after 14 years in Fort Worth serving as the Tarrant County agent. Fair Hall, shown in the background, was used for women's exhibitions when this photograph was taken. Dr. E.D. Fyke is shown in the below photograph with his grand champion Shetland Stallion. (Above, courtesy of DRC; below, courtesy of NTFR.)

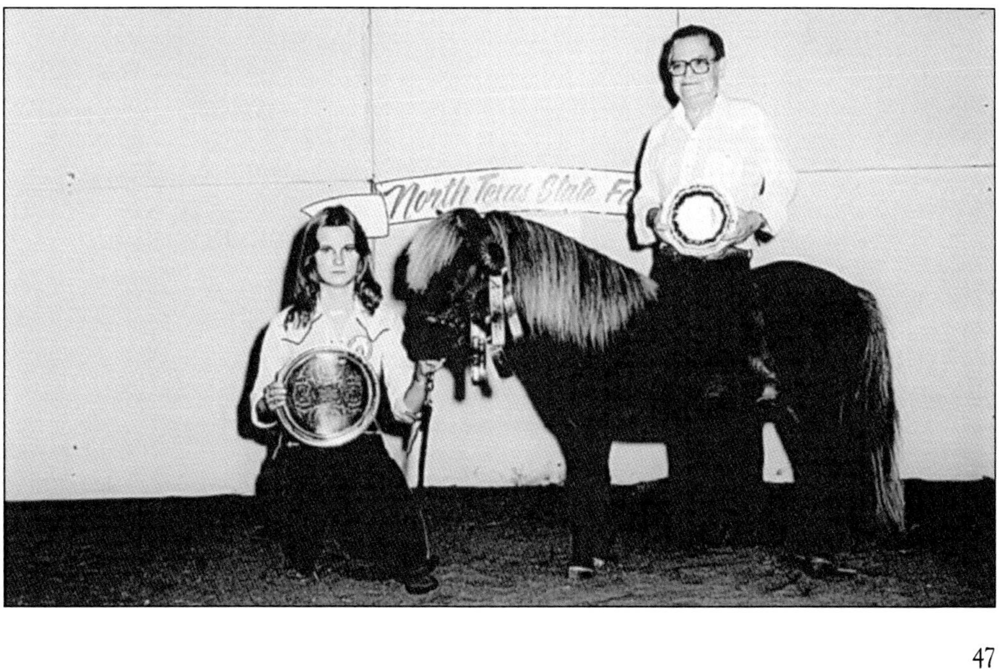

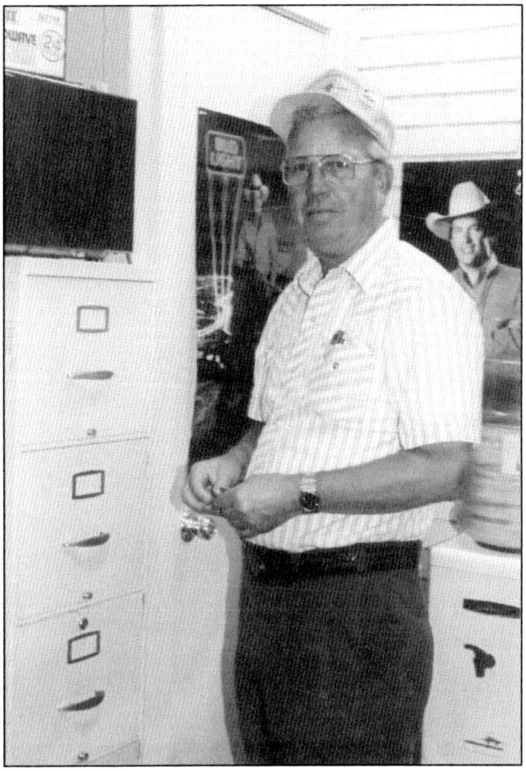

The Power of Service. Bobby "Bob" Calvin Powers (1932–1995), shown here in his signature white North Texas State Fair ball cap, joined the fair association in 1971 and was appointed director in charge of the first barbeque cook-off in 1975. Renowned barbeque cook Ed Bradford was one of the three cooks in the inaugural contest. Powers served as vice president of the association, and in 1980, he became the treasurer for the fair. (Courtesy of NTFR.)

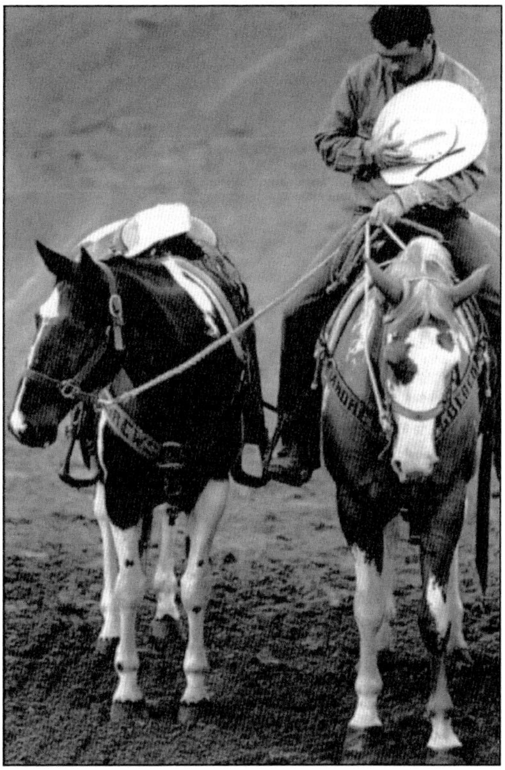

A Tribute to a Beloved Board Member. Bob Powers was at the fairgrounds when he suffered a massive fatal heart attack in 1995. In the photograph at right, Glenn Carlton, NTSFA board member and rodeo chairman, bows his head in tribute to Bob Powers during a riderless horse ceremony held at the beginning of the rodeo. (Courtesy of DRC.)

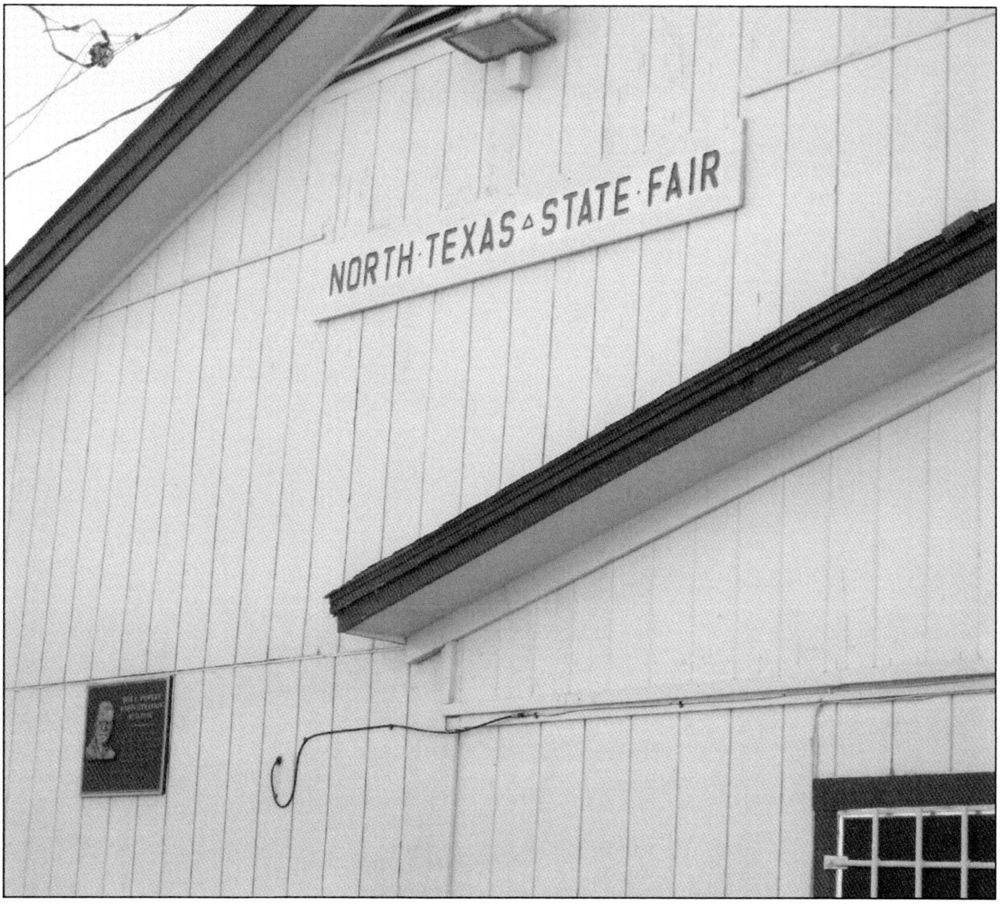

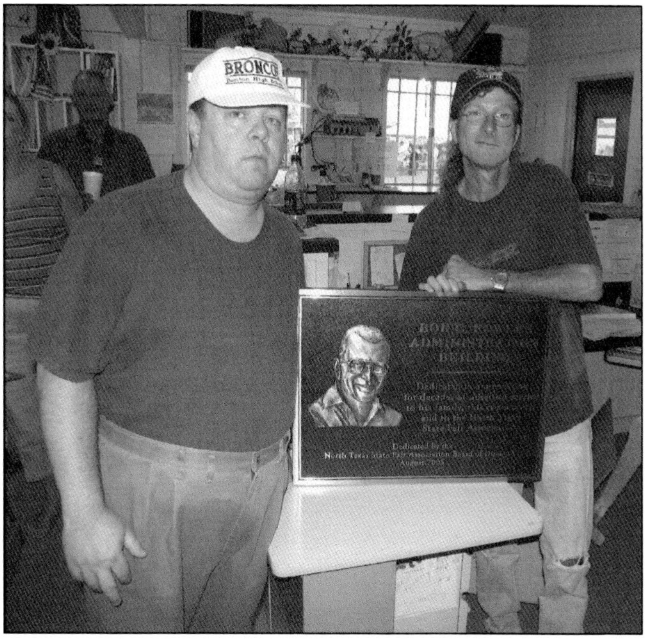

Honoring Bob C. Powers. Powers's wife, Gloria, and the fair board of directors created the Bob C. Powers Scholarship after his death to assist high school graduates with tuition at a junior college or university. Since that time, 10 annual scholarships have been given to deserving students. As further acknowledgement of Powers's contributions to the fair, the Bob C. Powers Administration Building was dedicated in his honor in 2005. At right, Powers's sons Michael (left) and Troy (right) are shown inside Bob's namesake building holding the plaque that is now mounted on the outside. (Both, courtesy of NTFR.)

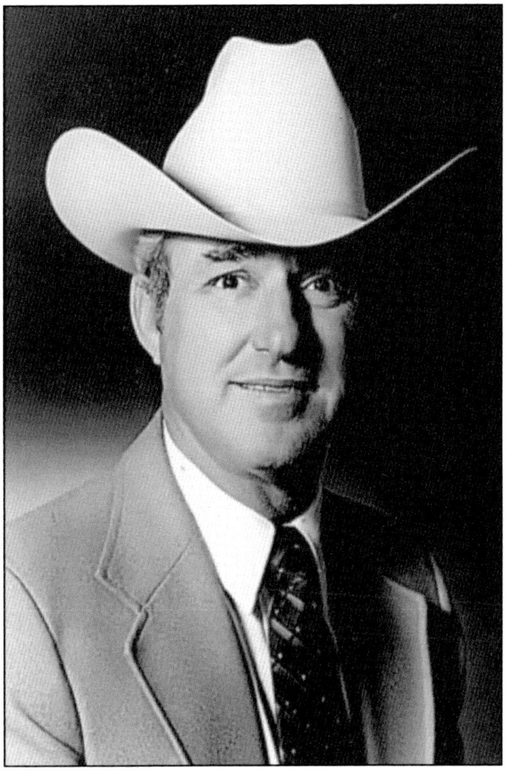

JAMES RODEN, FIRST EXECUTIVE DIRECTOR. James Roden was president of the Denton County Agricultural Fair Association (DCAFA) from 1973 until 1983 and served as president of the Texas Association of Fairs & Events (TAF&E). On June 16, 1981, the board amended the original articles of incorporation to officially change the name of the corporation from DCAFA to the North Texas State Fair Association (NTSFA). Roden, the first paid executive director of the NTSFA, served from 1983 until January 2000. (Courtesy of NTFR.)

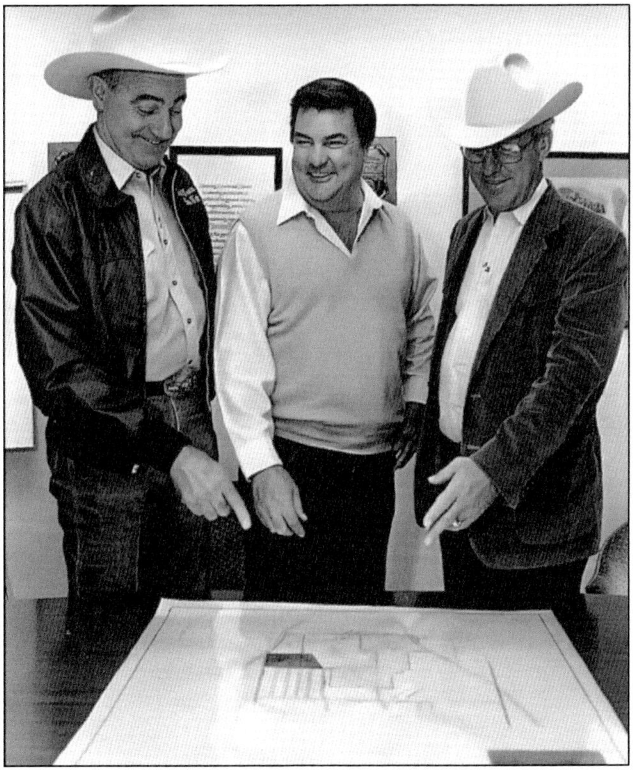

PLANNING FOR THE FUTURE. In 1986, James Roden sought a one-percent increase in Denton hotel occupancy tax funds to assist with securing a site and constructing a multipurpose exposition center on 125 acres in Denton's Denia area. Shown looking at the plat of the proposed location are Weldon Burgoon (left), Newton Rayzor (center), and Roden. The exposition center never came to fruition because the current fairgrounds property failed to sell. (Courtesy of DRC.)

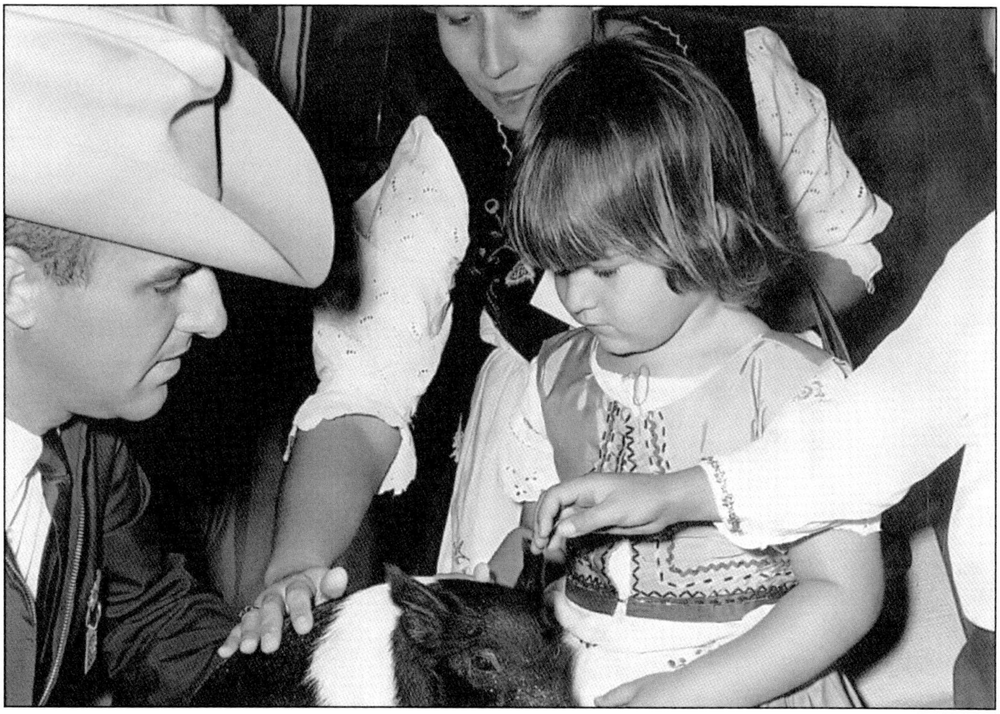

Roden's Children's Barnyard. James Roden delighted in having a children's educational area that included cow-milking demonstrations, chickens hatching, suckling piglets, and other farm animals in a lifelike agrarian setting. He understood the importance of youth involvement, including junior livestock shows such as those affiliated with FFA and 4-H programs. Roden poses above with costumed young dancers who performed on stage and a piglet from the children's barnyard exhibit. The 1985 photograph below shows an unidentified child hugging his beloved Charolais heifer. (Above, courtesy of NTFR; below, courtesy of DCOHC.)

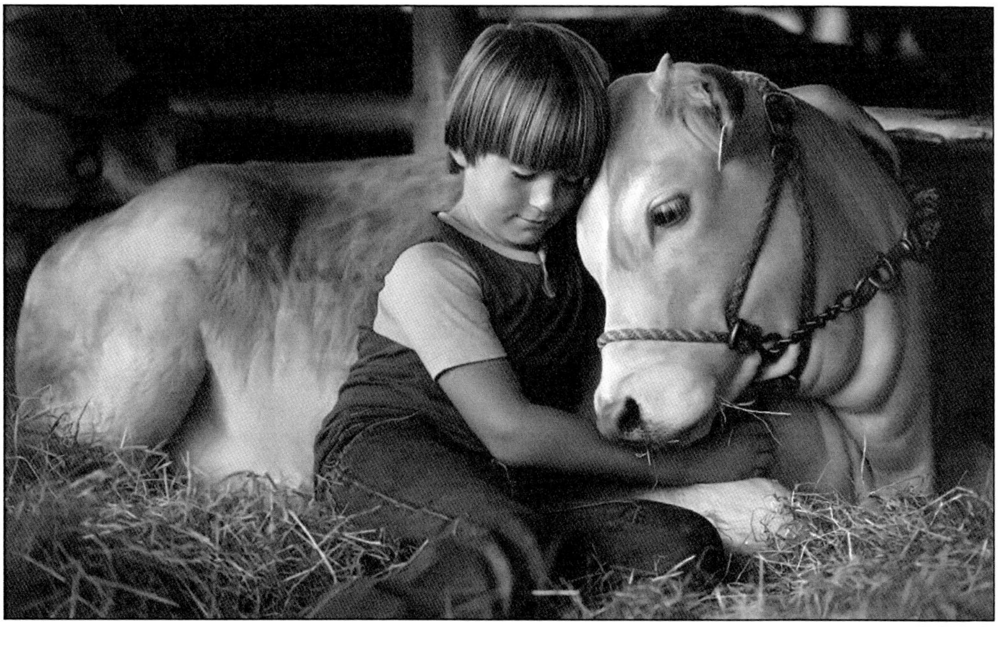

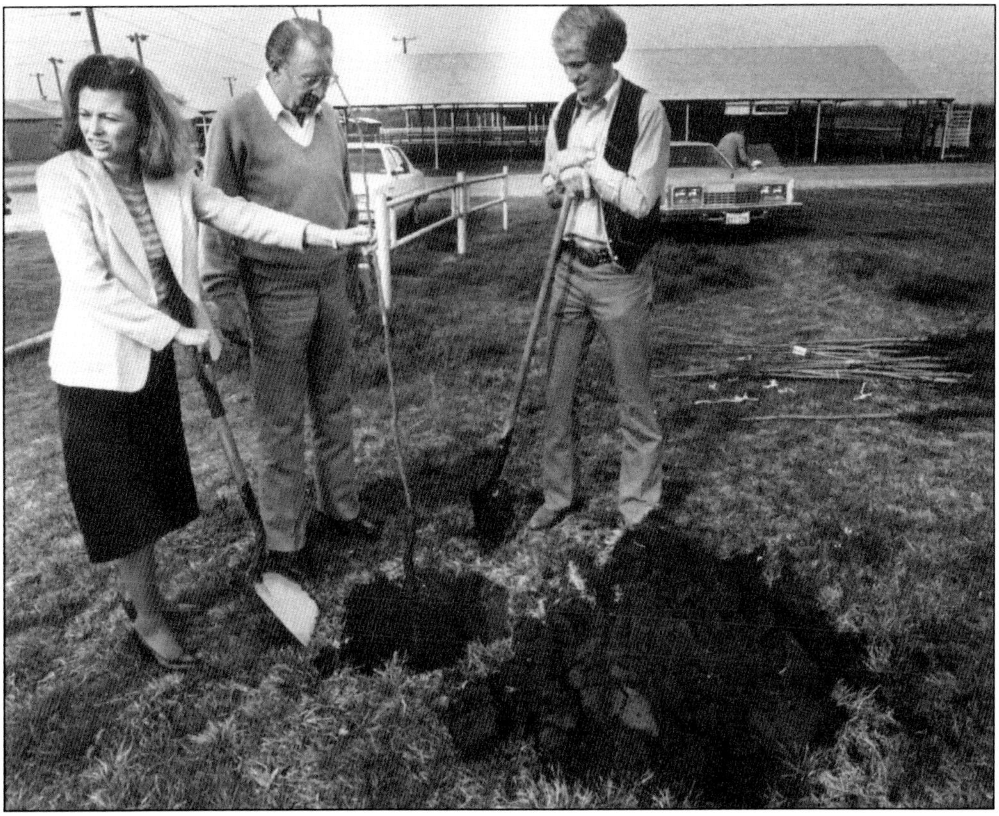

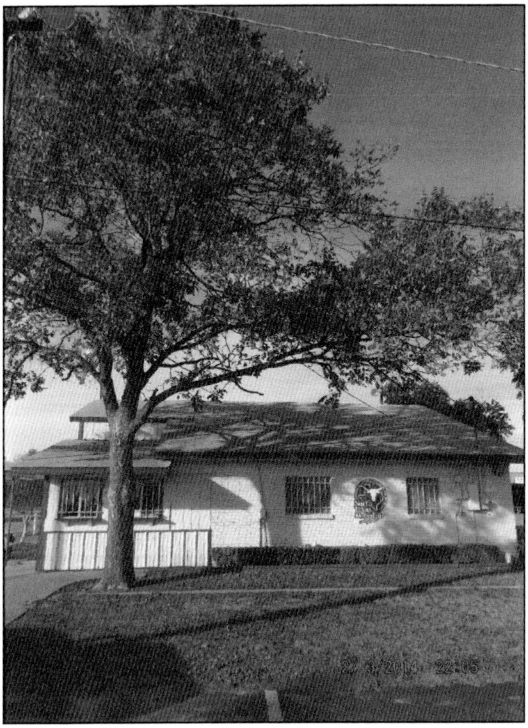

Planting Pecan Trees for Posterity. As shown in the above image, Kathy Orr (left), a member of the North Texas State Fair Association's board of directors, along with "Pinky" Harpool (center) and Stanley Lovelace, both members of the agribusiness committee of the chamber of commerce, planted a pecan tree outside the fair office in 1982. Harpool Seed donated the tree. The pecan tree is native to Texas and is the official state tree. This same pecan tree still shades the Bob C. Powers Administration Building and has provided pecans for many delicious pecan pies for fair officials. (Above, courtesy of DRC; left, courtesy of NTFR.)

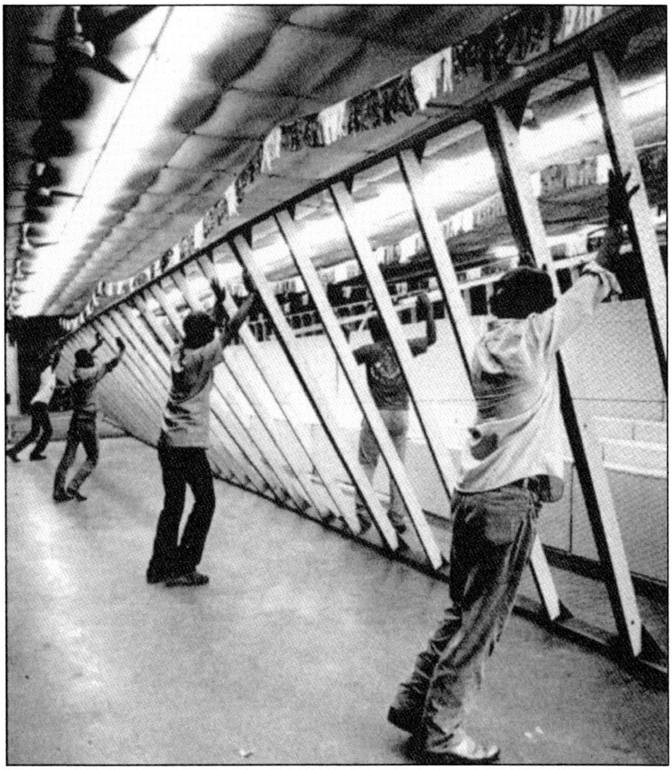

Displaying their Wares. It takes about four days to set up the commercial exhibit area and two days to decorate the exhibit hall. Volunteers and hired laborers secure structures for display areas and divide the building into commercial exhibit booth space for vendors. The number of vendors has grown to more than 80 over the years. Since the earliest days of the fair, the arts and crafts area has served as an important venue for women to show off their handiwork and compete for ribbons and premiums. Today's creative arts department is divided into needlework, arts and crafts, home-canned food, antiques, and junior entries. (Right, courtesy of DRC; below, courtesy of NTFR.)

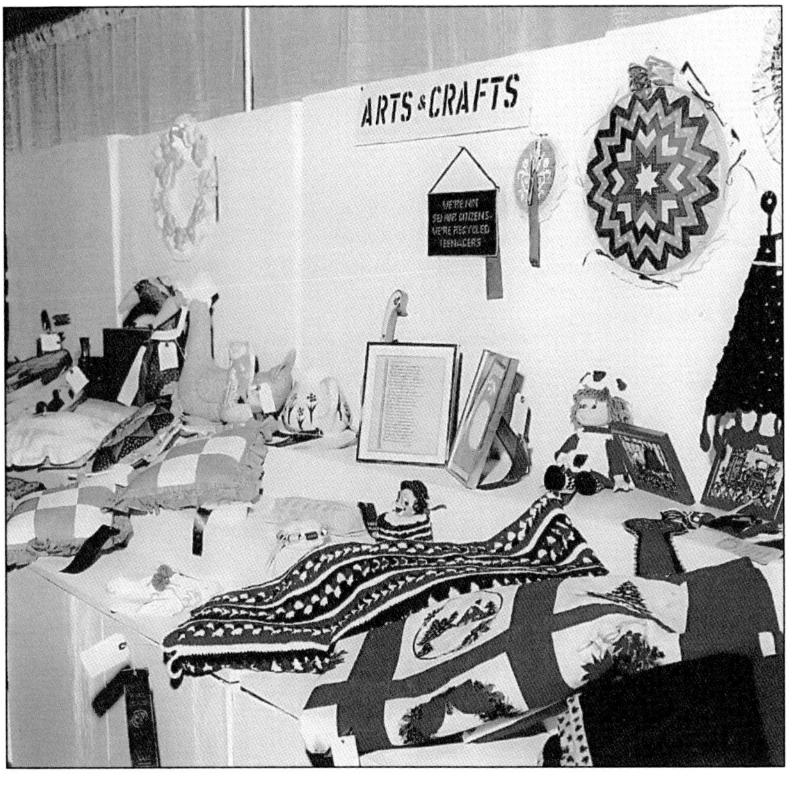

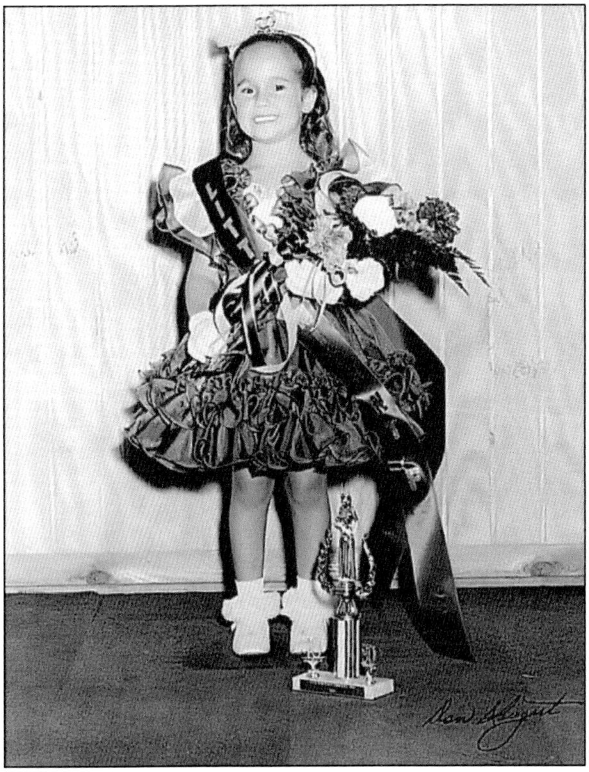

Beauty Pageant. Longtime fair advocate and board member Melvin Haisler and his wife, Joneen, started the North Texas State Fair Beauty Pageant in 1979. Categories included Little Miss, Miss Teen, and Miss North Texas State Fair. In 1986, Nanci Kimmey became chairman of the contests and added Junior Miss. The contestants are judged on beauty, poise, and personality, and the winner is given flowers, a savings bond, a sash, and a trophy, plus she represents the fair for a year at various community events, including the annual parade. At left, Little Miss Lindsay Knox proudly holds her bouquet and trophy. Casey Krueger (Jones) from Denton was crowned Junior Miss in the late 1980s. She and her husband, Ethan, appeared on The Learning Channel's program, *Quints By Surprise*, when they had five babies in 2009. (Both, courtesy of NTFR.)

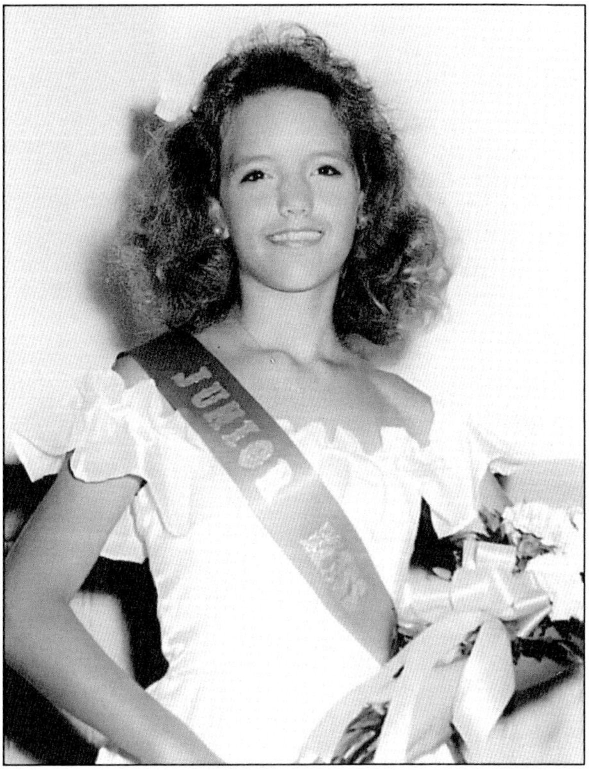

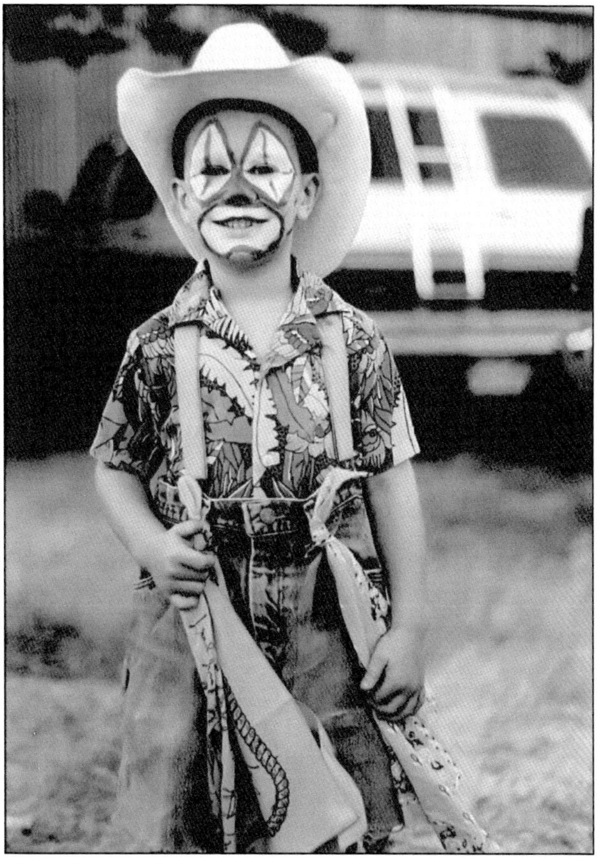

Rodeo Kids Clowns. The 1988 Rodeo Kids Clown contest attracted several children who dressed up like their favorite rodeo clowns. Moms and professional rodeo bullfighters help these kids to achieve an authentic look by creating costumes that mimic rodeo clowns, who, with their outrageous garb and courageous actions, get in front of bulls to divert them away from unprotected cowboys. Cody Bullock (right) is all dressed up for the judging. Five-year-old Cory Sanders (below), of Aubrey, stands with his father while waiting to enter the contest. Sanders took second place in the five-and-under category. (Right, courtesy of NTFR; below, courtesy of DRC.)

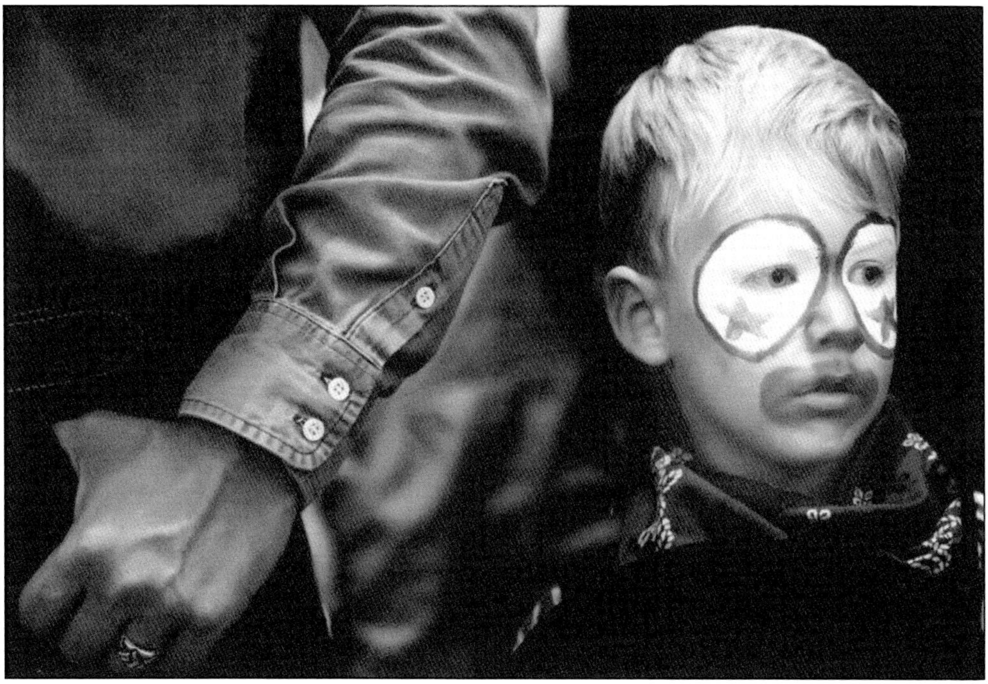

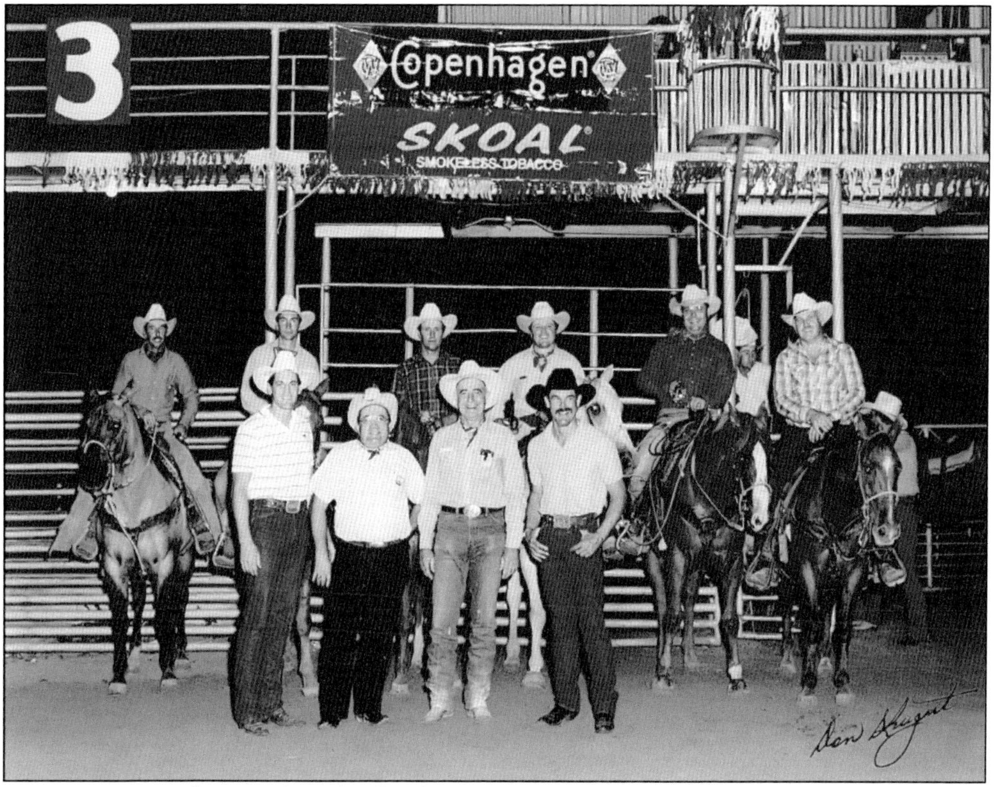

RANCH RODEO. The Ranch Rodeo has been an important part of the North Texas State Fair and Rodeo since the 1980s. In the Ranch Rodeo competition, cowboys from area ranches vie against each other for bragging rights in events such as team branding, team doctoring, maverick catch-in, team sorting, and bronc riding. Cowboys, like the three unidentified competitors shown below, demonstrate the day-to-day skills required for survival on a ranch in the Old West. Pictured above are, from left to right, (standing) Randy Vaughn, with Copenhagen Skoal; Al Croix, Denton County extension agent; Weldon Burgoon, rodeo chairman; and Darrel Barron, with Copenhagen Skoal; (on horseback) the Ranch Rodeo team of Jerry Blocker, Mike Bullock, Jimmy Brazil, Warren Hudspeth, Joe Powell, and Sam Voss. (Above, courtesy of NTFR; below, courtesy of DCOHC.)

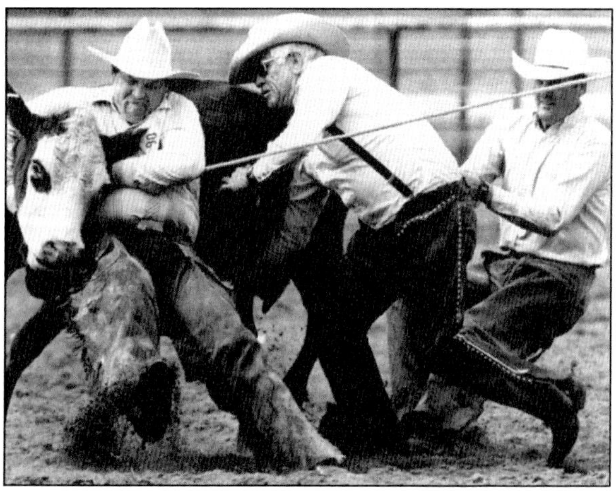

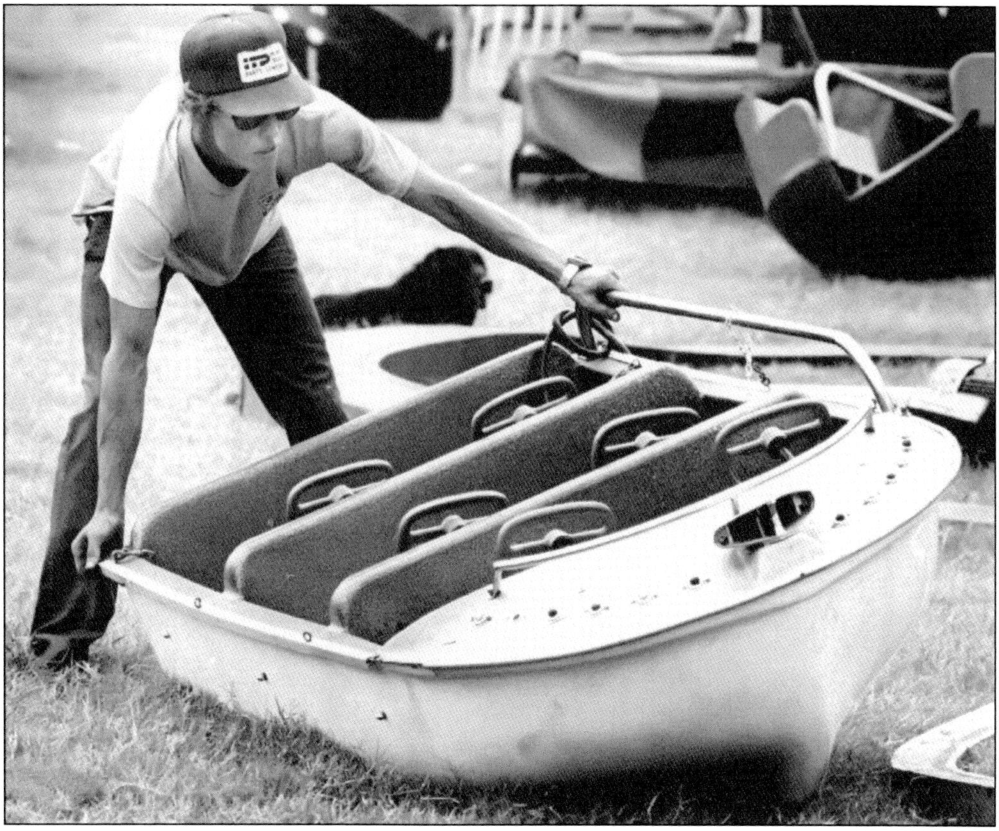

Boat Rides. Carnival or amusement rides provide thrills and spills and are an important part of any fair to provide fun entertainment for children and adults. These mechanical structures either spin on a vertical axis, like the carousel, or ride at ground level, like bumper cars. Other rides defy gravity, like the spindle top or round-up, and yet others move their passengers vertically around a fixed point, such as Ferris wheels. Curtis Erwin (above) is setting up a boat ride in the children's area. Below, Venus Gonzales is giving an elephant a bath in preparation for opening day. (Both, courtesy of DRC.)

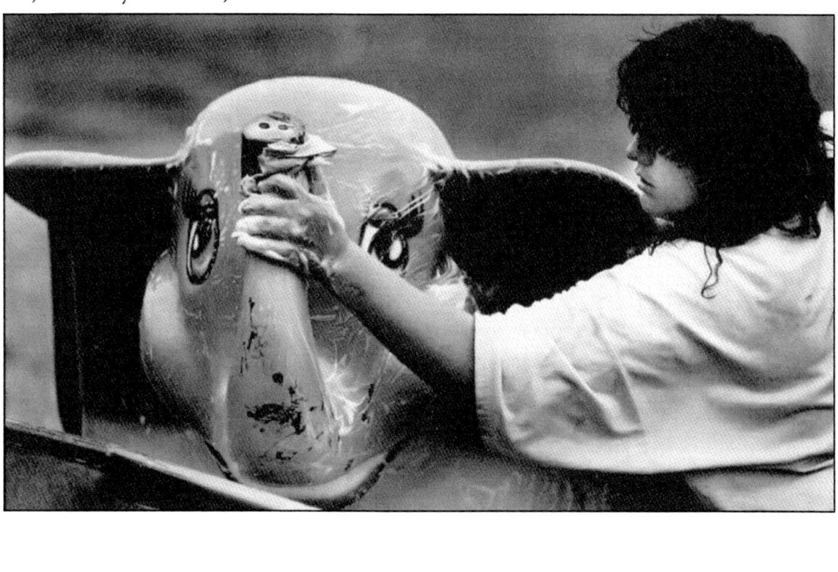

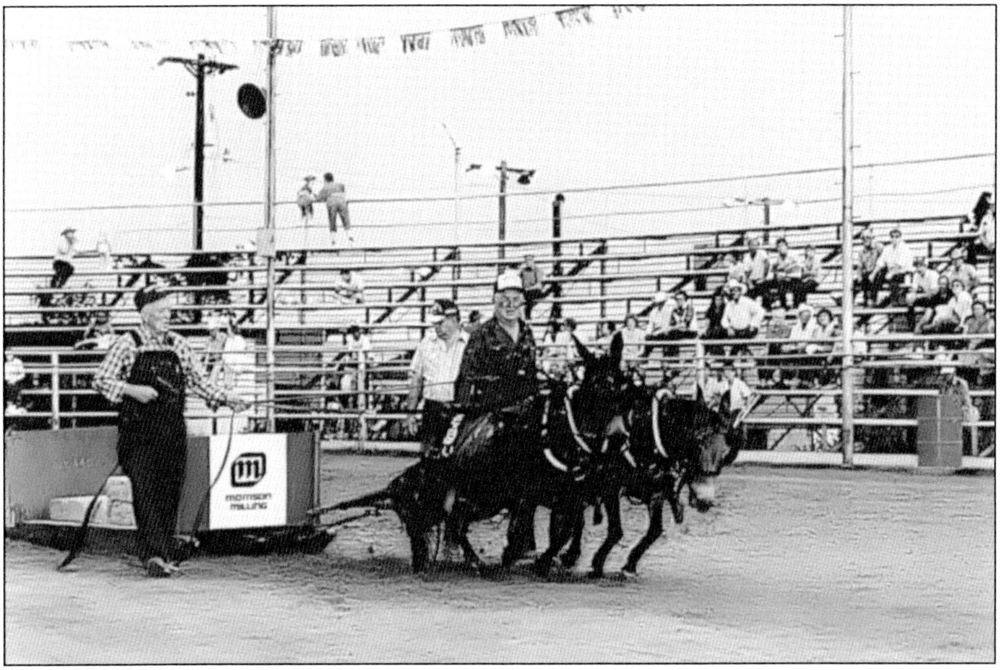

Mule-Pulling Competition. The mule-pulling contest is an opportunity for proud owners of these sure-footed, intelligent animals to claim bragging rights for whose mules are the strongest and have the ability to drag the heaviest weight. Mule trainer Wade London (pictured below) described these sturdy animals as "cantankerous, but [with] a heart of gold [that] will also kick your head off." These photographs show teams of mules pulling sleighs of concrete or salt blocks weighing more than twice their body mass. (Both, courtesy of NTFR.)

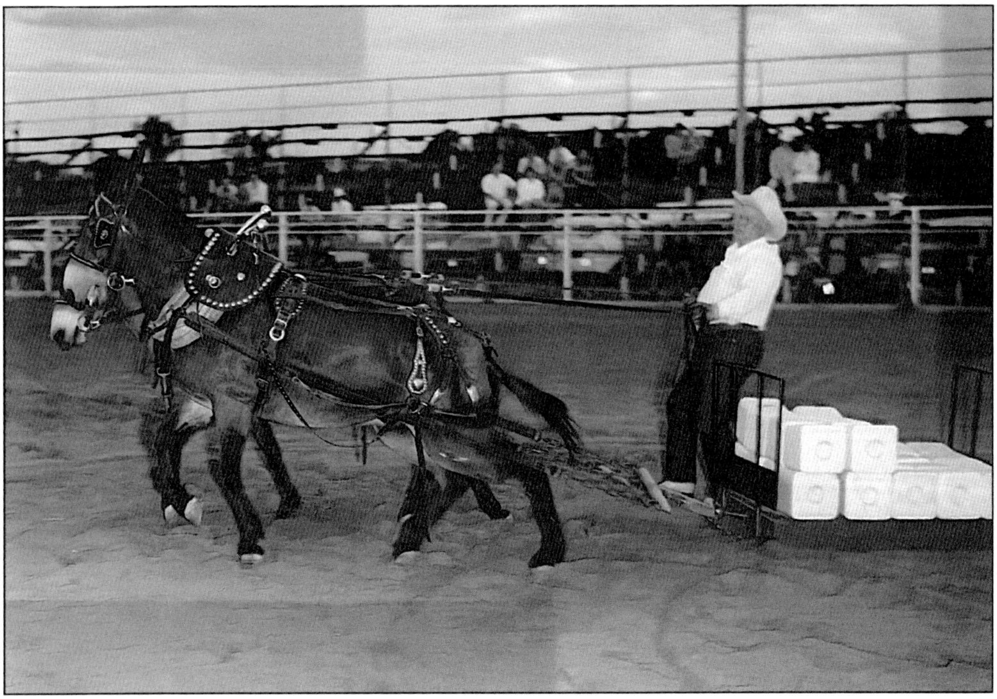

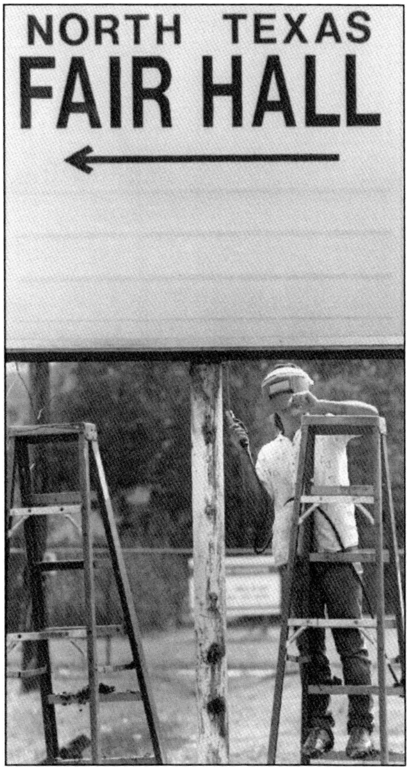

A Sign by Any Other Name. A controversy ensued between the City of Denton and the fair association in 1990, when the fair installed a new directional sign within the fairgrounds to point attendees toward Fair Hall. The city claimed that the sign did not meet city ordinances for height restrictions and was an advertising sign, not a directional sign. At right, Mike Gillan, of Starlite Sign Company, works on the new sign donated by Amyx Excavation, A&M Plumbing, and Starlite Sign. Eventually, the fair association prevailed, and the sign remained. James Roden is pictured below with the sign. (Both, courtesy of DRC.)

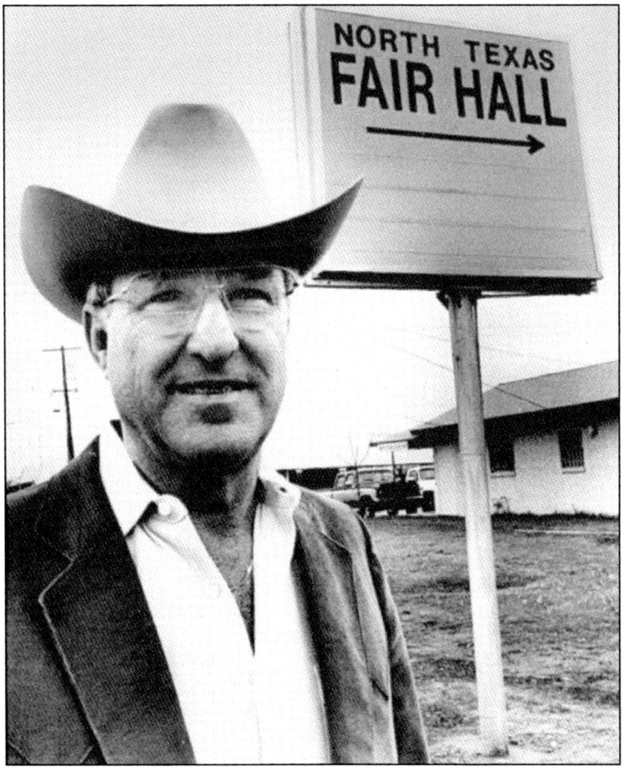

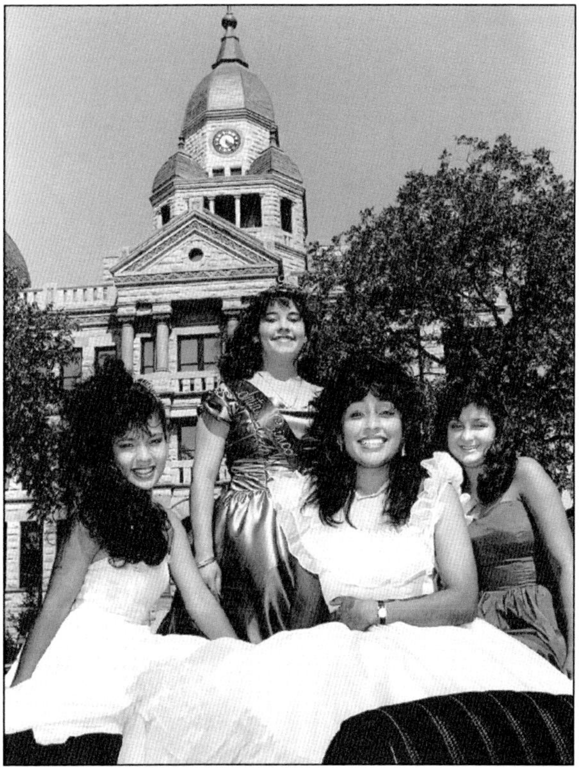

Hispanic Heritage at the Fair. The North Texas State Fair and Rodeo parade included the Srita Cinco de Mayo y Princesas float. The 1988 queen was Berenice Long (standing in the image at left). She is pictured with her court of princesses, from left to right, Trini Lopez, Minerva Simental, and Janie Silva. These beautiful young ladies were featured guests during Hispanic Heritage Day at the beginning of the fair. Fairgoers enjoy strolling mariachis, Hispanic musicians in traditional costumes, and a popular Latino performer on the main stage. Bobby Pulido (below), winner of Album of the Year and Male Entertainer of the Year at the 1997 Tejano Music Awards, has appeared at the fair. (Left, courtesy of DRC; below, courtesy of NTFR.)

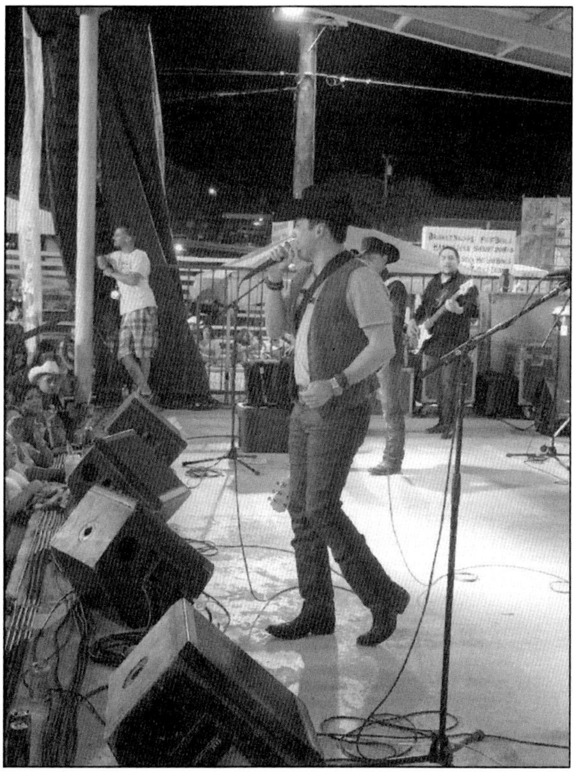

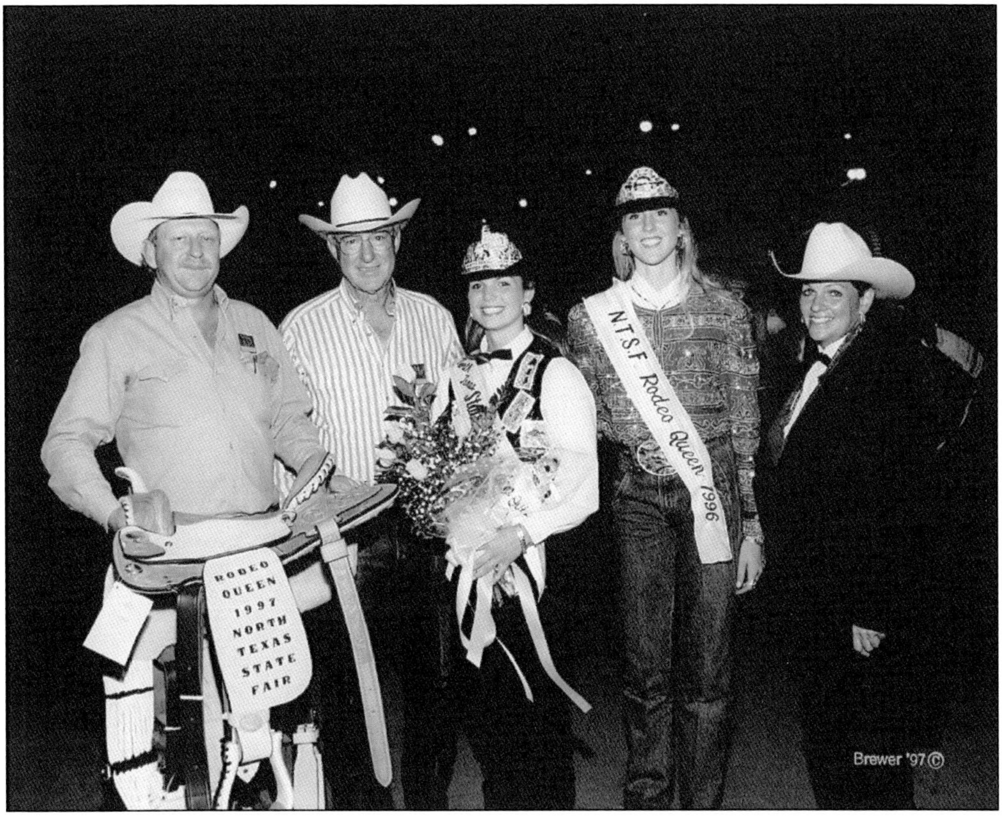

QUEEN AND QUEEN MUM. Becoming rodeo queen has been an ambition of many cowgirls. Codie Counts (at center in the above photograph) was named North Texas State Fair rodeo queen in 1997. Candidates for rodeo queen must compete in the areas of horsemanship, appearance, speaking ability, and personality. Counts is shown with, from left to right, board member Mark Foster, fair executive director James Roden, 1996 rodeo queen Jill Shaw, and rodeo queen coordinator Candice Clark. Clark's exemplary rodeo queen programs were recognized as a model for many other statewide competitions. Clark (pictured at right) served as rodeo queen coordinator from 1995 until her untimely death in an automobile accident in 2007. (Both, courtesy of NTFR.)

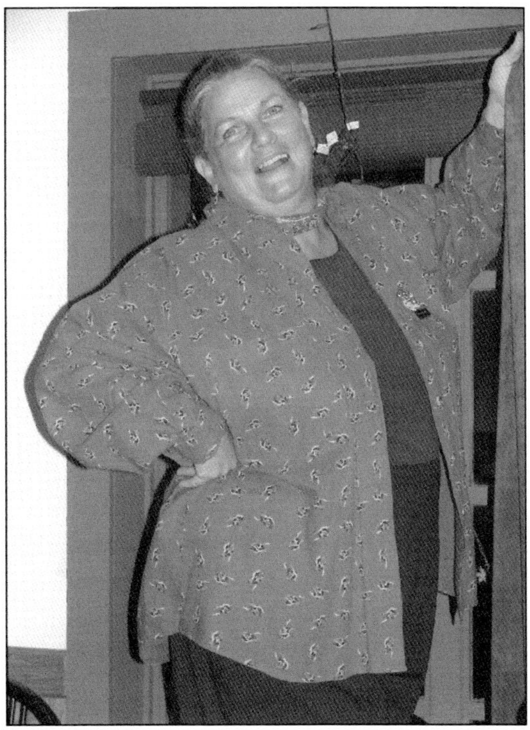

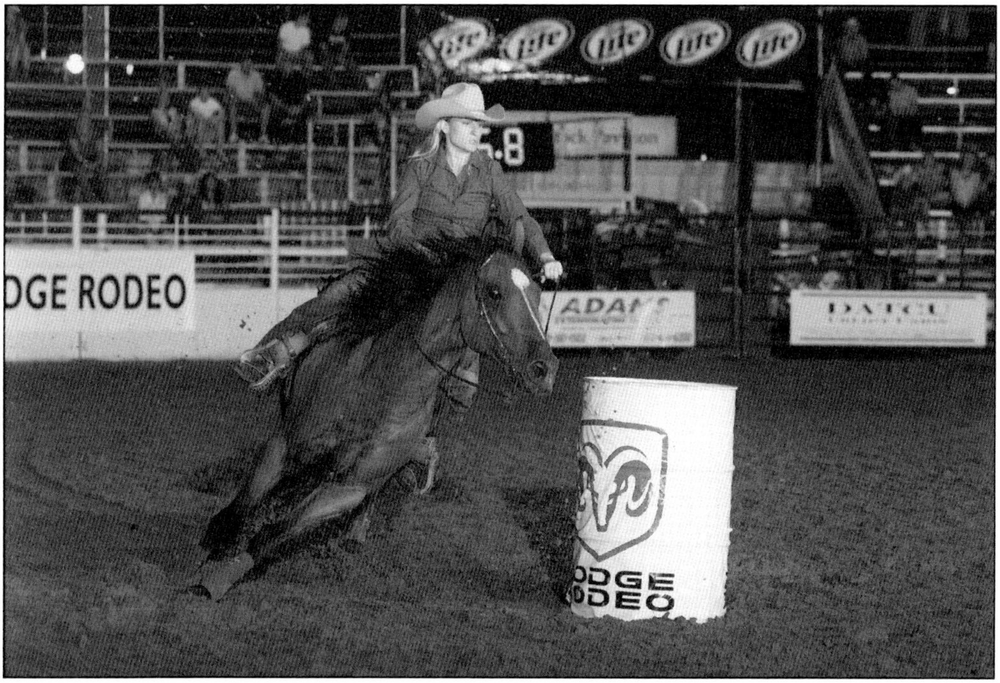

Barrel Racing. Barrel racing is primarily a rodeo event for women. It combines a horse's athletic ability and the horsemanship skills of the rider as he or she safely and successfully maneuvers a horse in a cloverleaf pattern around three barrels placed in a triangle in the center of the arena. The above photograph shows a racer in perfect form as she speeds around the last barrel. Unfortunately, the cowgirl in the below photograph knocked over one of her three barrels, adding a five-point penalty to her score. (Both, courtesy of NTFR.)

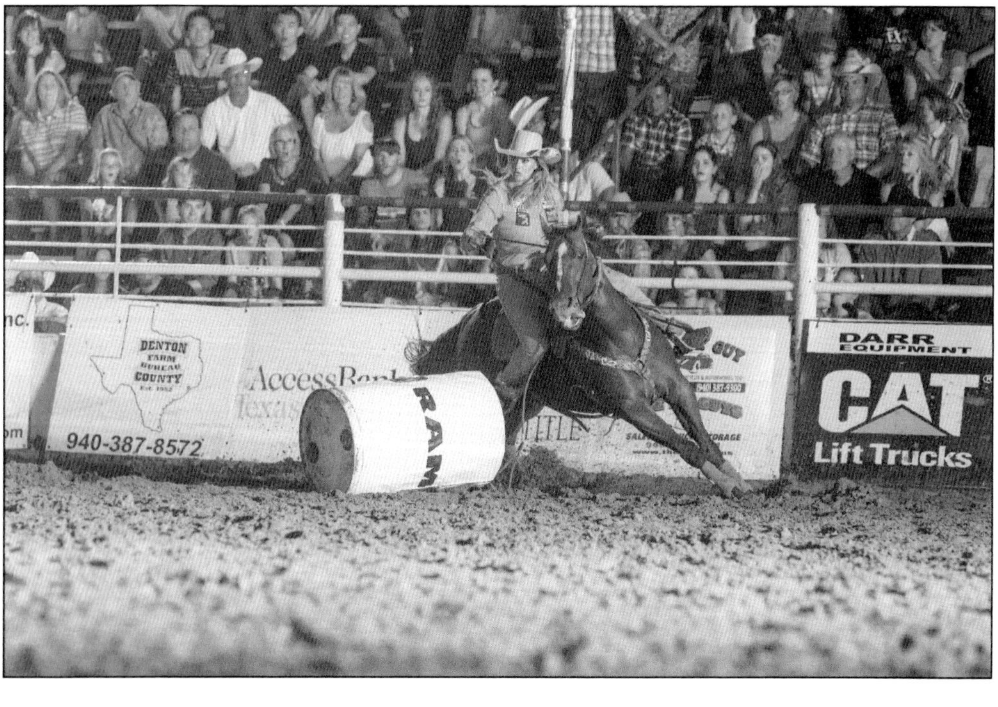

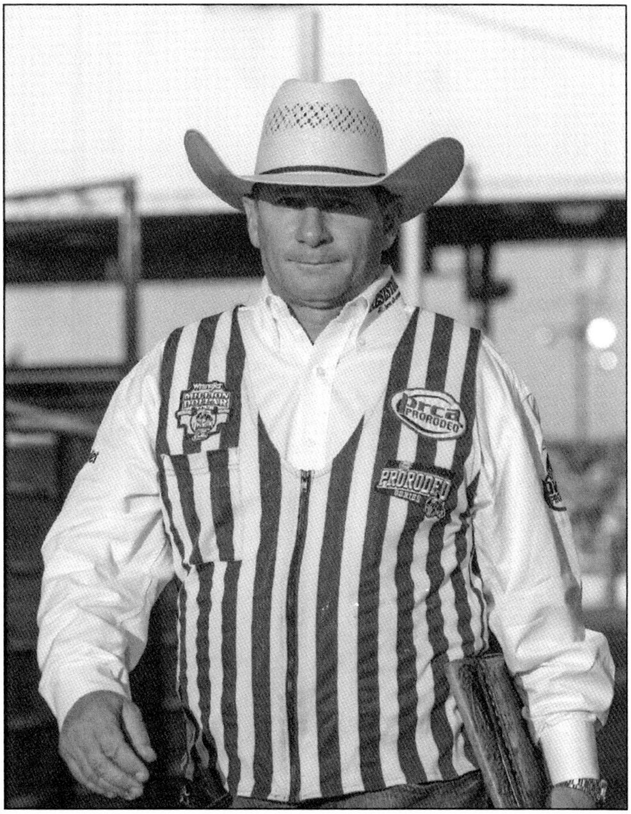

Professional Rodeo Cowboys Association (PRCA) Achievement. The NTSFR achieved PRCA sanctioning in 1989. The PRCA commands higher purses, which consequently attracts nationally known pro athletes and stock to their arenas. The PRCA endorses rodeos in 37 states and three Canadian provinces. All roads lead to the annual Wrangler National Finals Rodeo in Las Vegas. This photograph is of PRCA official Gary Case. (Courtesy of NTFR.)

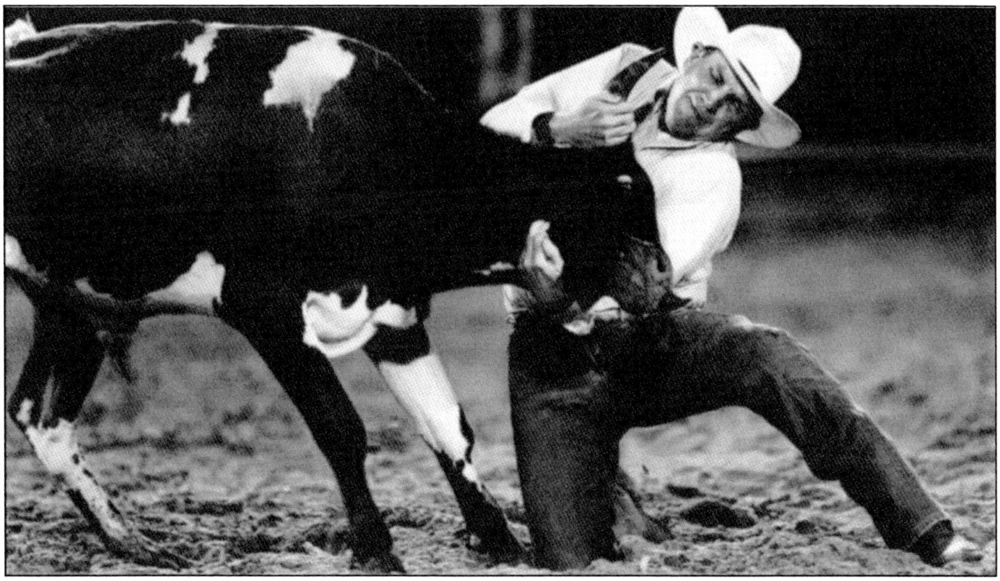

Steer Wrestling. Steer wrestling, also known as bull dogging, seems simple enough. Drop from a horse, grab a steer by the horns, and wrestle it to the ground, stopping the clock as quickly as possible. Timing, technique, strength, and the horsemanship of the hazer (a rider on horseback who guides the steer in a straight path for the cowboy) are necessary for a win. Brian Hudson is shown here wrestling a steer and hoping for a fast time. (Courtesy of DRC at DCOHC.)

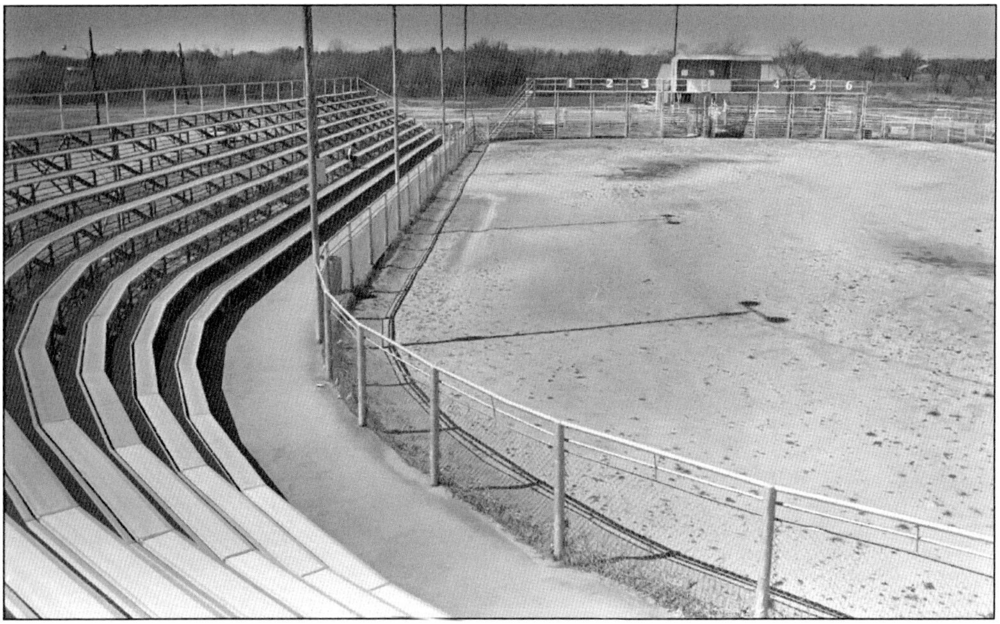

Oh, Chute! In the early 1980s, the original wooden bleachers were replaced with aluminum seating that held approximately 3,000 rodeo fans. The bucking chutes were updated with WW equipment, and the roping box was moved to the east end of the arena. Twenty separate back pens can now house the rodeo stock that arrives at fair time. The current arena measures 230 feet by 150 feet. (Courtesy of DCOHC.)

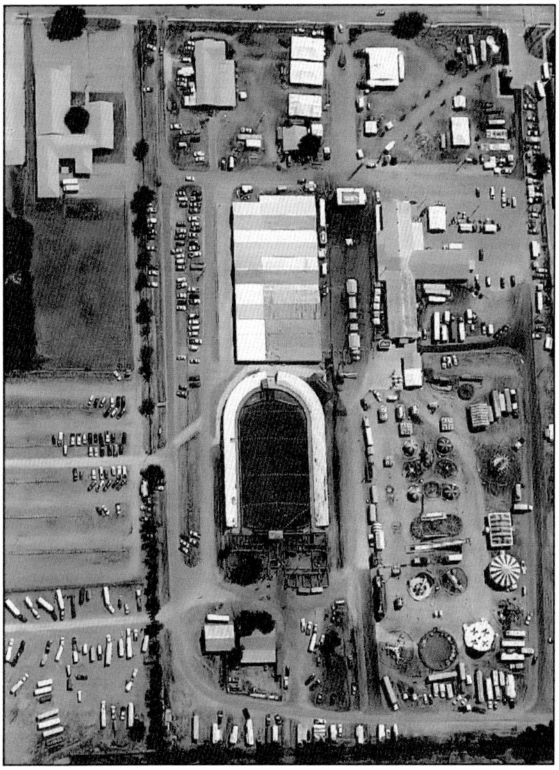

Overhead of Fairgrounds. This 1984 aerial view shows the existing 21-acre fairgrounds. Pictured are, from lower left (counterclockwise), the carnival, the T-shaped commercial exhibit building, the Kid's Zone, Fair Hall in the Fun Zone, the livestock barns, and the rodeo arena. The main stage and concession stands are at center. Eleven acres of parking space are north of the rodeo arena. (Courtesy of NTFR.)

Four

Saddle Up
Transition Years (2000–2004)

James Roden, the first paid executive director of the North Texas State Fair Association (NTSFA), developed the fair into a growing business of livestock shows, rodeos, and commercial exhibits. Upon Roden's retirement in 2000, Ken Burdick began the process of taking the fair and rodeo to the next level.

The Burdick years were some of the most productive years for the fair, with changes that included upgrading entertainment, increasing rodeo venues, enhancing the children's area, and updating the fair's facilities. Burdick created the Kid's Zone so that young boys and girls could experience what it was like to be a cowboy/cowgirl in a safe environment and with animals just their size.

Burdick brought his experience as an executive with Lone Star Gas, the Denton Chamber of Commerce's Economic Development department, and the Denton Area Teachers Credit Union to the job, as he oversaw more than $500,000 in improvements of fair facilities and doubled the fair's sponsorship program. Burdick also submitted several applications for Texas Association of Fairs and Events (TAF&E) awards, which the fair won in various categories.

With the increase in hotel occupancy tourism funds and sponsorships from the community and corporations, the advertising budget was put to use promoting the fair on a broader basis. In addition, scholarships and involvement with children's activities sparked interest from a younger audience and their parents.

Tom Hadley and Terry Starnes, rodeo announcers whose knowledge of the sport is unsurpassed, have devoted 45 and 30 years, respectively, to the profession and spent many years at the North Texas State Fair and Rodeo. Two more names became synonymous with the Denton County fair—stockman Sammy Andrews and rodeo clown/barrelman Rudy Burns. Andrews brought in a higher quality of bucking bulls that were a major draw for some of the top-ranked cowboys across the United States. His terror-inducing bull, Bodacious, struck trepidation in bull riders unlucky enough to draw him for their ride. Burns became a mainstay on the fair scene, where he has entertained crowds for the past 20 years.

The early 21st century brought good years for the fair—years of growth, years of stability, and years of progress.

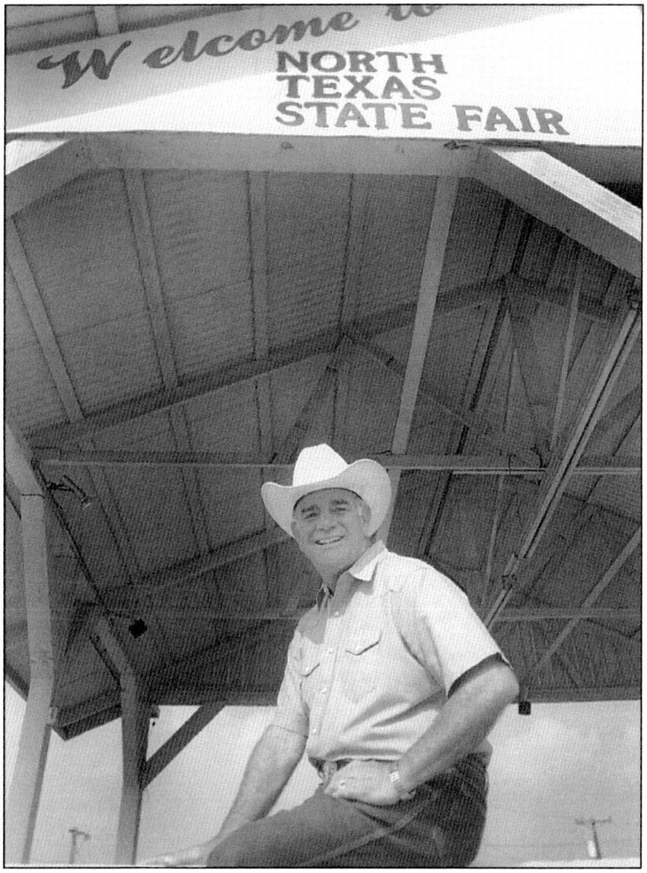

Ken Burdick, Executive Director. Kenneth DeWayne Burdick (1943–2007) served as executive director of the fair from 1999 until 2005. Under his direction, fair attendance increased, especially with the showcasing of major country music artists. Burdick also carved out a portion of the fairgrounds and dedicated it as the Kid's Zone. Burdick always felt that the Kid's Zone was his greatest accomplishment during his tenure at the fair. (Left, courtesy of DRC; below, courtesy of NTFR.)

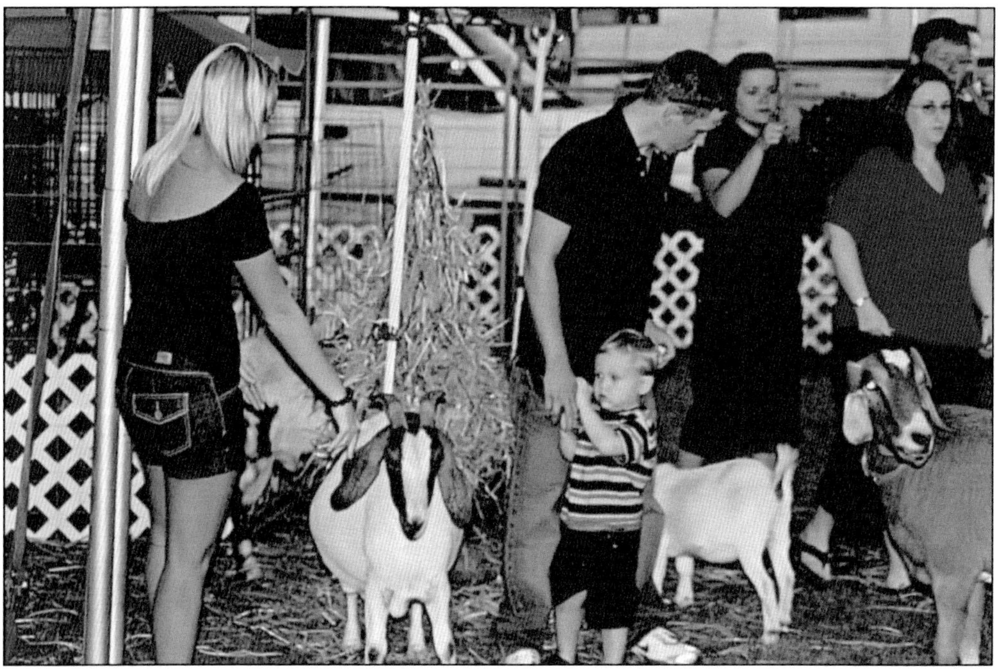

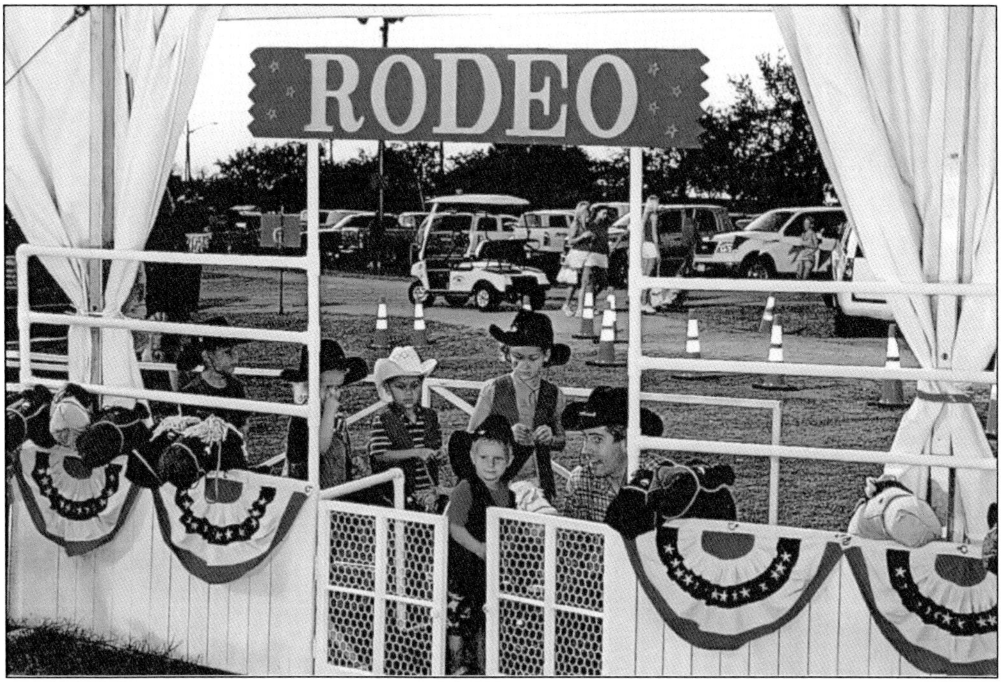

An Honored Community Leader. The attractions at the Kid's Zone included a petting zoo, a little folks' rodeo, and bounce houses, all of which were free for children to enjoy. At right, executive director Ken Burdick (wearing his signature Hawaiian shirt) is shown with his wife, Pat; granddaughter Madeline; and two beloved Sheltie dogs. Ken Burdick served on the board of the Texas Association of Fairs & Events (TAF&E) and was posthumously awarded the 2008 Otis Fowler Award for community leadership. His dedication to the fair and foresight into the future laid the groundwork for his successor, Glenn Carlton. (Both, courtesy of Ken Burdick family.)

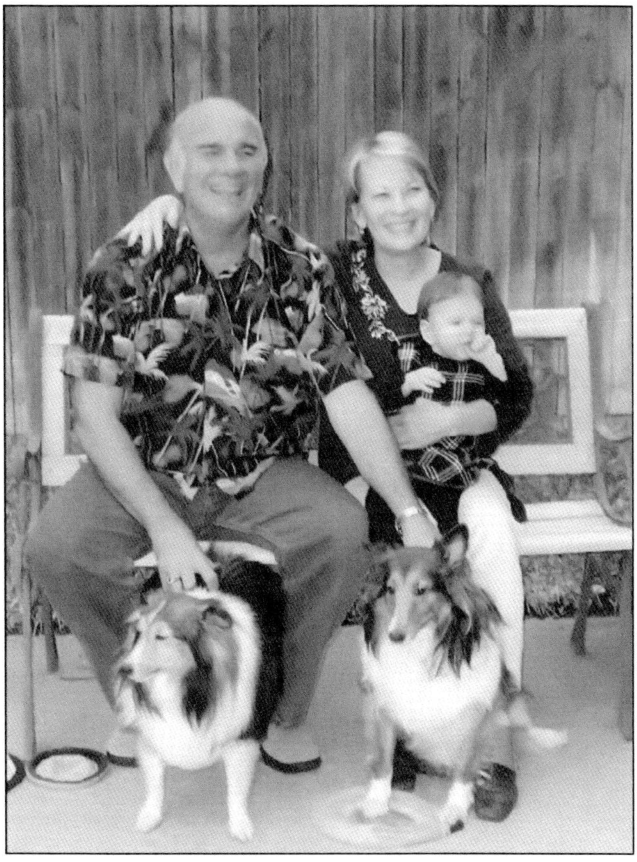

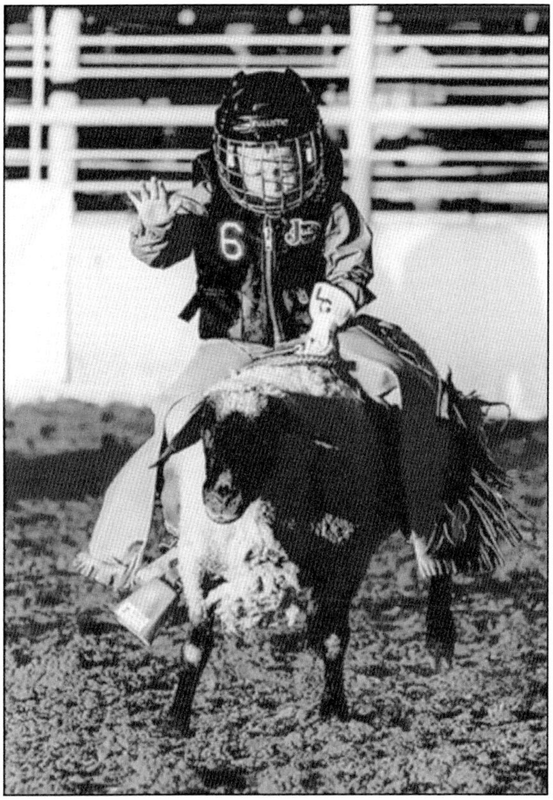

MUTTON BUSTIN'. Thousands of children participate in Mutton Bustin' every year in the United States. These sheep-riding events are an entertaining way to introduce young children to the rodeo "rough stock" events of bull riding, saddle bronc, and bareback riding. The young rider at left—in chaps, helmet, and a protective vest—is attempting to stay on the back of a wild and woolly sheep for the eight seconds required to win a trophy buckle. Rylee Holder (below), who was thrown off her woolly nemesis before the buzzer sounded, was not so lucky. (Left, courtesy of NTFR; below, courtesy of DRC.)

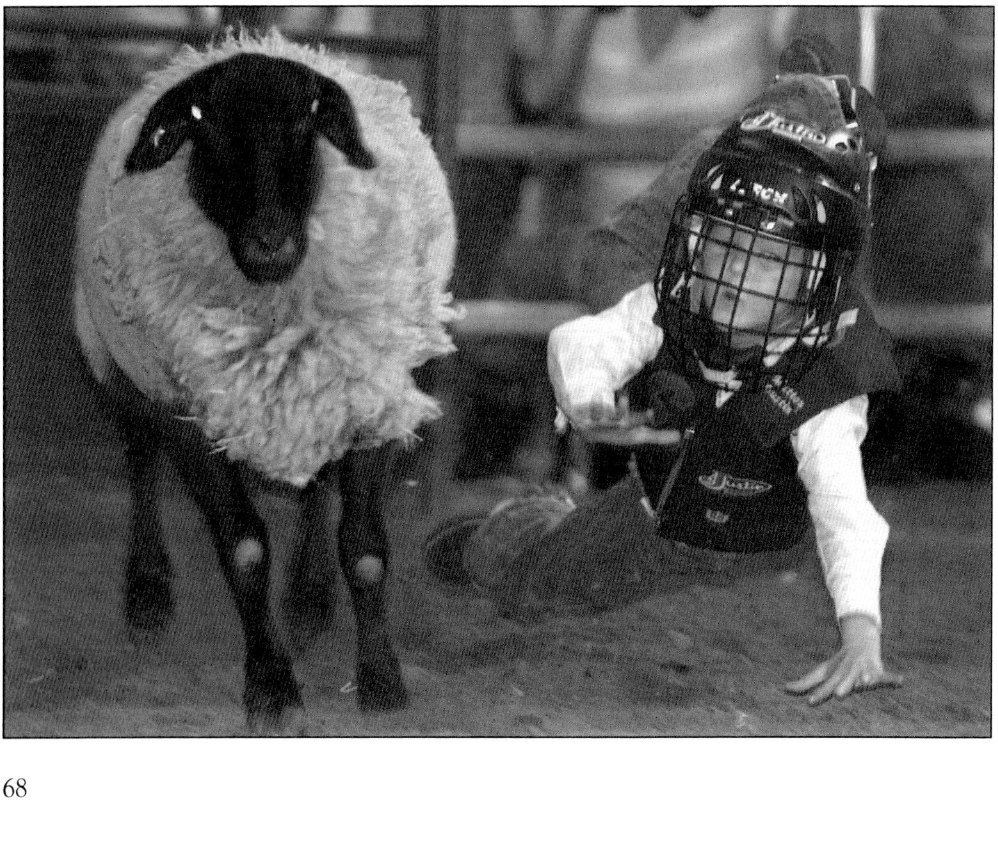

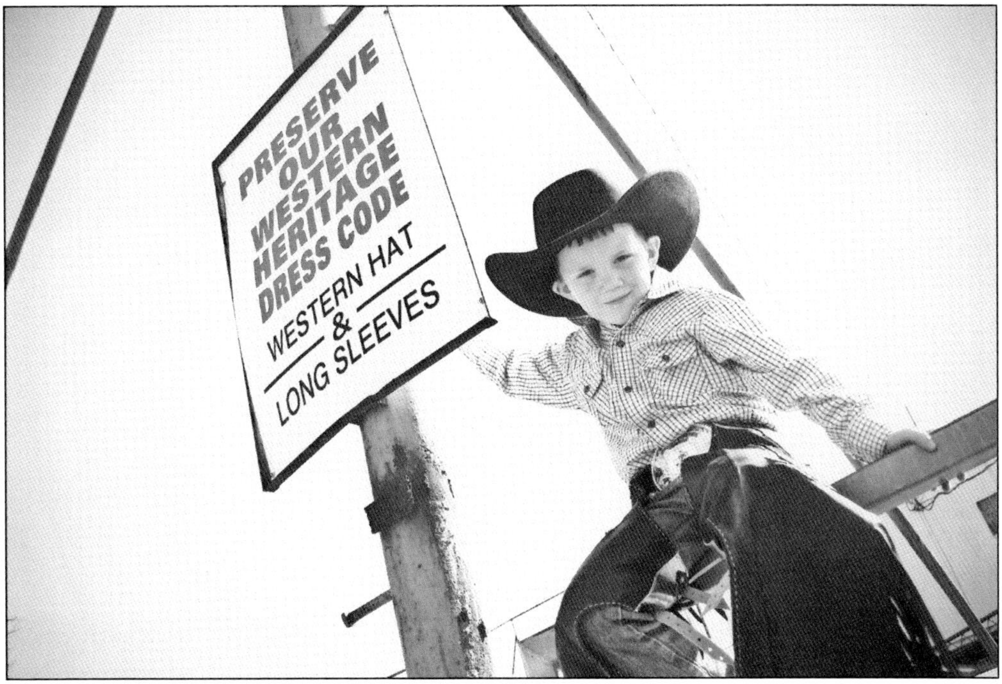

Western Heritage Dress Code. Wearing the appropriate attire in the rodeo arena is an important tradition of Western heritage. This young cowboy, Levi Nelson, learned early on that a western hat and long sleeves are required whether one is a contestant or a spectator. (Courtesy of NTFR.)

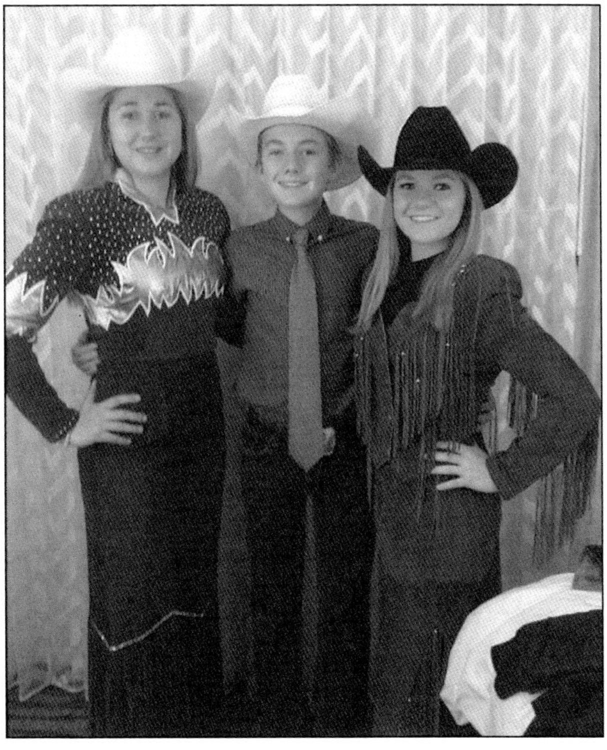

Rodeo Royalty. Taylor Sorrells (left) and her sister Brandy (right) are shown in their full "leathers," traditional attire for rodeo queens in modeling and formal competitions. Both girls have winning in their genes, having won several NTSFR titles, including Princess, Teen Queen, and many other categories. Contestants are required to presell tickets to the event; total ticket sales between the two girls equals more than $35,000—a record for the competition. Their brother Bret is escorting the accomplished young ladies. (Courtesy of the Sorrells family.)

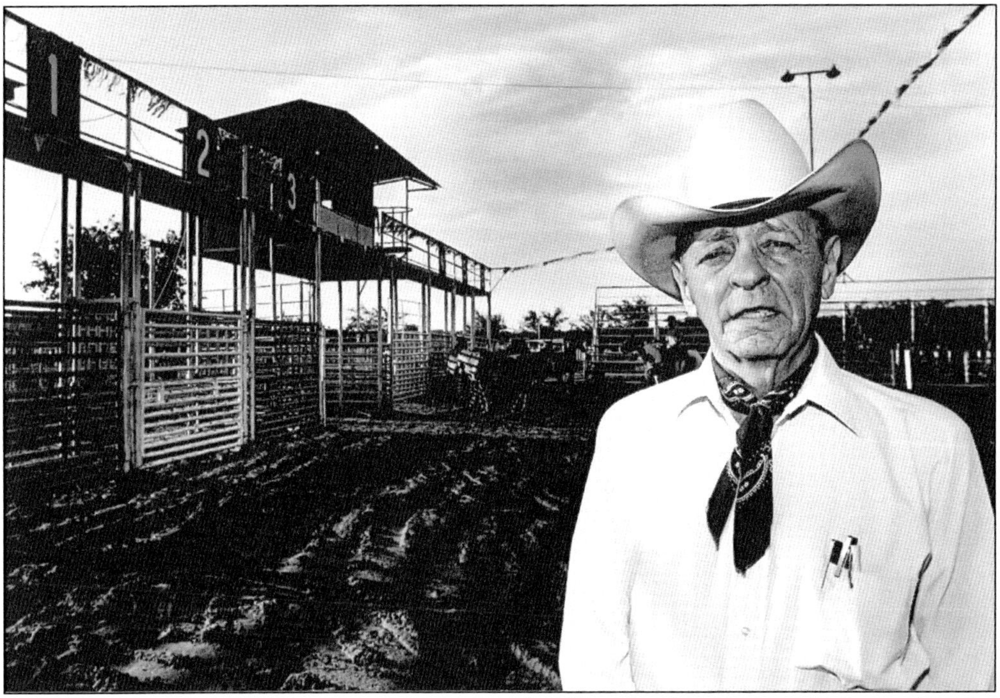

Rodeo Announcers Have Cowboy Fun. Tom Hadley (above), a former steer wrestler, made rodeo announcing his profession for more than 45 years. His book *Forty-five Years of Cowboy Fun* recounts his work experience. Working with just a program, Hadley became a pretty good "ad-libber" who knew how to entertain a crowd. Hadley announced three generations of cowboys and cowgirls, as well as three years at the National Finals Rodeo. He was inducted into the ProRodeo Hall of Fame in 2001. Terry Starnes (below) has been a rodeo announcer for 30 years, traveling all over the United States to ply his trade. Sixteen of those years have been at the NTSFR. Using his sharp wit, he has developed a special technique that holds the crowd's attention while he explains the rules and informs them about what the cowboys were doing. (Above, courtesy of DRC; below, courtesy of NTFR.)

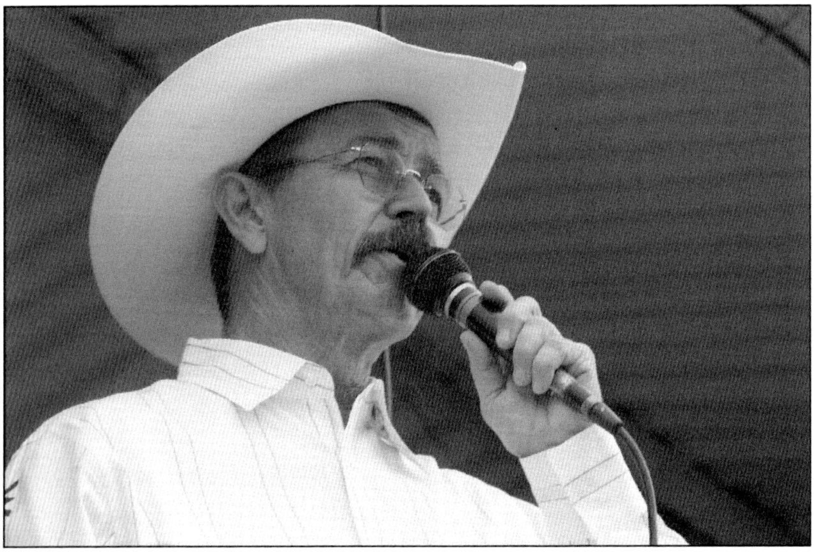

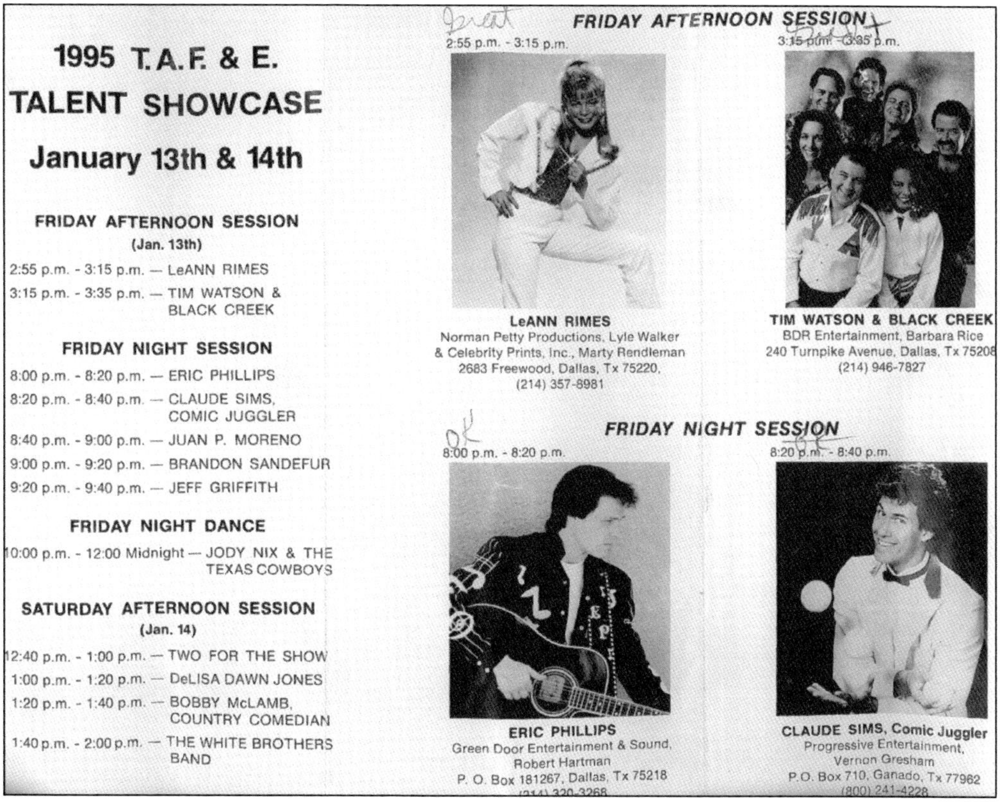

1995 T.A.F. & E.
TALENT SHOWCASE
January 13th & 14th

FRIDAY AFTERNOON SESSION
(Jan. 13th)
2:55 p.m. - 3:15 p.m. — LeANN RIMES
3:15 p.m. - 3:35 p.m. — TIM WATSON & BLACK CREEK

FRIDAY NIGHT SESSION
8:00 p.m. - 8:20 p.m. — ERIC PHILLIPS
8:20 p.m. - 8:40 p.m. — CLAUDE SIMS, COMIC JUGGLER
8:40 p.m. - 9:00 p.m. — JUAN P. MORENO
9:00 p.m. - 9:20 p.m. — BRANDON SANDEFUR
9:20 p.m. - 9:40 p.m. — JEFF GRIFFITH

FRIDAY NIGHT DANCE
10:00 p.m. - 12:00 Midnight — JODY NIX & THE TEXAS COWBOYS

SATURDAY AFTERNOON SESSION
(Jan. 14)
12:40 p.m. - 1:00 p.m. — TWO FOR THE SHOW
1:00 p.m. - 1:20 p.m. — DeLISA DAWN JONES
1:20 p.m. - 1:40 p.m. — BOBBY McLAMB, COUNTRY COMEDIAN
1:40 p.m. - 2:00 p.m. — THE WHITE BROTHERS BAND

FRIDAY AFTERNOON SESSION
2:55 p.m. - 3:15 p.m.
LeANN RIMES
Norman Petty Productions, Lyle Walker
& Celebrity Prints, Inc., Marty Rendleman
2683 Freewood, Dallas, Tx 75220,
(214) 357-8981

3:15 p.m. - 3:35 p.m.
TIM WATSON & BLACK CREEK
BDR Entertainment, Barbara Rice
240 Turnpike Avenue, Dallas, Tx 75208
(214) 946-7827

FRIDAY NIGHT SESSION
8:00 p.m. - 8:20 p.m.
ERIC PHILLIPS
Green Door Entertainment & Sound,
Robert Hartman
P. O. Box 181267, Dallas, Tx 75218
(214) 320-3268

8:20 p.m. - 8:40 p.m.
CLAUDE SIMS, Comic Juggler
Progressive Entertainment,
Vernon Gresham
P.O. Box 710, Ganado, Tx 77962
(800) 241-4228

FROM THE FAIR TO A GRAMMY. The North Texas State Fair and Rodeo was an instrumental venue in several contemporary performers' careers. Thirteen-year-old LeAnn Rimes was one of the musical and variety acts that performed at the TAF&E showcase in 1995. Fair officials signed her, and she performed at the 1995 fair. At age 14, Rimes became the youngest person to win a Grammy, both for Best New Artist and Best Female Country Vocal Performance (for her song "Blue"). (Courtesy of TAF&E.)

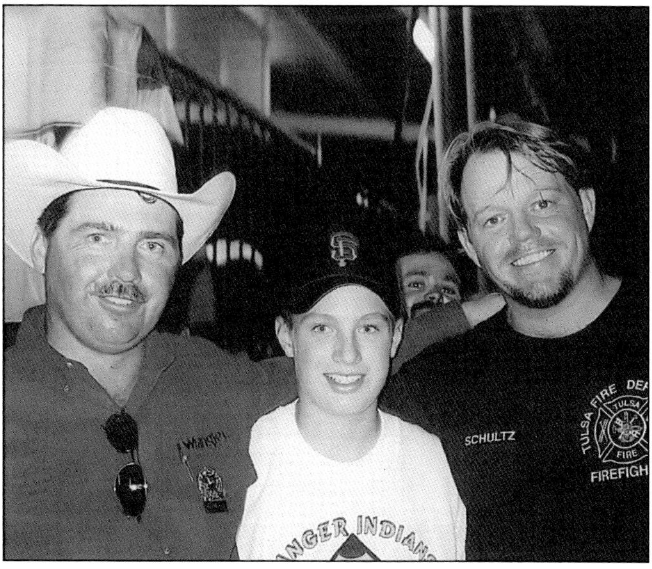

PAT GREEN. Green is a Texas country singer whose list of achievements includes three Grammy nominations and sales of more than two million albums. Green has released 10 albums since 1995, with his single "Wave on Wave," from his gold-certified album with the same title, earning one of those Grammy nominations. Green (right) is shown here with Glenn (left) and Chance (center) Carlton after Green's performance on the main stage at the fair. (Photograph by Mickie Miller Blagg; courtesy of the Carlton family.)

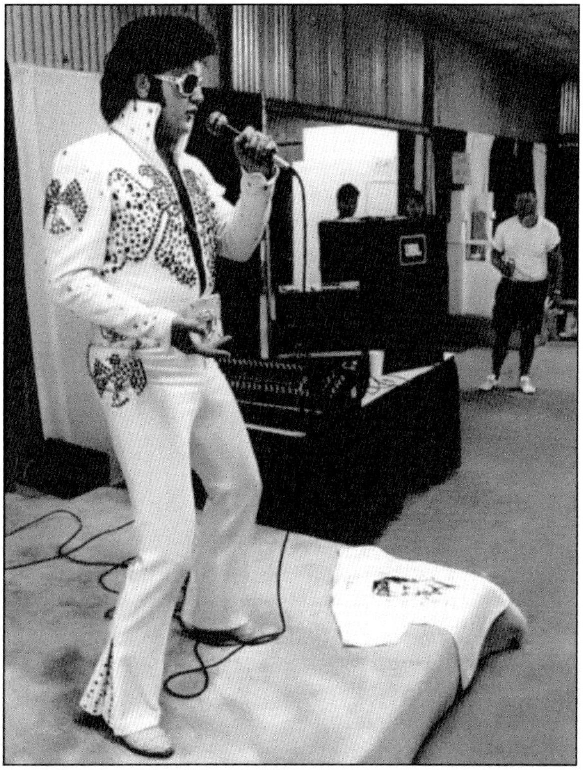

The King is Back. In 1991, Elvis impersonator Dave Tapley, of Dallas, performed four nightly shows at the North Texas State Fair and Rodeo as the king of rock and roll. Elvis—er, Tapley—impressed fairgoers with his fake sideburns, a studded white polyester jumpsuit, and dark sunglasses, as well as his voice. The King may be dead, but Tapley is alive and well and currently acts as an agent for dozens of fellow impersonators. (Courtesy of DRC.)

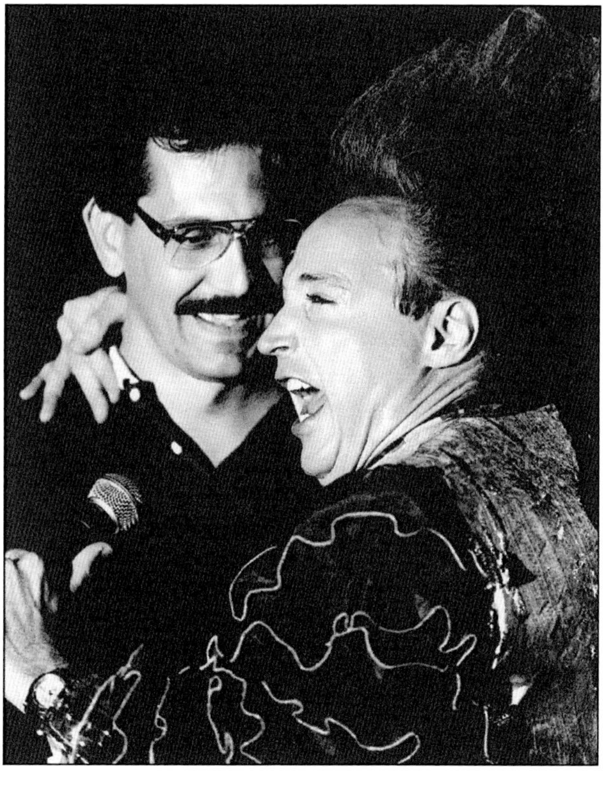

Hair! Vince Vance & the Valiants became a mainstay at the fair for several years. Dedicated followers reveled in singing along with the rockin' tunes of the 1950s and 1960s and delighted in the antics of Vance. The lead guitarist of the group was Bob Powers's son Troy, also known as the "teenage heartthrob." Vance (right) is shown here having fun with Woody Woodward during a performance. (Courtesy of DRC.)

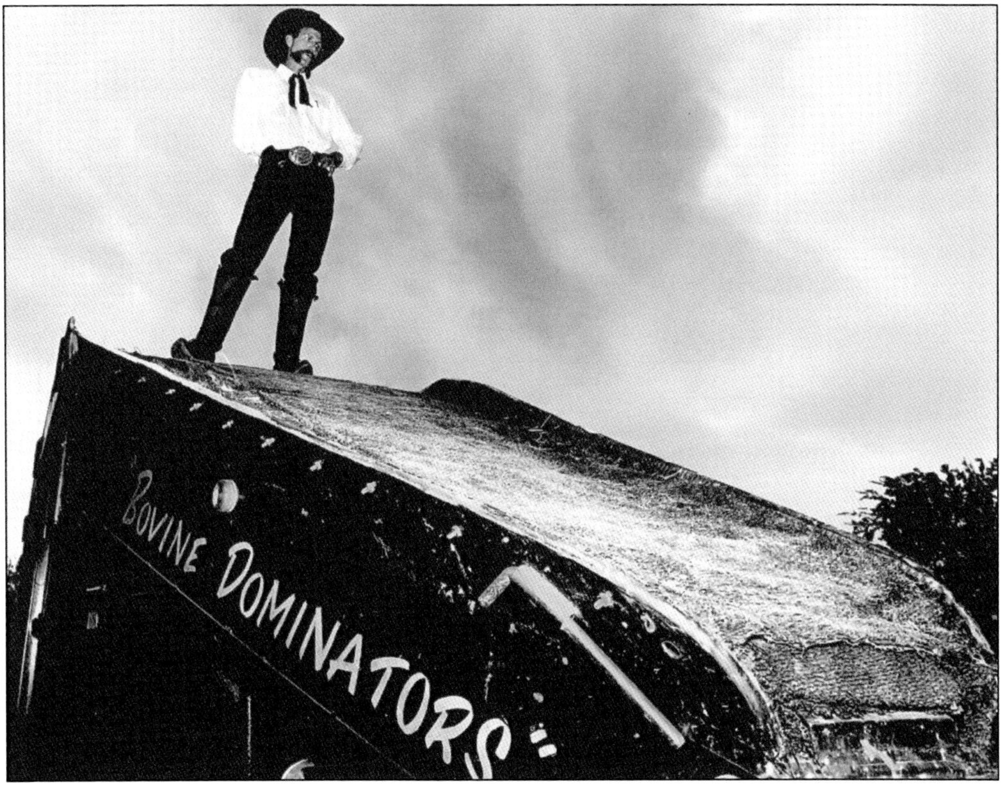

"One-Arm Bandit." One of the many specialty acts in the rodeo world is John Payne, an Oklahoma performer without a right arm. Payne worked for years training Black Mouth Cur dogs and cattle and quarter horses, incorporating them into his one-of-a-kind act. Signaling with a bullwhip and his voice, he guides his unbridled horse and four steers to the top of a cattle trailer. True trust and understanding of his animals has led to his success. (Courtesy of DRC.)

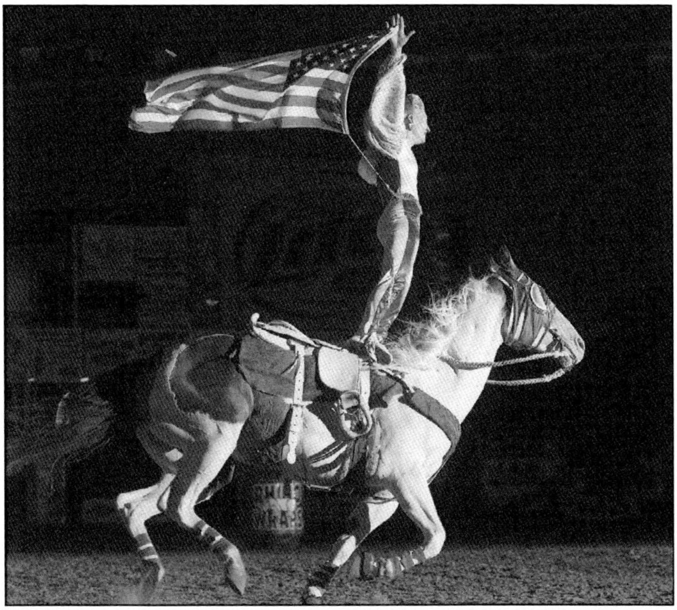

All-American Trick Rider. Trick riding originated in the early days of rodeos and Wild West shows. Cowboys and cowgirls would compete for prize money by performing death-defying stunts on the back of galloping horses. Today, this sport includes jumping on and off of a fast-moving horse or hanging upside down off the side of the horse. This unidentified trick rider proudly displays an American flag as the horse gallops around the arena. (Courtesy of NTFR.)

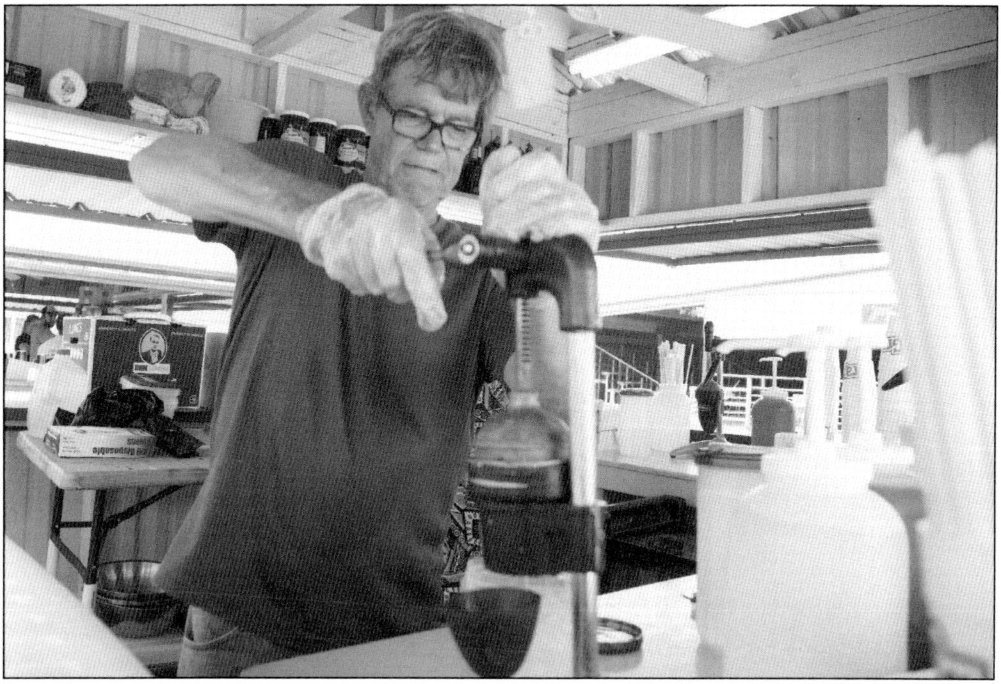

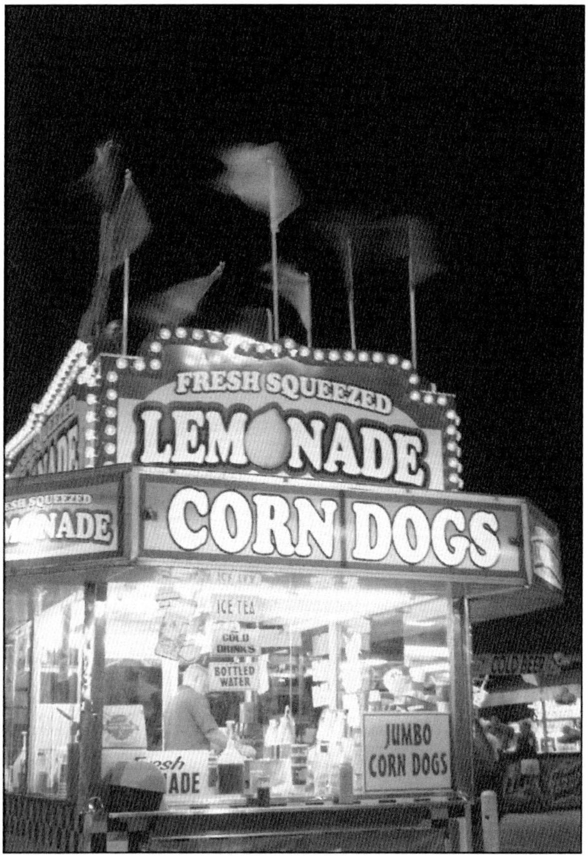

Making Lemonade from Lemons. Don Olson, purveyor of lemonade, holds the record as one of the longest-running commercial vendors at the fair, with 27 continuous years under his belt. He held a corporate job while enjoying his fruitful hobby and retired to pursue this mouth-puckering business, proving that when life gives you lemons, you make lemonade. Olson has expanded his business enterprise to include making handmade trays from repurposed wood. (Courtesy of DRC.)

McKinney's Corn Dogs. The McKinney family is known for its colorful and profitable stands, which shine brightly on the midway. In addition to their hand-dipped jumbo dogs, they offer tasty funnel cakes, hand-squeezed lemonade, and hot and zesty nachos. After the untimely death of Tim McKinney, his wife, Michelle, their three daughters, and other family members continued to provide customers with delicious fair fare. (Courtesy of NTFR.)

WHERE'S THE BEEF? Ed Bradford and Bob Powers argued over who could cook the best barbecue and what type of cooker was superior. That argument resulted in the fair's first barbecue cook-off, held in 1975, which has become one of the most popular traditions at the fair. These boastful aficionados often travel all over the country plying their culinary skills. They produce finger-lickin', smokin'-good 'cue. Sometimes they win a little bread to cover their expenses, along with bragging rights for having the tastiest grub. Not everyone uses a traditional smoker to produce their barbecue, as shown in these photographs of Joe Amyx's Texas Jack cooker (at right) and Lonnie Green's armadillo smoker "Bubba" (below). (Right, courtesy of NTFR; below, courtesy of DRC.)

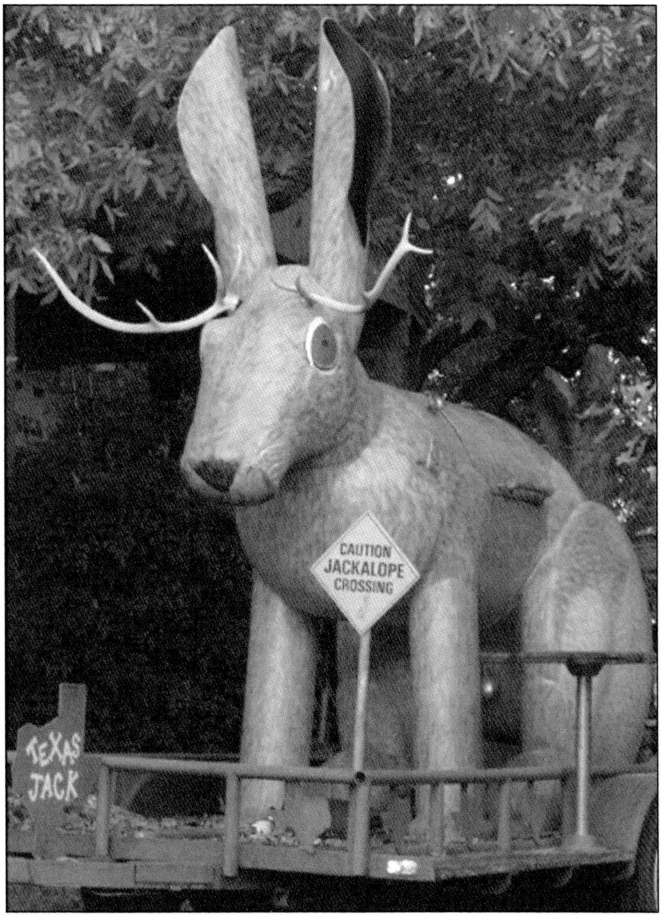

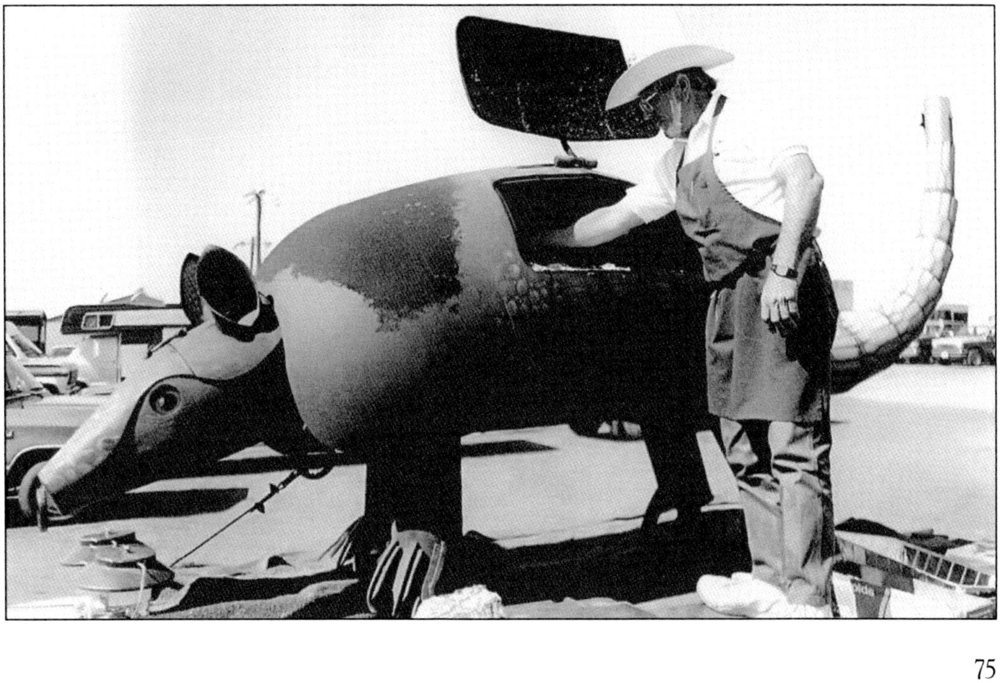

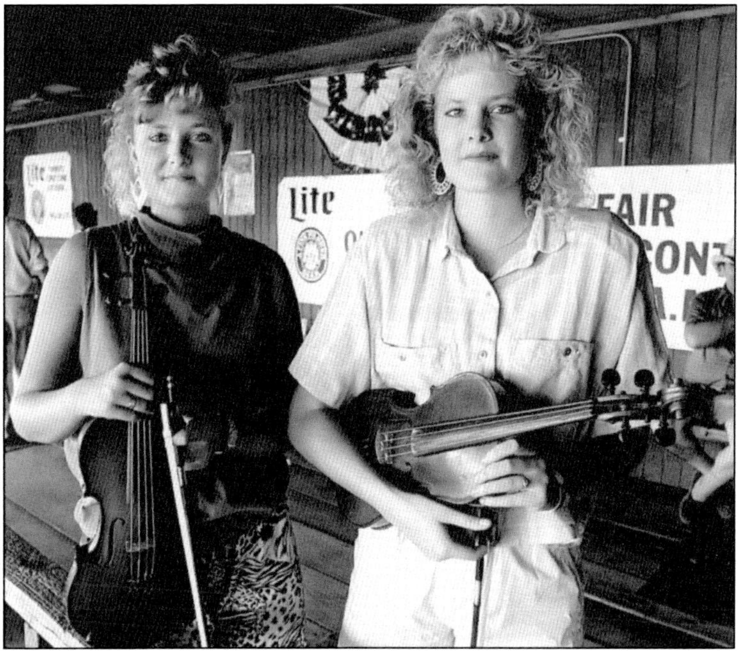

Fiddle-dee-dee! It would be fair to say these gals are just fiddlin' around at the fair. The annual fiddler contest at the NTSFR has attracted some of the most talented artists in this field. Michelle Kolbrek (left) and her sister Heather (right) participated in the North Texas Old Time Fiddlers Contest in 1988, competing against more than 30 fiddlers of all ages from across the United States. (Courtesy of DRC at DCOHC.)

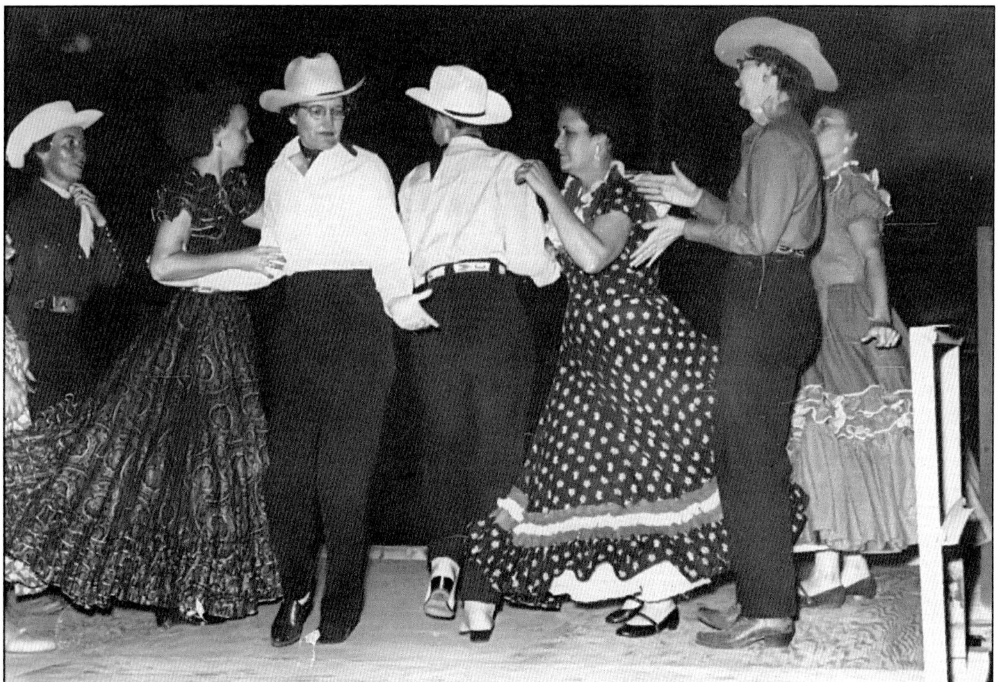

Do-si-do. In 1982, Pres. Ronald Reagan signed a Congressional act proclaiming square dancing the official national folk dance. Its origins began in the Colonial period of rural America. Although urbanization and newer dance forms nearly led to the demise of this folk dance, square dancers—including these dancers at the Denton fair—enthusiastically continue with their do-si-dos, spin chain the gears, and Ferris wheels at competitions held at county and state fairs throughout the United States. (Courtesy of NTFR.)

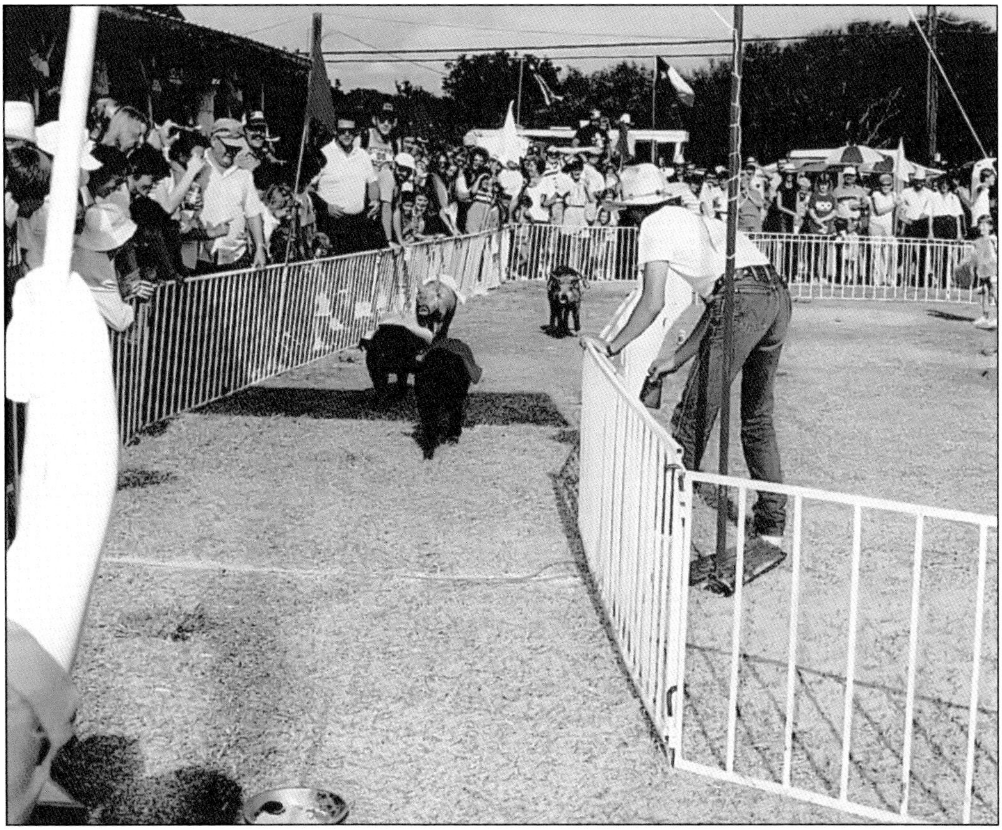

Wee-Wee-Wee All the Way Home. Pig racing is an entertaining sport that is popular at most county fairs. In this event, pigs race around a small, enclosed track. There is no betting on the bacon in Porkchop Downs races, and winners grunt their pleasure while oinking for joy. Cheerleaders' pom-poms match the colors of the racing pigs' silks, and the winning pig is awarded with Oreo cookies at the finish line. (Courtesy of DRC at DCOHC.)

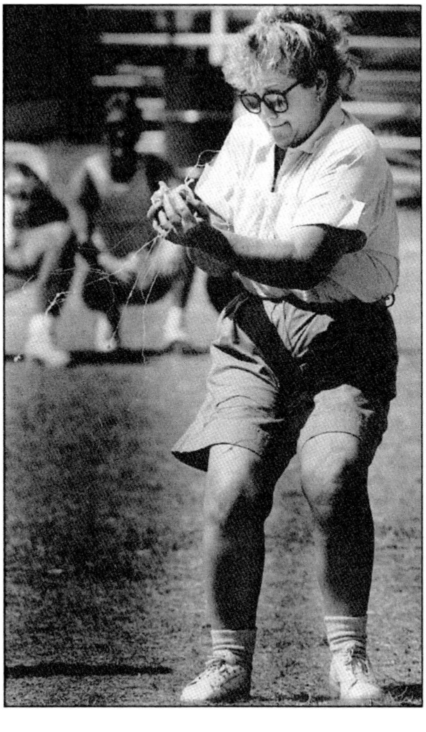

Eggs-actly right. The egg-tossing competition is a contest of daring and dexterity. Competitors definitely do not want fellow contestants to say "the yolk's on you!" At right, Joy McManus, of Aubrey, mishandles an egg tossed to her in the North Texas State Fair and Rodeo egg toss; she even cut off her fingernails to give her an edge in the competition. (Courtesy of DRC at DCOHC.)

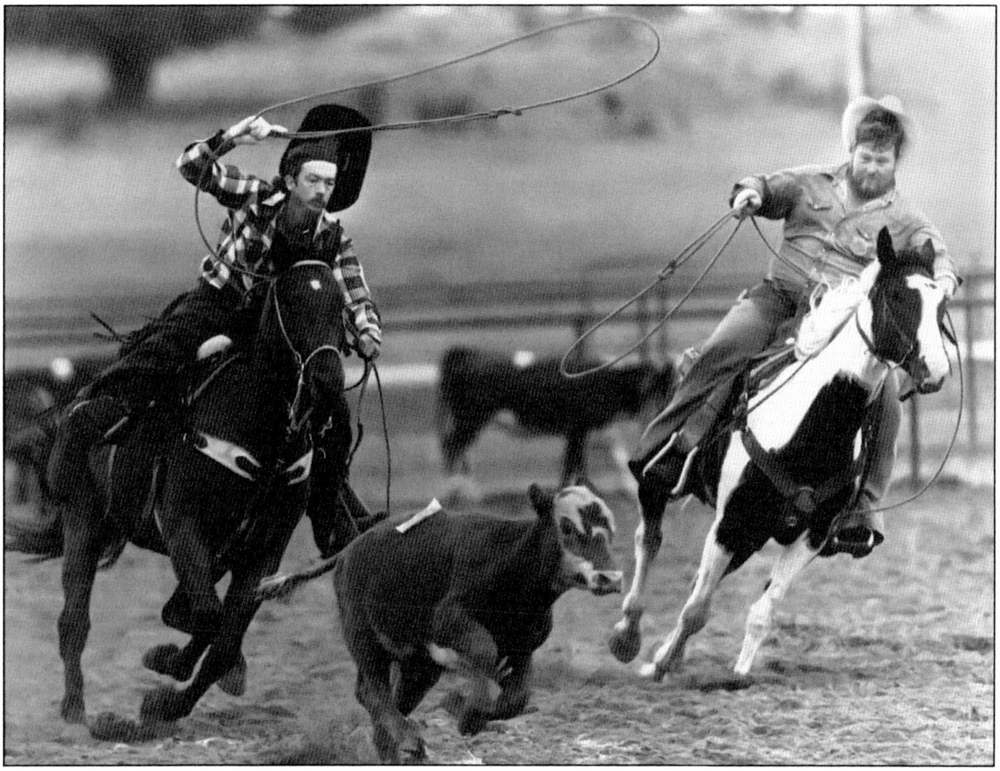

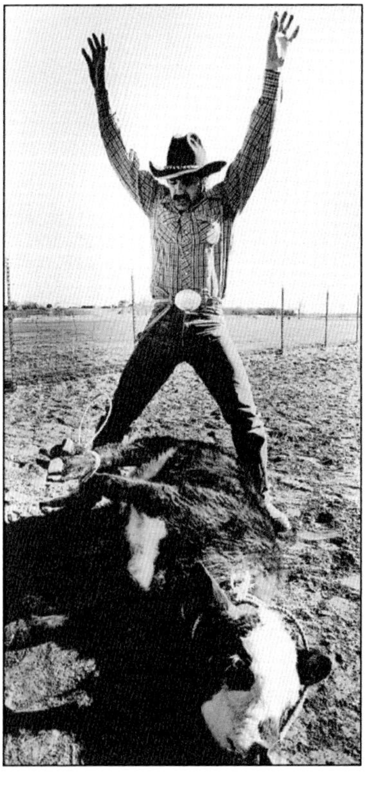

Two for Two. Team roping requires precise timing and anticipation between the header and the heeler, making it the rodeo's only true team sport. A header must rope a steer around the neck or horns and turn it so that the heeler can rope both hind legs. A five-second penalty is assessed if only one leg is caught. In this image, the unidentified cowboy on the left is the header; and the unidentified cowboy on the right is the heeler. (Courtesy of DRC at DCOHC.)

Tying Three On. Tie-down roping, also known as calf roping, begins with a mounted cowboy giving a head start to a calf, roping the calf, then tying any three of the calf's legs together. This timed event requires a great athlete to accomplish this in a matter of a few seconds. Here, David Wilkinson throws both hands in the air to celebrate his successful tie-down roping practice. (Courtesy of DRC at DCOHC.)

Bull Blowout. The Bull Blowout tests the skill, strength, and endurance of every cowboy and the agility, power, speed, kicks, and drops of every bull that participates in this annual event at the fair. Riders must stay on the back of bucking, rearing, kicking, spinning, and twisting bulls weighing as much as 2,000 pounds for a minimum of eight seconds. Bull riders are also judged by their constant control and rhythm with the bull. It is no wonder that bull riding has been called the most dangerous eight seconds in sports. Here, Matt Ward found the sweet spot for a successful eight-second ride. (Courtesy of NTFR.)

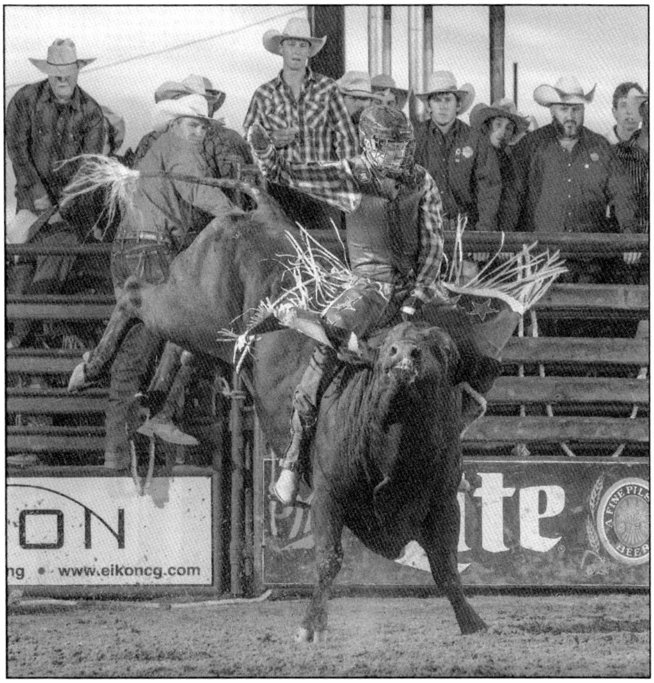

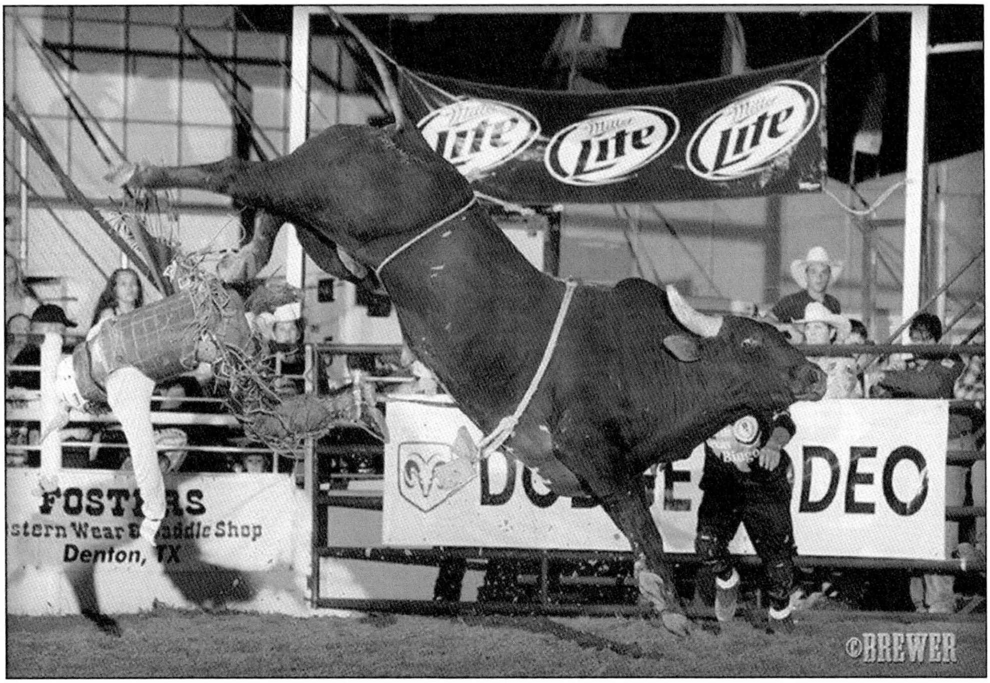

Carlton Cattle Company. Glenn Carlton not only serves as executive director of the fair but is also a rancher who raises world-class bucking bulls. His bulls compete in—and have won—many national events, including a year-end championship with the National Bucking Bull Association. Carlton Cattle Company's bulls also participate in PRCA and PBR events. Pictured here is 690 Cowboy Colt, a Carlton bull, throwing off Sam Wyatt at the Bull Blowout. (Courtesy of NTFR.)

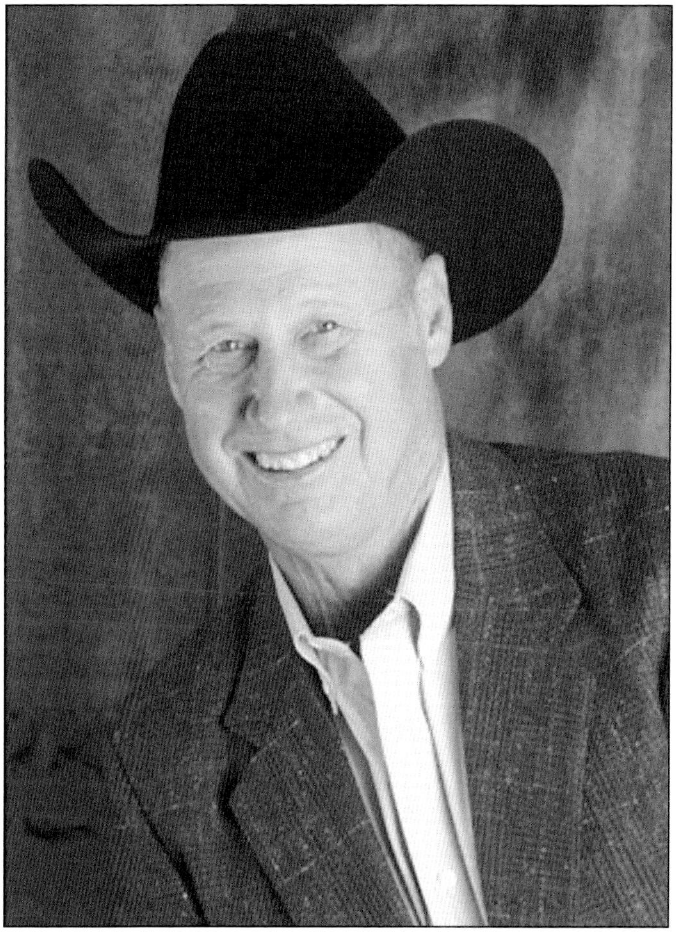

Sammy Andrews, Stock Contractor of the Year. Andrews, a third-generation stock contractor, started producing outstanding amateur rodeos in 1980 and has operated an award-winning breeding program for bucking bulls and horses at the Andrews Ranch for more than 35 years. Andrews was nominated for Stock Contractor of the Year in 2000 and 2004 and selected by the PRCA as 2002 Stock Contractor of the Year. Andrews has produced multiple bull and bronc winners and hundreds of National Finals Rodeo qualifiers. Below, Andrews is shown with his son James (at right) and his saddle bronc, Roaney Wiggles (at left) in 1992. (Left, courtesy of Sammy Andrews; below, courtesy of DRC.)

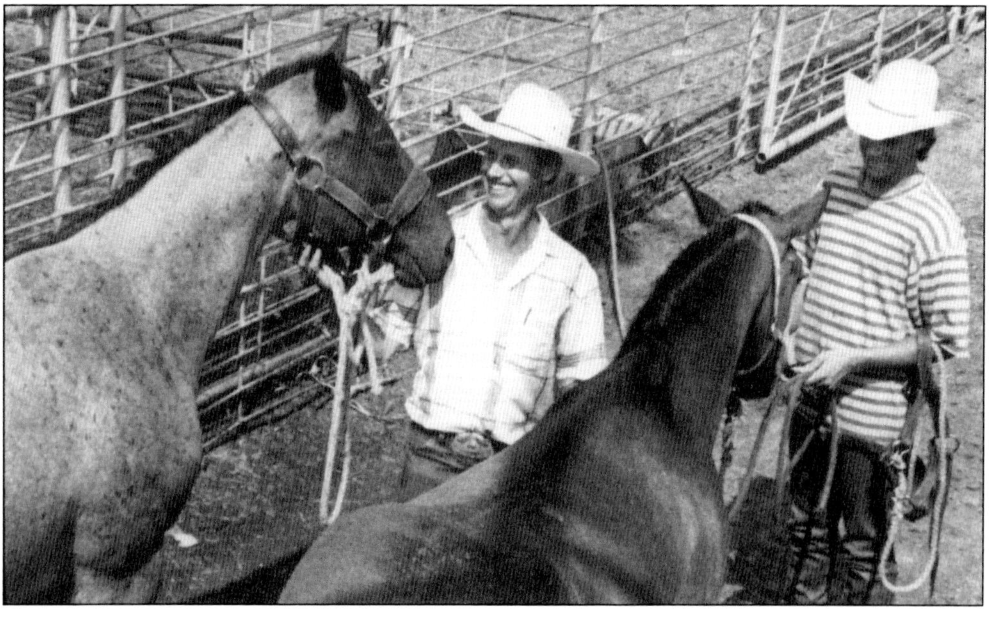

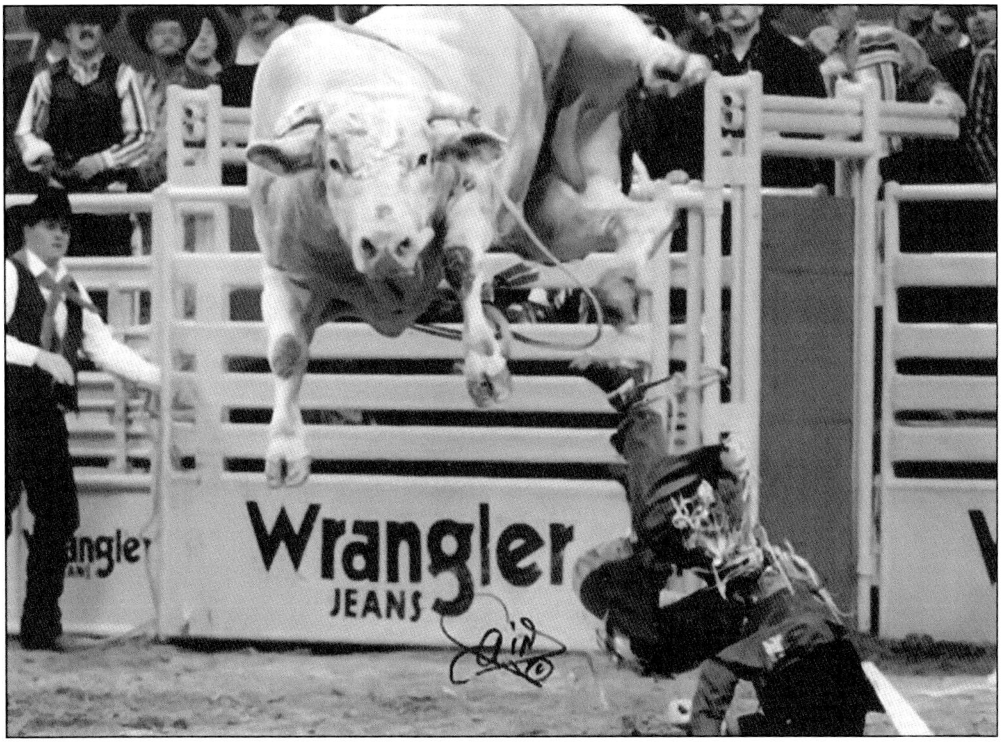

"World's Most Dangerous Bucking Bull." Sammy Andrews' ability to produce quality stock is well noted in regard to 1999 Hall of Fame Bucking Bull Bodacious (aka Bo), who has 135 outs and only 8 qualified rides. Bodacious (above) won Bucking Bull of the Year in 1994 and 1995 and Bucking Bull of the National Finals Rodeo in 1992, 1994, and 1995. "Bo" (1988–2000), a Charbray, developed a trick of unbalancing a rider, then lifting up his head with full force, injuring the rider. This head-butting trick eventually resulted in Bo's retirement from professional bull riding, as he was deemed too dangerous to ride. In 1999, Bodacious was inducted into the ProRodeo Hall of Fame. (Photograph by Aaron Semas; courtesy of Sammy Andrews.)

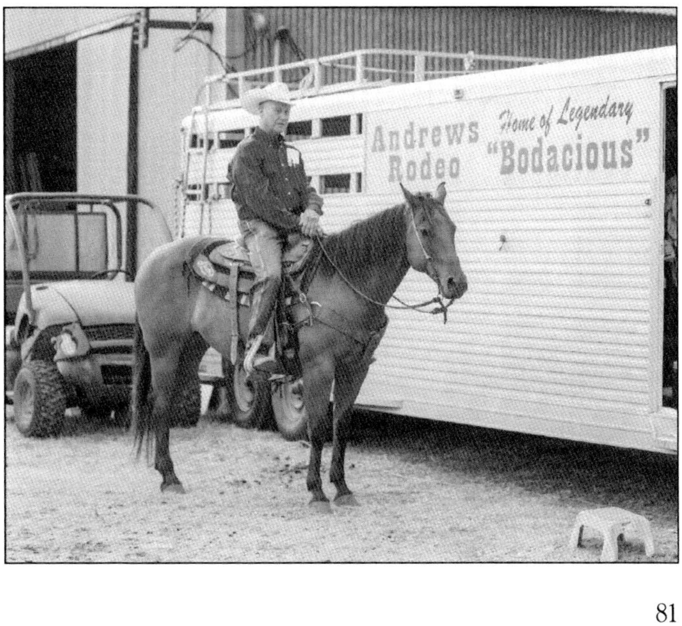

Bodacious. The Houston Rodeo and Livestock Show honored Sammy Andrews in 2004, awarding him with a bucking chute—the last one Bo bucked out of—to use as a memorial for Bo's grave. (Photograph by Aaron Semas; courtesy of Sammy Andrews.)

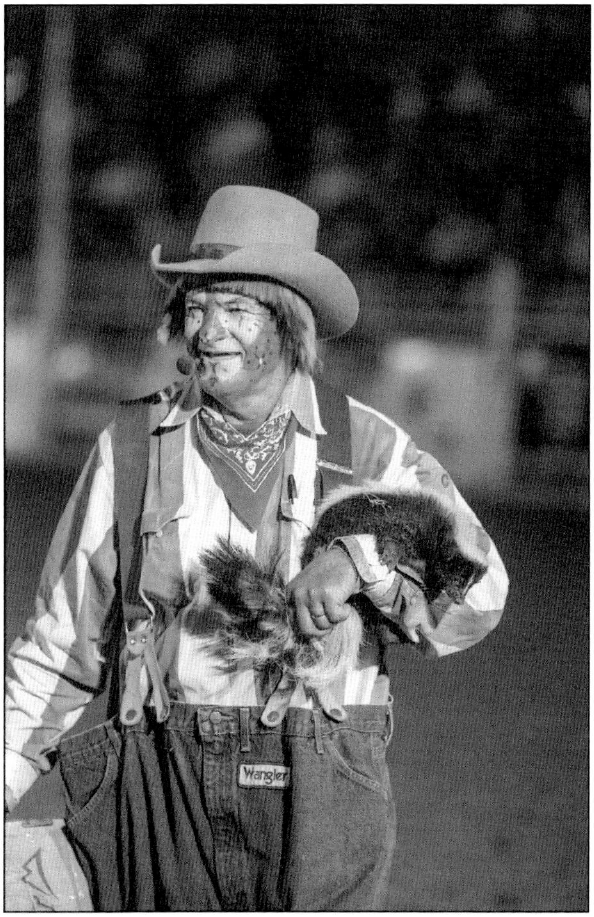

"**Do Something Funny.**" Rudy Burns started his rodeo career by accident in 1970 after being dared to ride a bull and suffering a broken nose. After his first incident with a bull, he started riding bulls in various rodeos. When one of the clowns did not show up for work, the rodeo manager told Burns to "get out there and do something funny." From then on, Burns was asked to come back as a clown and not a bull rider. Burns uses various animals in his act. This skunk shown at left came from a Mississippi prison road crew that captured it, de-scented it, and sold it to Burns—drum roll, please—for a few scents. It stinks that he had to buy it! (Both, courtesy of NTFR.)

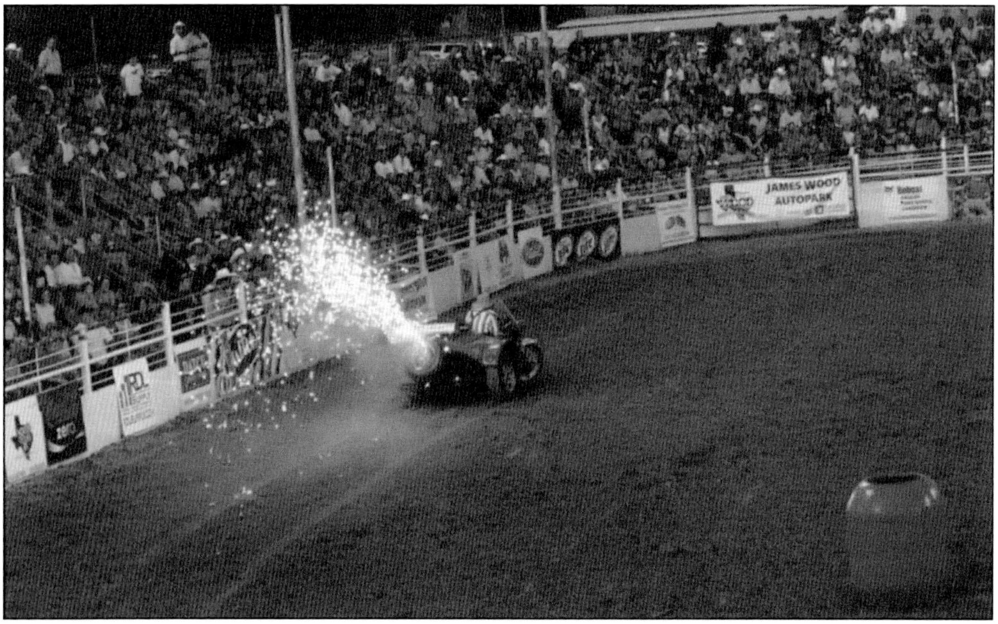

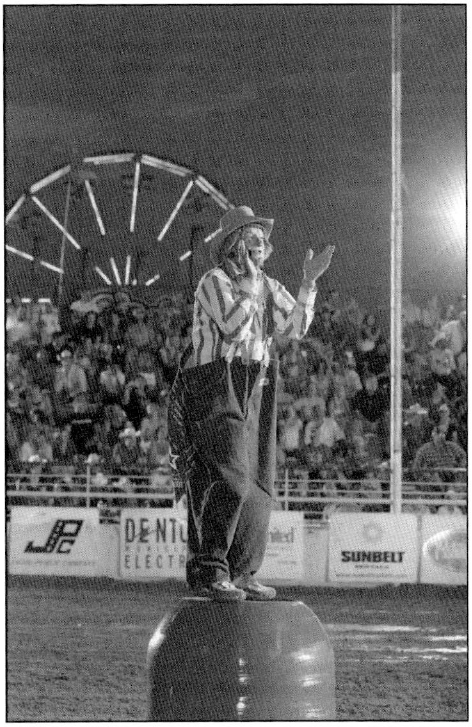

PRCA Barrelman of the Year. In 1995 and 2000, Rudy Burns was named PRCA Barrelman of the Year, a title voted on by bull riders, cowboys, and various rodeo participants. Burns, who is now semiretired, considers this acknowledgment to be his greatest professional achievement and continues to entertain crowds at the North Texas State Fair and Rodeo. For 46 years, Burns has been painting his face the same way and wearing his trademark pink hat and rainbow wig. He has been the "face" of the NTSFR on several occasions, appearing on billboards, business cards, posters, and brochures. (Both, courtesy of NTFR.)

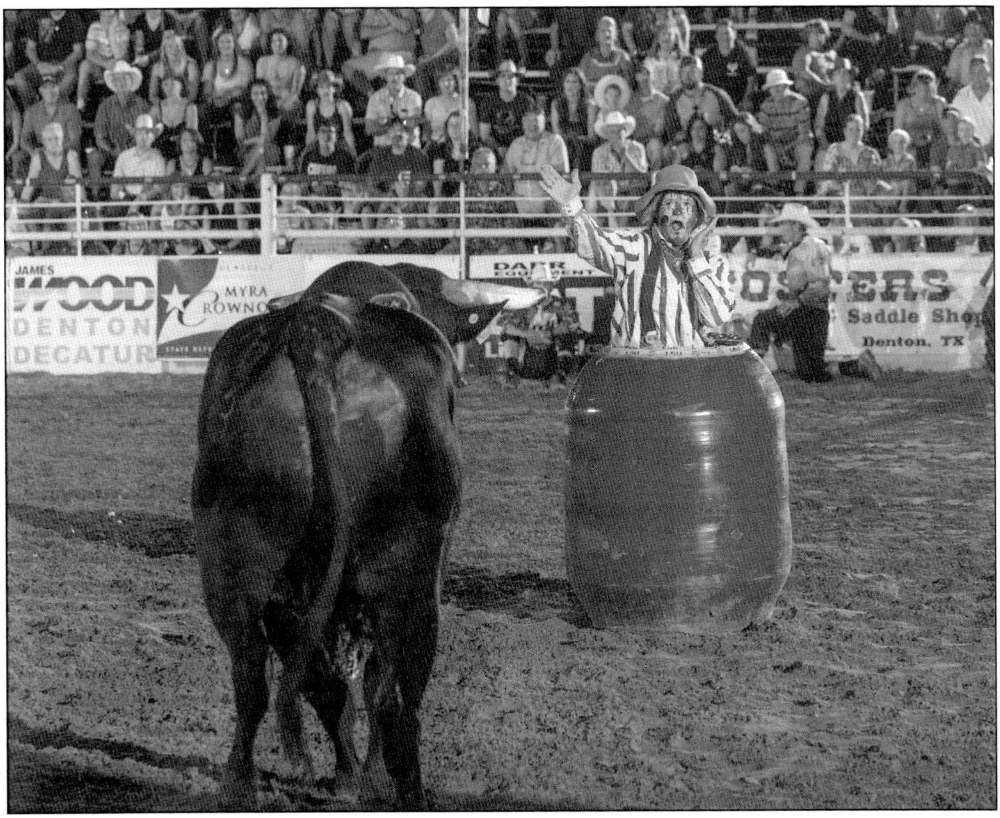

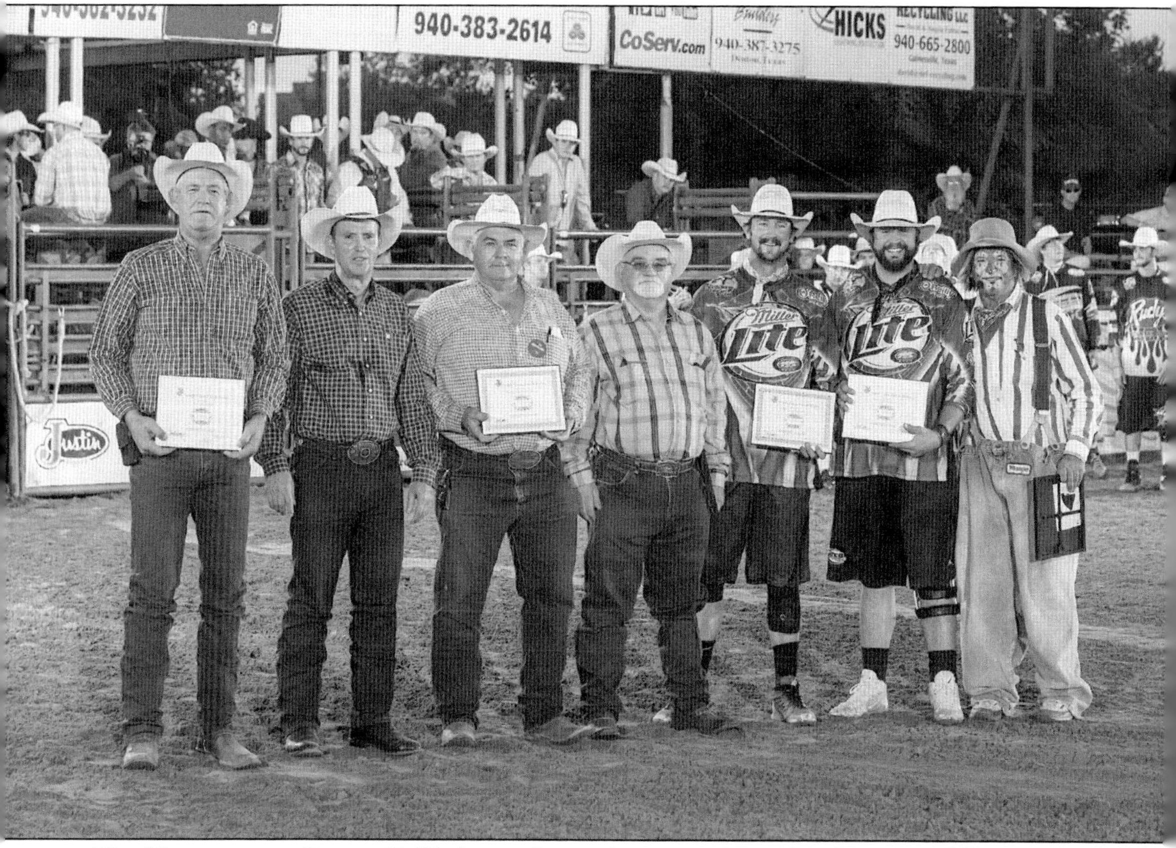

The Heroes of the Rodeo. Bullfighters, whose job is to put themselves between a fallen cowboy and a rampaging bull, are required to be both gifted athletes and fearless competitors. Their job is to distract a bull from a fallen cowboy and allow the cowboy to get to safety; many times, bullfighters actually place themselves between the bull and the rider. Barrelmen, sometimes referred to as rodeo clowns, also protect cowboys by luring a bull away from a rider—but that is not their only job They also entertain crowds during breaks in the action. Clowns, with their painted faces and funny costumes, also provide entertainment. Ronny Collins organized the first Rodeo Clown and Bullfighter Reunion in 2014. The North Texas State Fair and Rodeo bullfighter, barrelman, and clown alumni pictured here are, from left to right, Jimmy Council (who performed at the fair in 1988 and 1989); Collins (1974); Randy "Nubbin" Oliver (1972, 1973); Bill "Snuffy" Lamb (1970–1974, 1976); Weston Rutowski (2013–2015); Zach Arthur (2014); and Rudy Burns (1996–present). (Courtesy of NTFR.)

Five

The Cowboy Way
A New Era (2005–2015)

Building upon the work of executive director Ken Burdick, the North Texas State Fair Association (NTSFA) board of directors hired executive director Glenn Carlton and executive assistant Nanci Kimmey in 2005 to carry forward and expand his legacy. Carlton and Kimmey have taken the fair to new heights through innovative advertising, attracting national entertainment performers, ramping up fundraising, and expanding rodeo venues. In 2009, the University of North Texas conducted an economic impact study that revealed that the fair had a $6 million impact on Denton County (and an approximately $3.5 million impact on the city of Denton).

In 2009, the North Texas State Fair and Rodeo (NTSFR) won its first Texas Association of Fairs and Events (TAF&E) Award of Excellence. This honor reflects the NTSFR's advancements in professional rodeo, quality of entertainment, financial success, and attendance. The fair is a member of the International Association of Fairs and Expositions, as well as the TAF&E.

The next two years accelerated at a pace that raised the fair's stature not only in Texas but also in the nation. The NTSFR was recognized for excellence again in 2012, when the Texas State Historical Commission honored the fair with a historical subject marker—the first one given to a fair in the state.

After almost 40 years of using the words "State Fair" in its name, it became apparent that the names for the Denton and Dallas fairs needed to be more strongly differentiated, and since rodeo was a strong component in the success of the Denton fair, it needed to be recognized in the name. In 2013, the fair association's board of directors adopted the name North Texas Fair and Rodeo, deleting the word "State." The ensuing years trended toward more growth in attendance, higher standards in rodeo events, larger purses, and unsurpassed entertainment venues.

In 2015, the fair broke all attendance records as more than 175,000 fairgoers took part in the nine-day event. However, the principal achievement that year was the purchase of 109 acres of land for the proposed new fairgrounds and rodeo. The land, located at the northern edge of Denton, provides the acreage needed to build new arenas, stages, barns, multi-use buildings, and meeting facilities. Indeed, good times are ahead for this valued and valuable entertaining and educational institution.

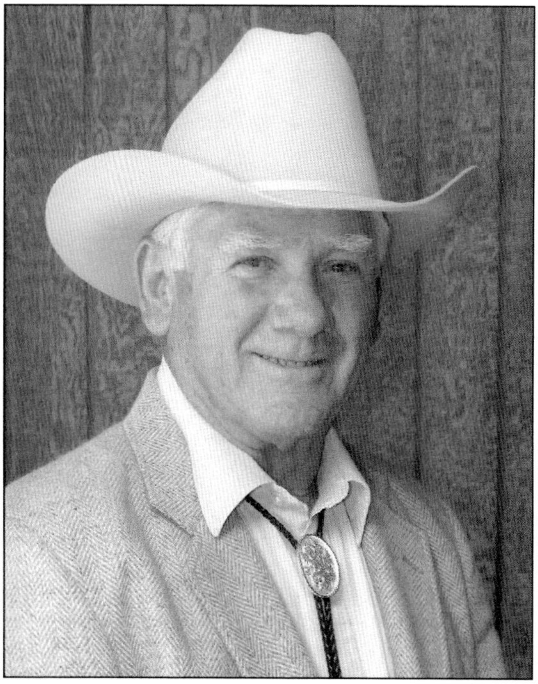

R.D. MARTIN, STRAIGHT SHOOTER. During the six years (2006 to 2012) when R.D. Martin served as North Texas State Fair Association (NTSFA) president, the event doubled in size and marked its first million-dollar fair. Martin was known for his honesty and integrity in supporting volunteers and members of the NTSFA. He always attended Youth Fair, Grand Champion Club, and Blue Ribbon Club meetings and was the first to support a child in need. (Courtesy of NTFR.)

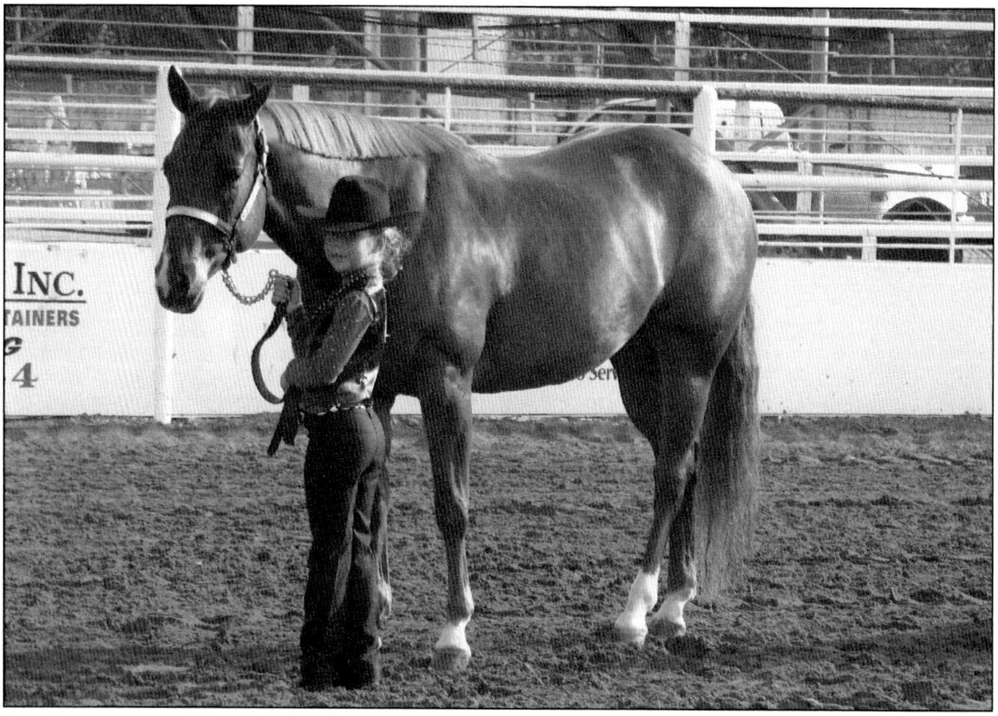

AN EQUESTRIAN WINNER. Eight-year-old Brooke Bancroft is showing her American Quarter Horse Association mare, Miss ZZ Snip, in this photograph from the 2005 NTSFA horse show. Bancroft had a successful youth career, becoming a multiple Appaloosa Youth World Champion with the Appaloosa Horse Club. She is currently a student at Baylor University in Waco and on the Baylor Bears equestrian team. (Courtesy of NTFR.)

Twisting with Chubby Checker. Ernest Evans, better known as "Chubby Checker," got his start at the Philadelphia Fresh Produce Market and made the top of the charts with his hit song "The Twist." Checker performed at the fair in 2005, but the Texas heat proved too much. After a 20-minute performance, he called it a night, got into his limousine, and departed, leaving many fans twisting in the wind. (Courtesy of NTFR.)

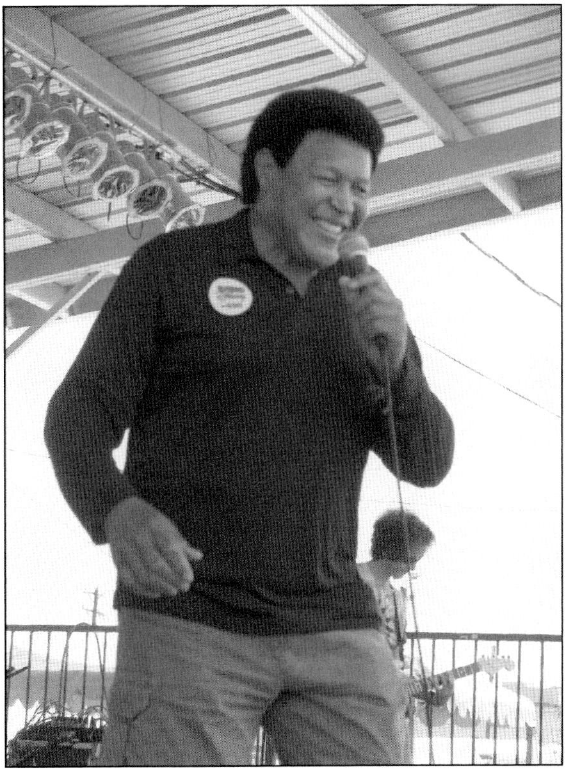

New Second Stage. In an effort to expand the musical entertainment and feature up-and-coming artists from this music-rich region, the fair added a second stage close to the rodeo arena so that patrons could enjoy music before the rodeo. This stage created a venue for additional concerts to be held from open to close, except during the rodeo. (Courtesy of NTFR.)

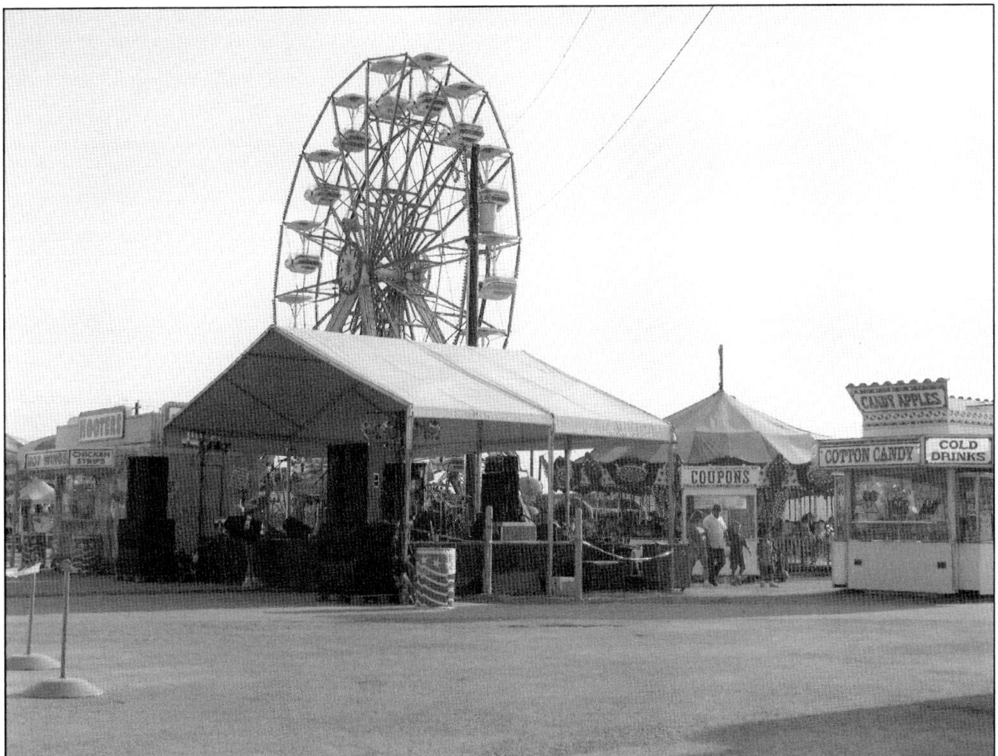

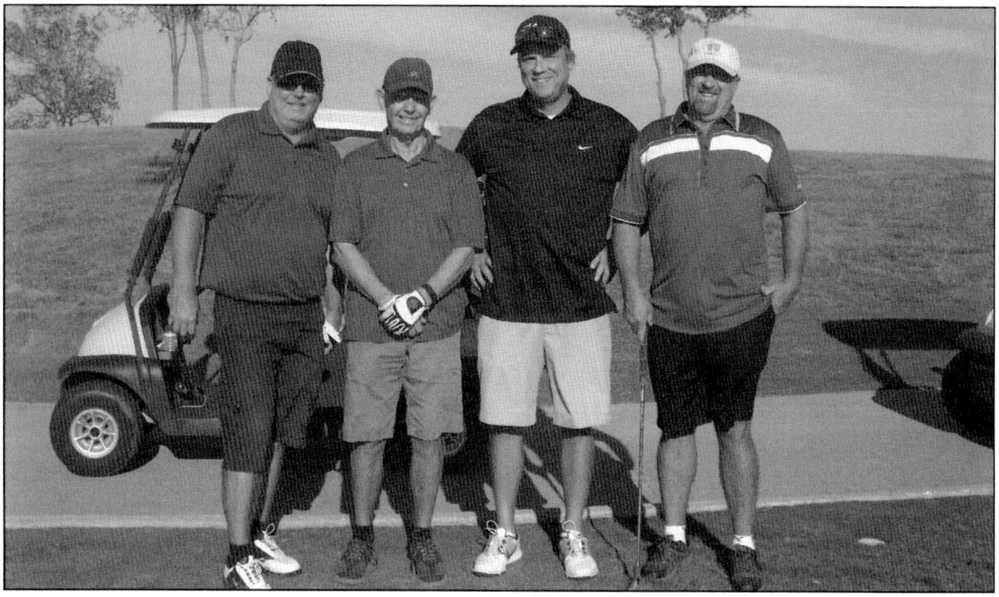

Four for Fore Fundraiser. This annual golf tournament, held since 2002, draws teams of community supporters who play to earn trophies, prizes, and bragging rights for the lowest score. Entry fees and hole and team sponsorships go toward scholarships and to support Denton County youth. Approximately $85,000 has been raised since the first tournament was held. The 2007 tournament winners, Team Reddy Ice (pictured), included, from left to right, Robert Pierce, Jim Davis, Ron Simpson, and Pete Farmer. (Courtesy of NTFR.)

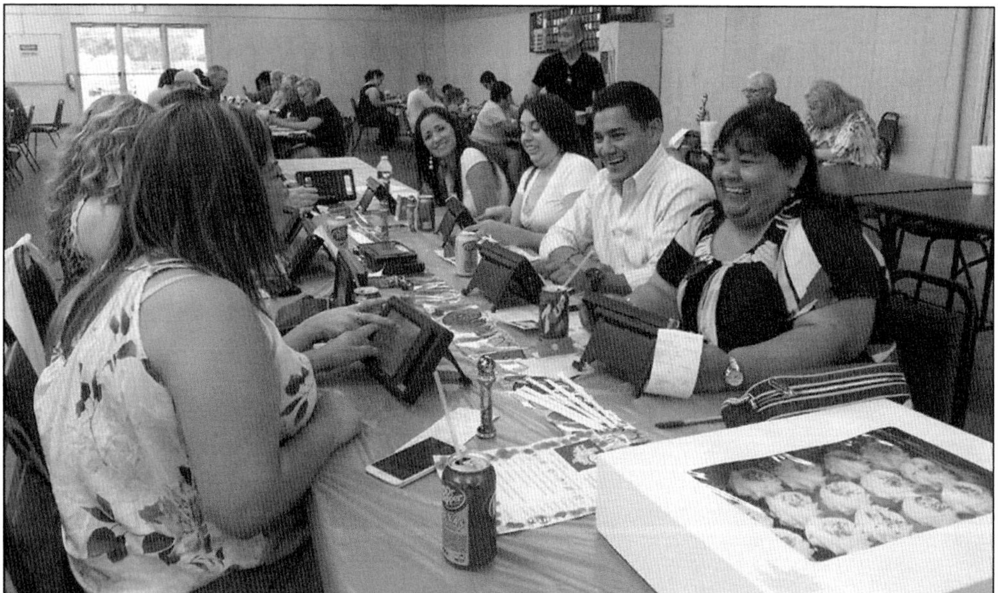

Bingo! Bingo became a Catholic church fundraising opportunity, giving it acceptability as a game of chance. Charity bingo has been a nightly fundraiser at the fairgrounds since 2009, with funds benefiting the NTSFA, Fair 2000 Inc., the Blue Ribbon Club, and the Elks Lodge and raising about $150,000 per year for these organizations. These birthday celebrants appear to be having fun (and hopefully yelling "Bingo!"). (Courtesy of North Texas Bingo Archives.)

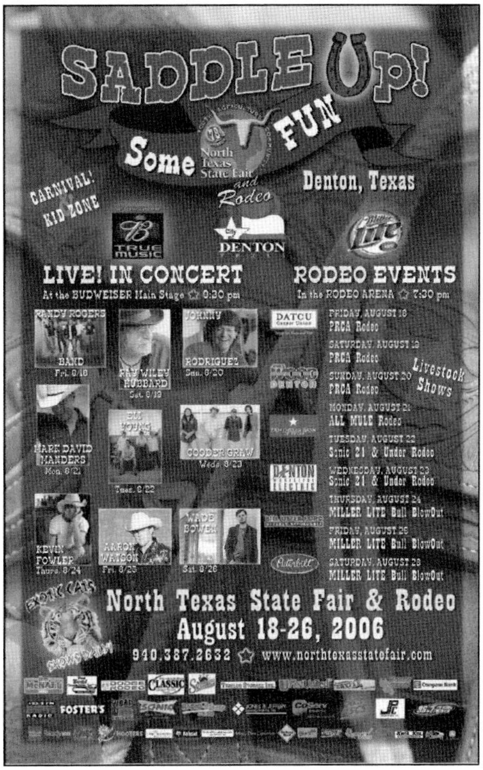

"SADDLE UP SOME FUN." The fair's theme for 2006 was "Saddle Up Some Fun." This clever slogan invited folks to enjoy the rodeo, concerts, carnival, and Kid's Zone. Many sponsors received top billing along with the numerous rodeo events and musicians. This poster was the first to be designed by the new managers of the fair and graphic artist Stephanie Taylor. A thematic advertising tradition has been in place ever since. (Courtesy of NTFR.)

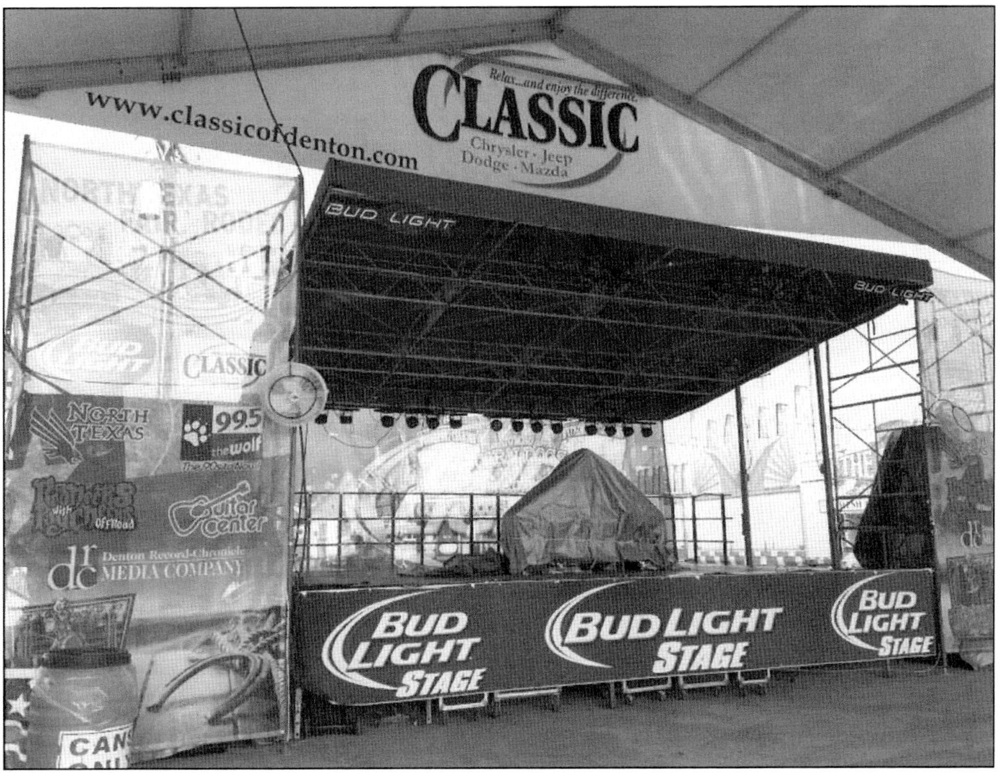

UNDER THE BIG TENT. In 2006, the "big tent" was added over the smaller stage to provide more shade and seating areas for the comfort of fairgoers. The first year, there was not a sponsor for the tent; however, a sponsorship for this highly visible entertainment and concessions location was sold in the second year, and the cost has been underwritten ever since. (Courtesy of NTFR.)

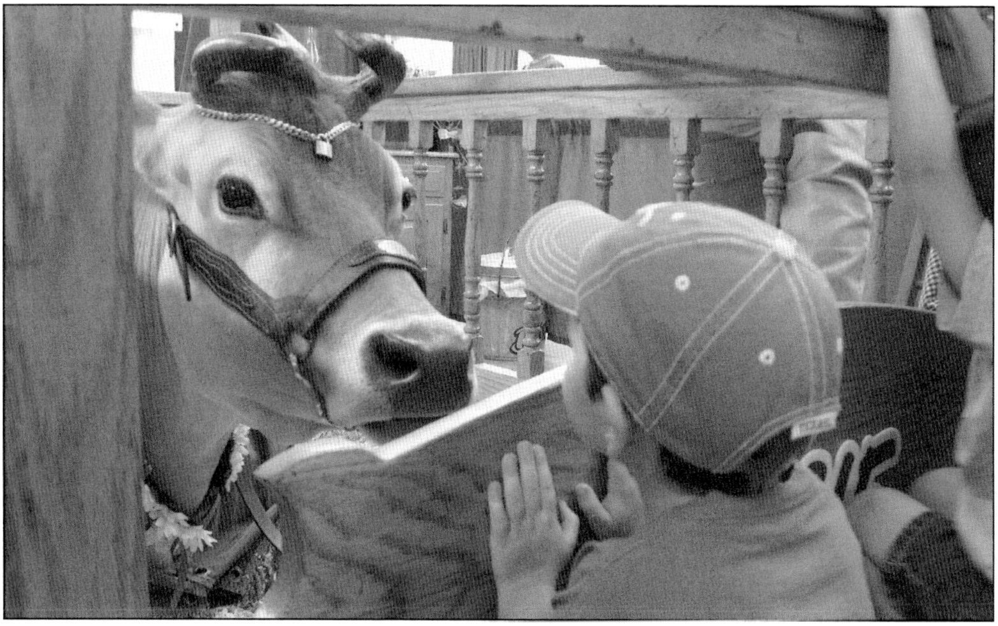

Elsie the Cow. Elsie the Cow, the Borden Dairy Company mascot since 1936, is meant to symbolize the "perfect dairy product." The original Elsie was a Jersey heifer, like the cow in this photograph, who made a special appearance at the commercial exhibit building for several years to the delight of young and old. Elsie has received humorous honorary awards, such as Doctor of Ecownomics, Doctor of Bovinity, and Queen of Dairyland. (Courtesy of NTFR.)

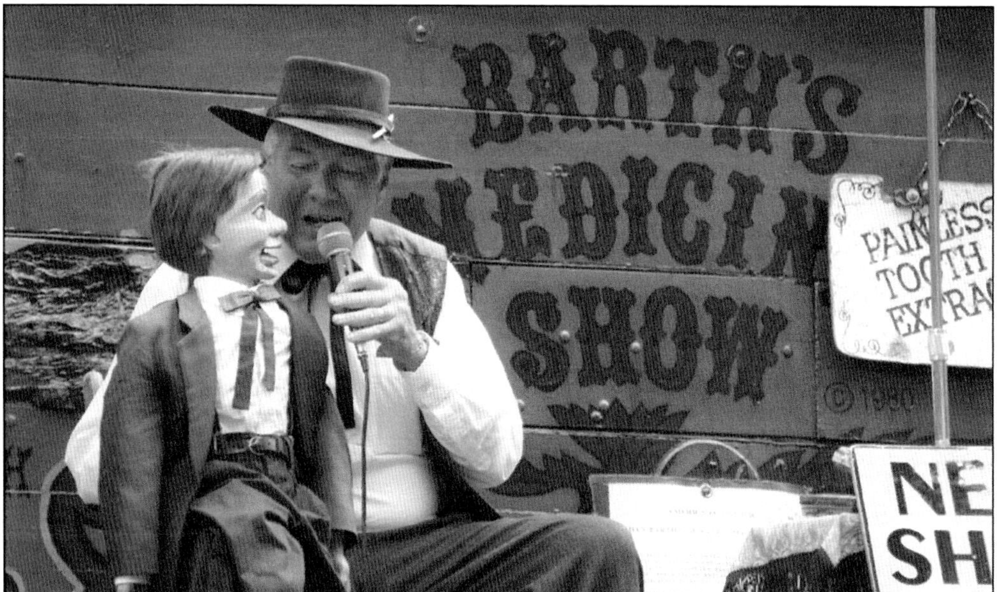

Dan Barth Medicine Show. Dan Barth—storyteller, humorist, and historian—brought his living history performance and medicine show exhibit to the NTSFR. Barth created and coproduced the nationally aired television series *America on Tour* with cohost Bill Garlow Cody, who was, at that time, the last living grandson of William F. "Buffalo Bill" Cody. Barth never failed to please a crowd. (Courtesy of the Dan Barth website: www.angelfire.com/biz4/danbarthshows/.)

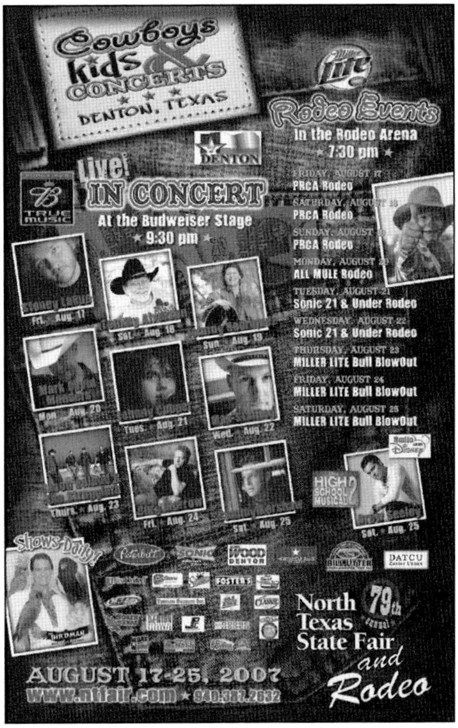

"Cowboys, Kids, and Concerts." At upper right on this 2007 "Cowboys, Kids, and Concerts" theme poster, Rudy Burns, barrelman and rodeo clown, gestures his positive "thumbs up" message to let the crowd know that all is well at the North Texas State Fair and Rodeo. Burns was featured because he embodies the essence of the fair. (Courtesy of NTFR.)

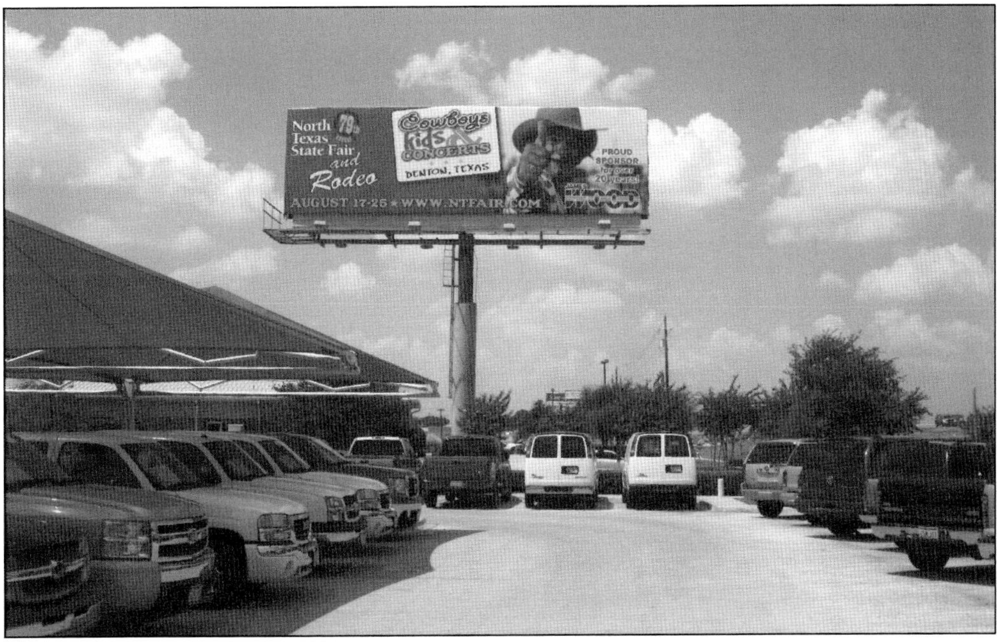

Advertisements in the Air. Billboard advertising for the fair was jump-started by a partial sponsorship through James Wood Autopark and Ben E. Keith Distributors. This cooperative advertising featured both the headlining entertainment and logos of the sponsoring companies. The exposure of the fair began to expand with this outdoor advertising. Interest in the fair was growing to reach outside of the Denton area, and these billboards helped attract the traveling public. (Courtesy of NTFR.)

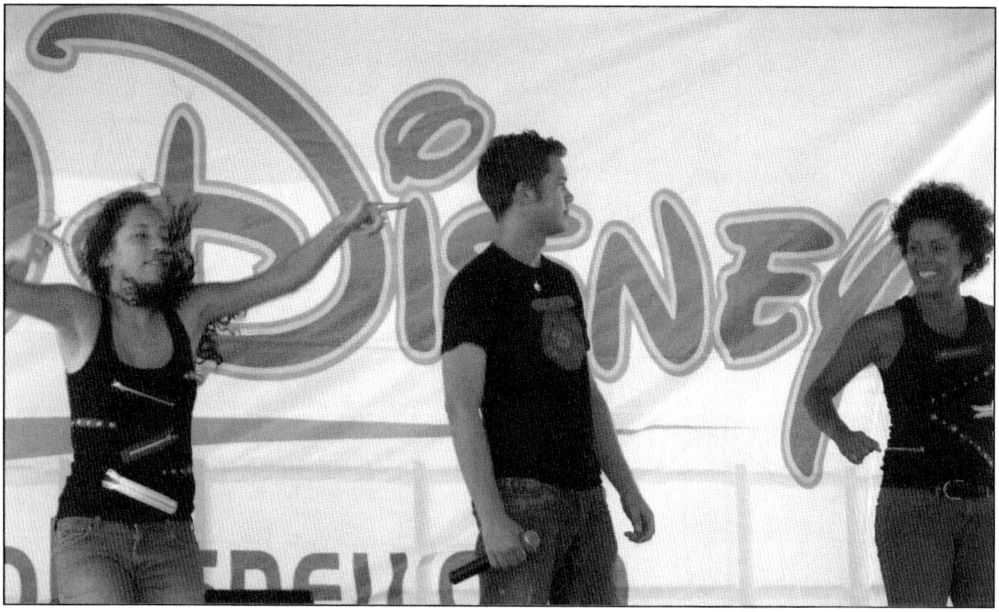

JUMP5. Formed in 1999, Jump5 was an American dance-pop contemporary Christian music touring group that enjoyed a string of hits on Radio Disney. Jump5 released a final album in 2007, stopping at the North Texas State Fair and Rodeo before ending their promotional tour in Nashville. (Courtesy of NTFR.)

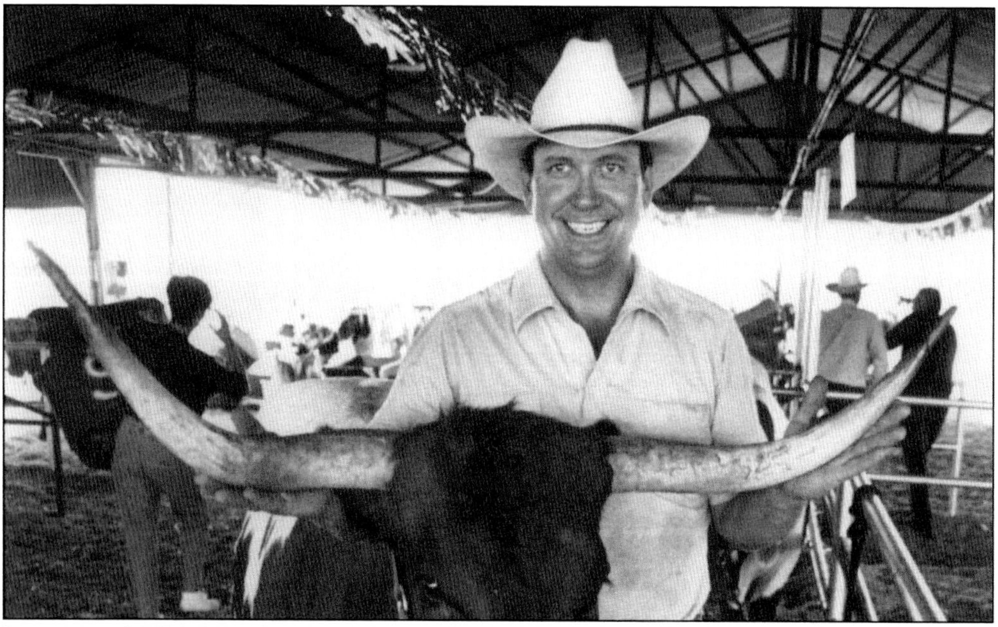

LONGHORN LIK-A-MELODY. Texas Longhorns are a popular attraction due to their size, diverse coloration, folkloric history, and immense horns. The horns of these animals can extend up to seven feet from tip to tip for steers and exceptional cows and from 36 to 80 inches for bulls. The grin on David Nance's face is typical of owners of these gentle but spirited beasts. LIK-A-MELODY, Nance's prize Texas Longhorn, has a 52-inch horn span. (Courtesy of DRC at DCOHC.)

"THE COWBOY WAY." "The Cowboy Way," the theme during the fair's 80th anniversary in 2008, summarized the cowboy ethics of everyday living. At right, Cade Pennington is learning the ropes from seasoned cowboy Weldon Burgoon in the Ron Bonge drawing that was used for the fair's advertising campaign. Pennington, who participated in the 2007 Mutton Bustin' contest, was chosen to represent the fair in its 2008 marketing program. James P. Owen's bestselling book, *Cowboy Ethics*, defines 10 principals to live by: 1) live each day with courage, 2) take pride in your work, 3) always finish what you start, 4) do what has to be done, 5) be tough but fair, 6) when you make a promise, keep it, 7) ride for the brand, 8) talk less and say more, 9) remember that some things are not for sale, and 10) know where to draw the line. Below, longtime supporter and volunteer Tom Shaw has handed down these traditions and ethics to his daughter Jill Shaw, current chairman of the North Texas Fairgrounders. (Both, courtesy of NTFR.)

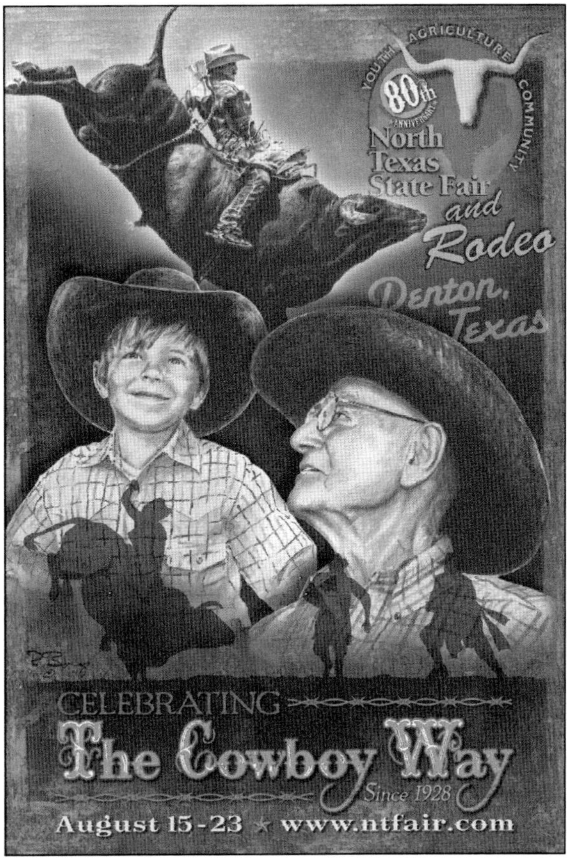

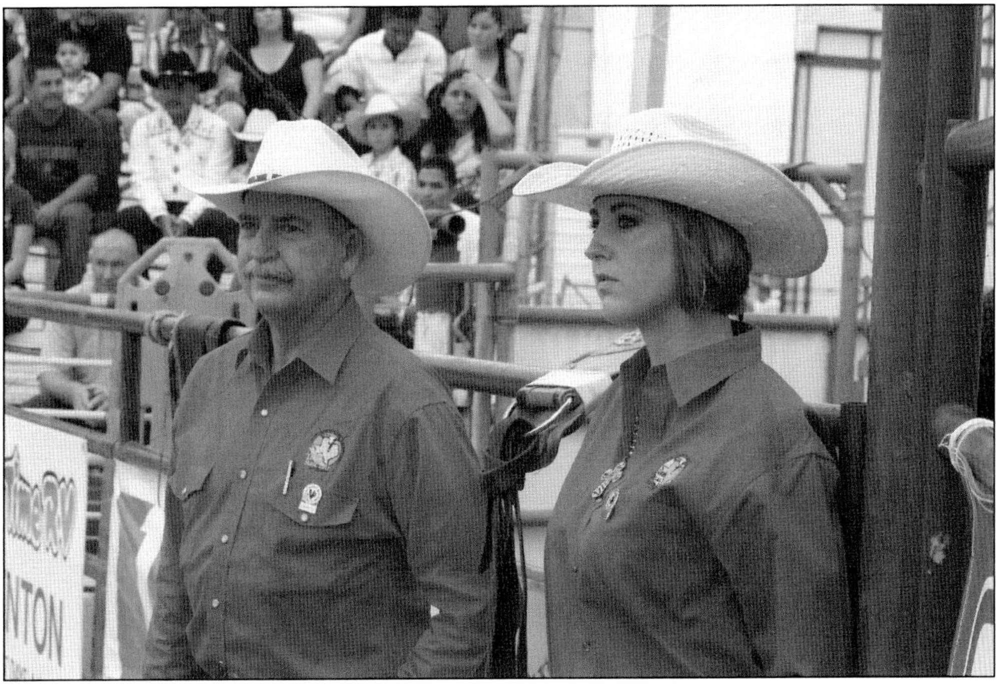

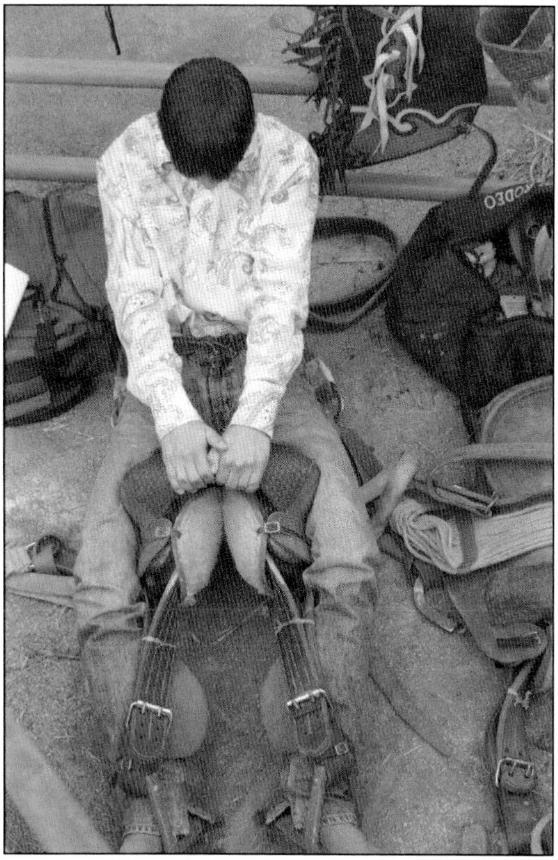

Ranking the Rider. The saddle bronc riding competition is a throwback from the old Wild West days. Cowboys mount the rankest broncs, whose sole purpose is to buck off their riders. A bronc rider must start the ride with his feet placed over the bronc's shoulders. During the eight-second ride, the cowboy must synchronize his spurring with the movements of the bucking horse in order to achieve a high score. The unidentified cowboy at left is mentally preparing himself before riding in the saddle bronc competition. Tol Cawley (below) displays perfect form on Sugar Shack as the PRCA judge scores his ride. (Both, courtesy of NTFR.)

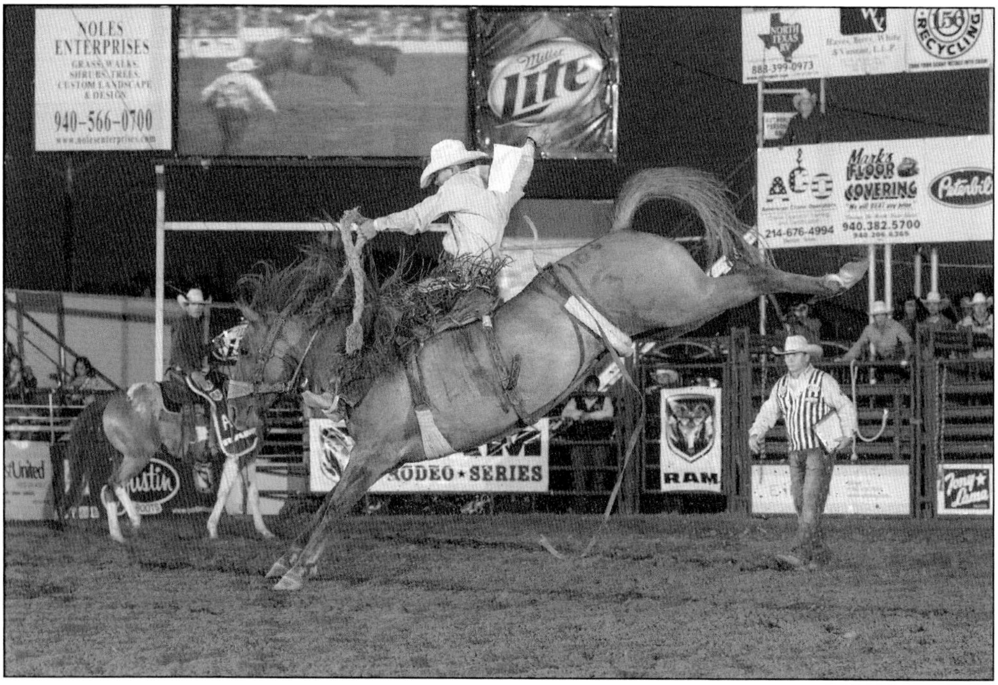

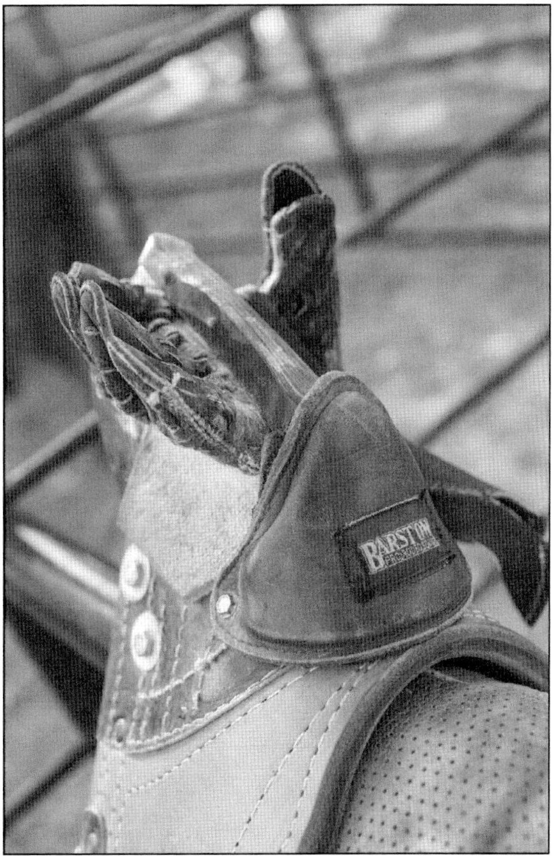

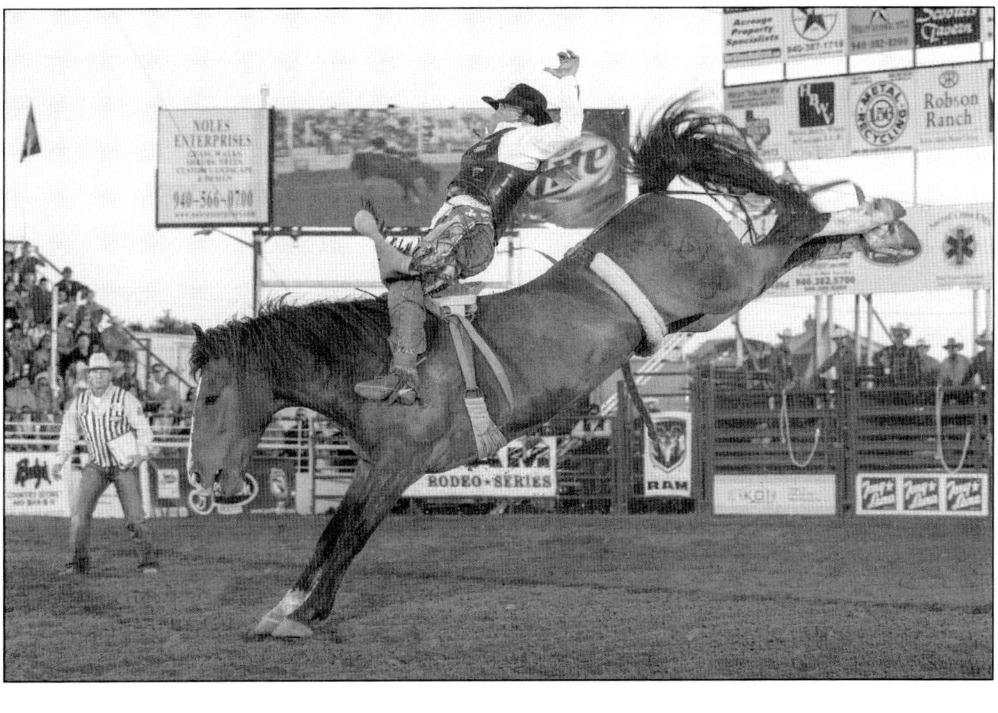

Break for Eight. Rough and explosive bareback bronc riding is one of rodeo's most physically demanding events. Cowboys have to ride fiery rough stock for eight seconds with nothing but a single handhold rigging cinched around the horse's girth. The special leather rigging has a hard, rawhide, suitcase-type handle (pictured at right). Custom leather gloves are coated in resin to aid with the grip. Below, Chad Rutherford's draw, Andrews Rodeo Company's Walk Hard—a volatile, bucking bronc—is kicking high in an attempt to dismount his rider. Rutherford is showing perfect form for a high-scoring eight-second ride. (Both, courtesy of NTFR.)

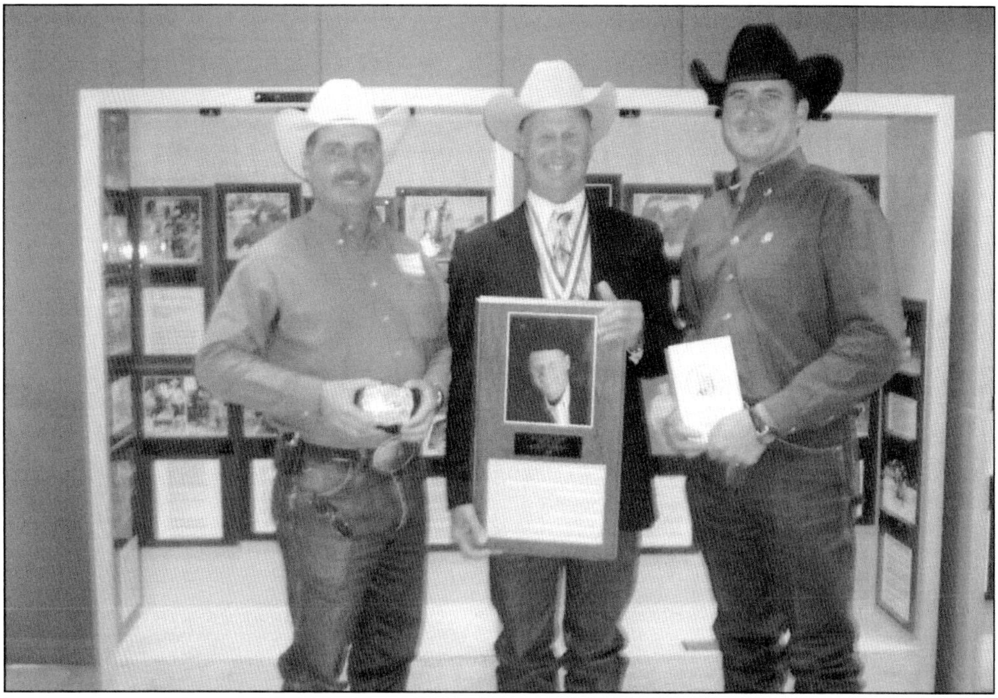

TEXAS RODEO COWBOY HALL OF FAME (TRCHF) INDUCTEE SAMMY ANDREWS. Glenn Carlton (left) and James Andrews (right) congratulate Andrews on his induction into the Texas Rodeo Cowboy Hall of Fame in 2008. Andrews was recognized for his contribution to the sport of rodeo as a stock contractor whose expertise produced championship bucking bulls for many years. A rare event occurred in Denton when the TRCHF traveling display appeared at the fair in 2008; the display arrived just in time to include the photograph taken when Andrews was inducted into the TRCHF. This display is now permanently housed in the Cowtown Coliseum in Fort Worth. (Above, courtesy of Andrews Rodeo Archives; below, courtesy of NTFR.)

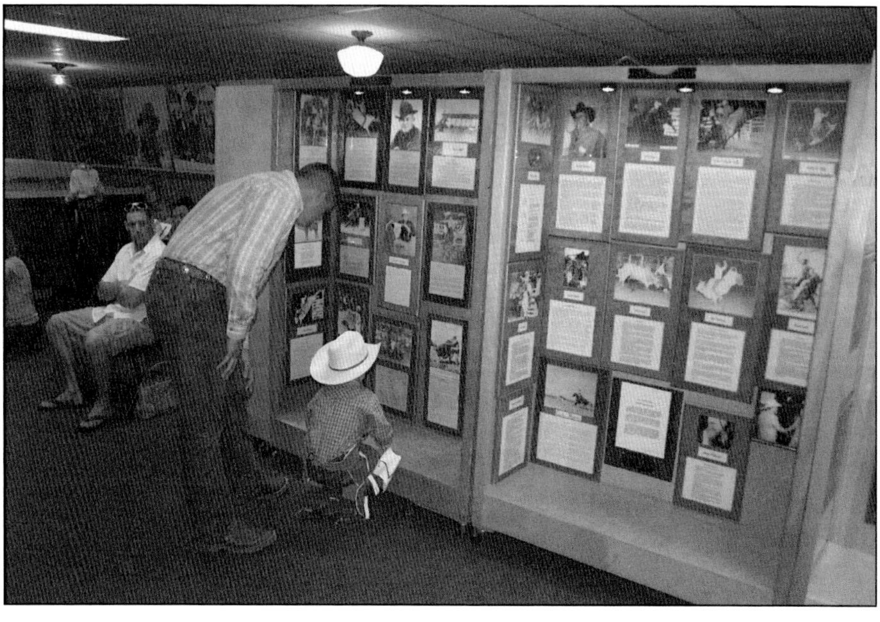

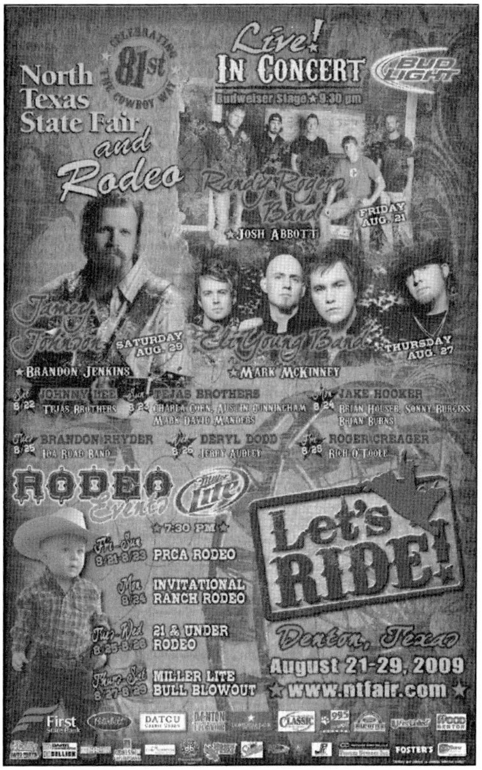

"Let's Ride." "Let's Ride" was the theme for the 2009 fair. The entertainment lineup included the Eli Young Band and Jamey Johnson. Also featured on that year's poster was Ty Grayson Purcell, the two-year-old son of Ryan and Ryan L. Purcell, who was selected not only for his cuteness but because of the cowboy attitude he already exhibited at his young age. Atwood Hat Company used this image in their advertising campaign along with the slogan, "If you start them out with the very best." (Both, courtesy of NTFR.)

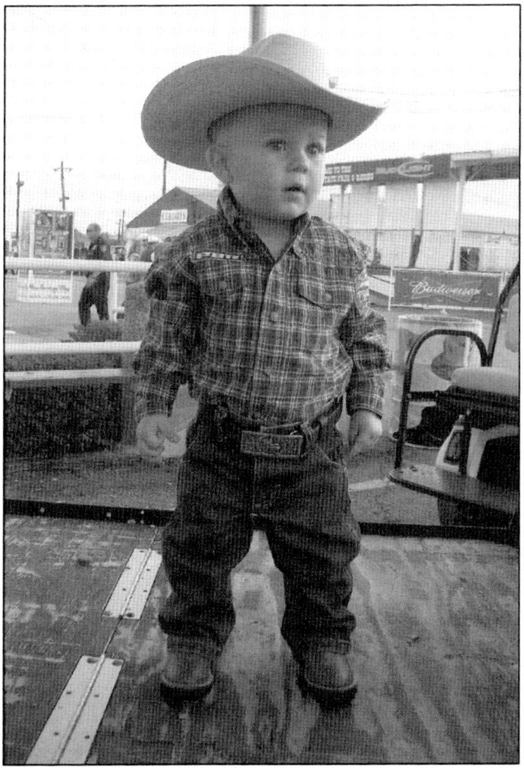

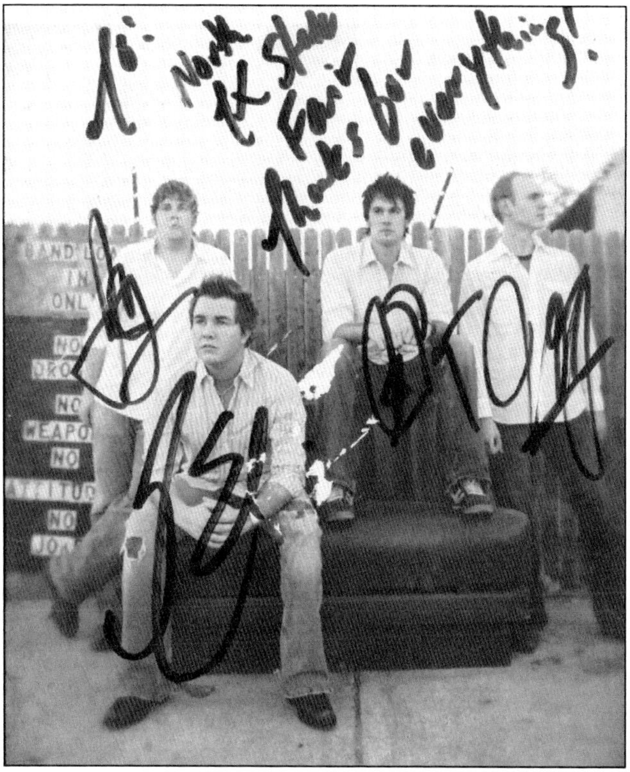

ACM Winners at the Fair. The Eli Young Band, featured at the fair in 2009, met at the University of North Texas in the late 1990s. They were nominated for a 2009 Academy of Country Music (ACM) Award as New Vocal Group. The band earned its first platinum record and the American Country Awards Song of the Year in 2011 and was nominated for a Grammy in 2013. (Courtesy of NTFR.)

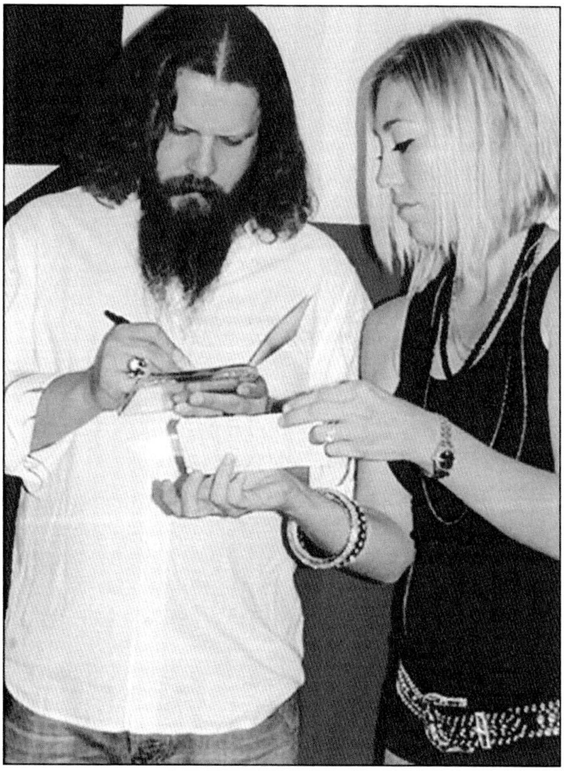

Jamey Johnson. Jamey Johnson—shown here autographing a CD for Ryan L. Purcell—is considered a restless maverick songwriter who not only records his own songs but also writes songs performed by country stars such as Trace Adkins, George Jones, and Joe Nichols. Johnson was the 2009 winner of Academy of Country Music (ACM) Song of the Year for "In Color," and cowriter of the County Music Awards and ACM 2007 Song of the Year, "Give It Away," recorded by George Strait. (Courtesy of NTFR.)

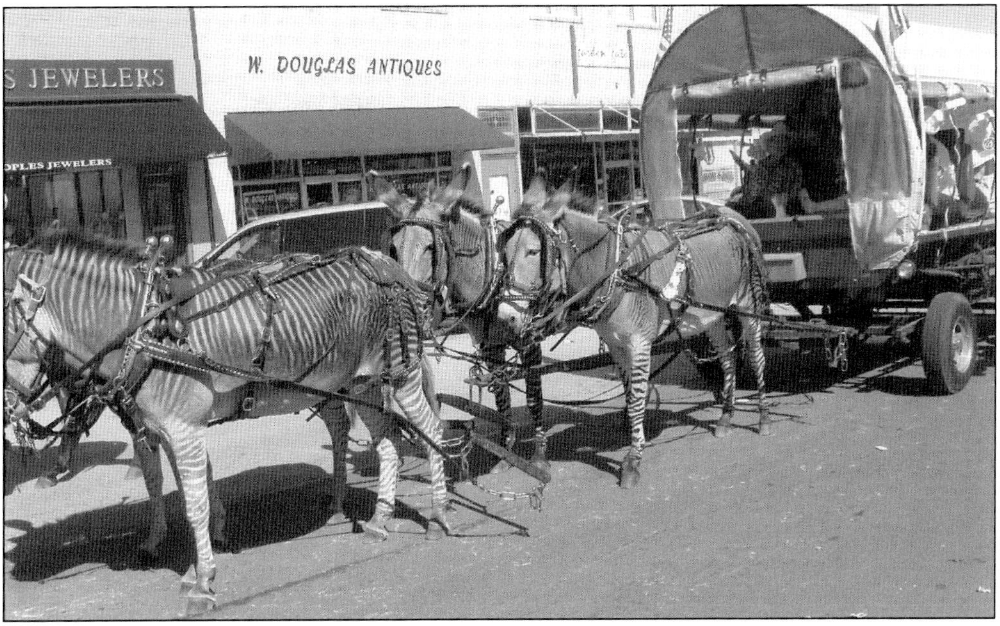

A Donkey of a Different Color. Hammie Boyd and his team of zeedonks were a hit at the fair parade in 2009. A zeedonk (also known as a zedonk, zebrass, zebronkey, zonkey, zebadonk, zenkey, or deebra) is a rare interspecies zebra mule—a cross between a zebra stallion and a horse mare or donkey mare. Boyd was as colorful as his zeedonks and a favorite at the annual parade. (Courtesy of NTFR.)

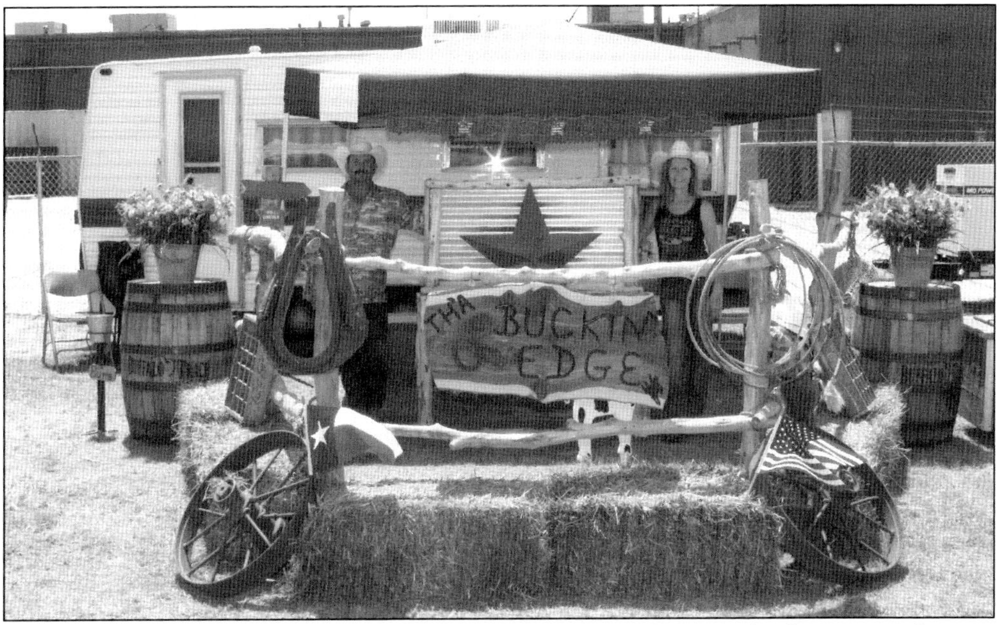

All Roads Lead to Terlingua. Chili heads gathered at the fair to make the meanest, hottest, tastiest chili in the county. This contest was a Chili Appreciation Society International (CASI)–sanctioned event whose winners garnered points to qualify for the CASI Terlingua Chili Championship. A portion of the chili cook-off entry fee is designated for local charities. Jody and Yvonne Wilkins are shown in their booth at the fair's chili competition. (Courtesy of NTFR.)

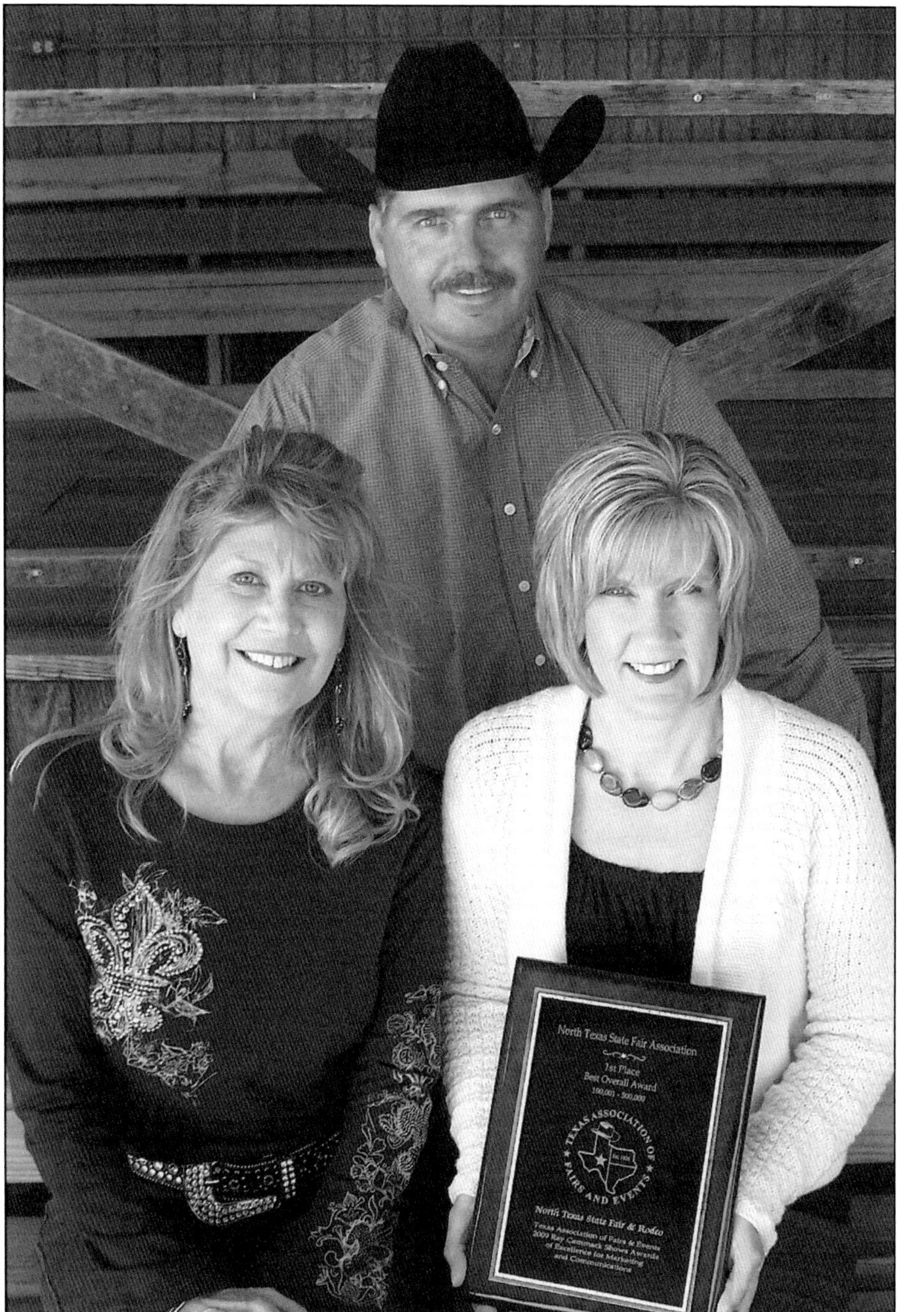

TAF&E Award of Excellence. The North Texas State Fair and Rodeo won its first Texas Association of Fairs & Events Best Overall Award of Excellence (for fairs with attendance of 100,001–500,000) in 2009. Pictured here are Nanci Kimmey (left), Stephanie Taylor (right; graphic artist with the Crouch Group), and Glenn Carlton. The NTSFR won this prestigious award from 2009 through 2011 and was runner-up in 2012 and 2013, when a member of a competing association made the remark, "Well, thank goodness, someone else had a chance to win." The NTSFR won first place again in 2014 and 2015. (Courtesy of NTFR.)

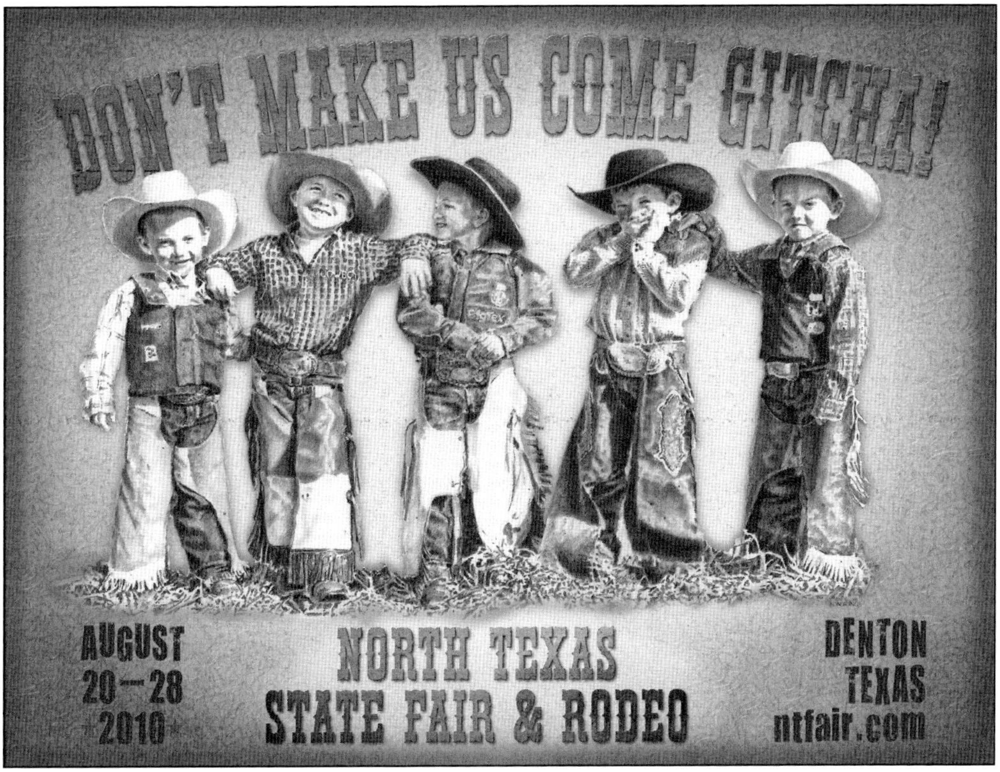

"Don't Make Us Come Gitcha!" The 2010 fair theme—"Don't Make Us Come Gitcha!"—was a tongue-in-cheek play on words about this posse rounding up thousands of people to attend the fair. The limited-edition art by Ron Bonge (above) was inspired by this rowdy group of five young buckaroos (below)—from left to right, Levi Nelson, Clay Akins, Tyler Akins, Riley Webb, and Ronnie Sellers—who are dressed to honor the cowboy tradition. (Both, courtesy of NTFR.)

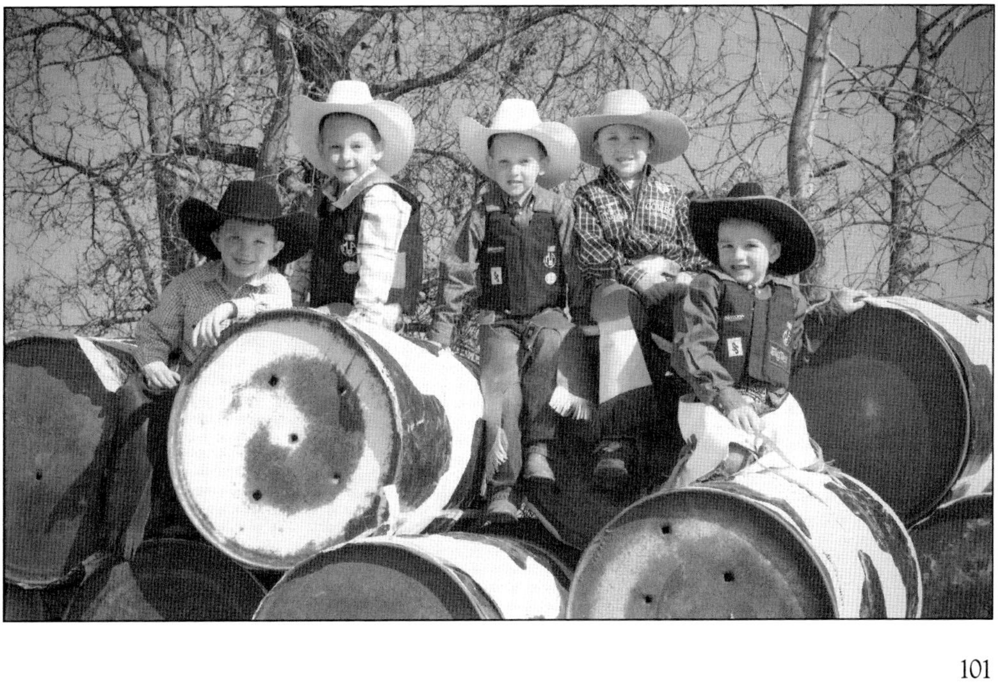

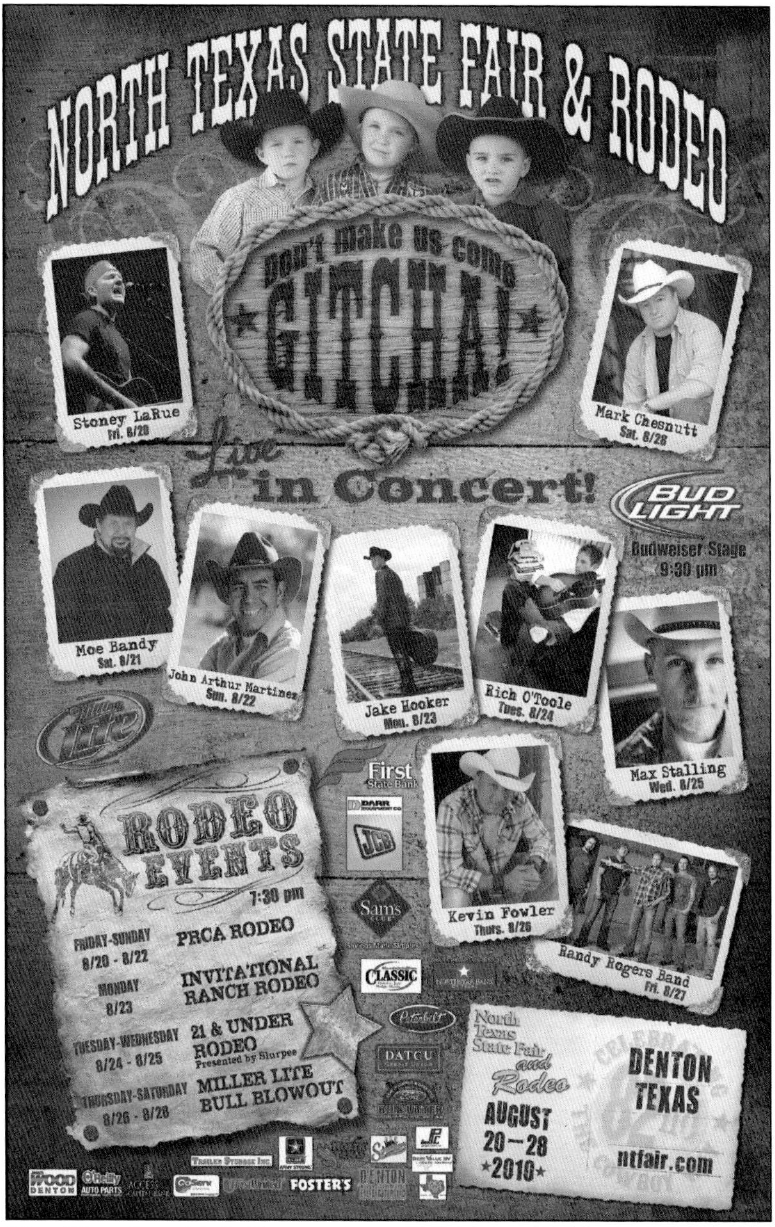

Mark and Moe. Texas-born Mark Chesnutt (upper right) is a country music artist who is passionate about keeping country music alive. He made his debut in 1990 with the hit single "Too Cold at Home" and has had eight No. 1 hits. Chesnutt earned a certified gold album with his 1994 effort, *What a Way to Live*. "Moe" Bandy (second row, far left) began his country music career in 1962 after trying bronco-busting and bull riding. The height of his popularity came in the late 1970s when he scored several hit songs, both alone and with his singing partner Joe Stampley. Two of his hit songs are "I Just Started Hating Cheatin' Songs Today" and "Bandy the Rodeo Clown." Bandy summed up his music by saying, "My songs are about life. There's cheating, drinking and divorcing going on . . . that's what country music is about." Moe Bandy and his brother Mike, a six-time NFR bull-riding qualifier, were inducted into the Texas Rodeo Cowboy Hall of Fame in 2007, three years before Moe performed at the fair. (Courtesy of NTFR.)

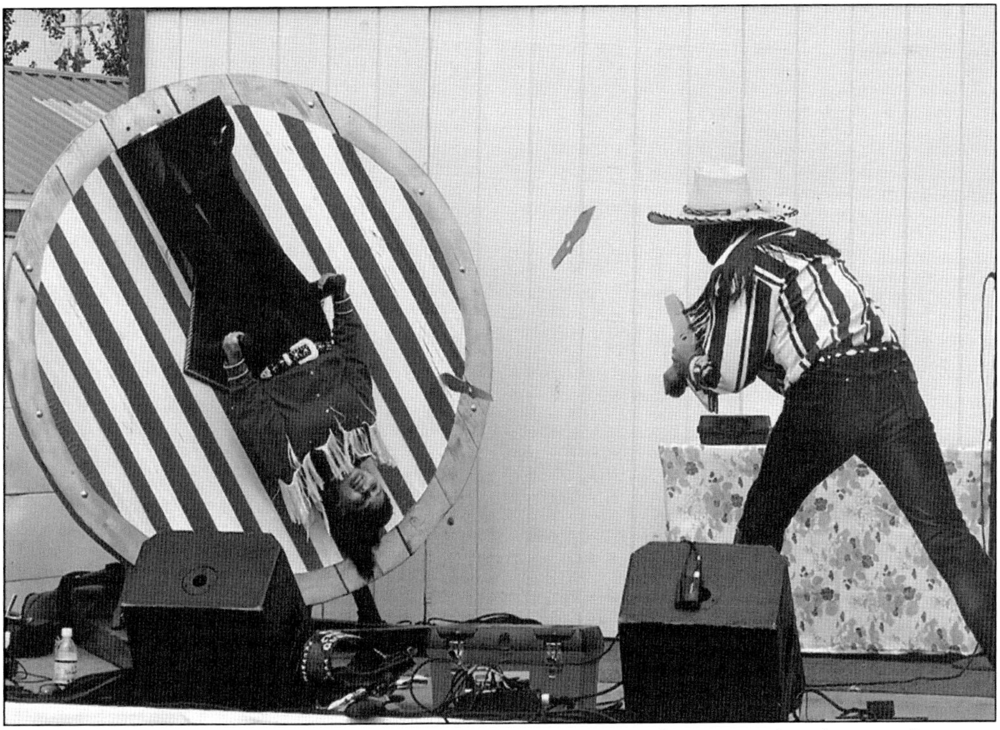

Rhinestone Roper. Dan Mink, the Rhinestone Roper, gives performances that showcase his rope, whip, knife, and gun skills and tricks. The Rhinestone Roper decided that to have an all-out Wild West show, he had to include a talented horse. His paint horse, Lucky Joe, fits the bill, performing humorous and unusual tricks. Teaching gun education and safety to children is important to Mink, so he interweaves these lessons into every program. (Courtesy of Dan Mink.)

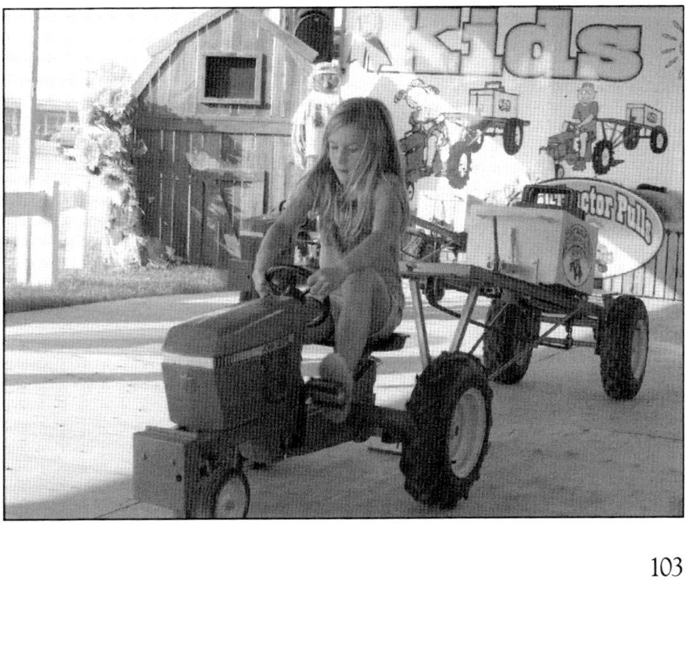

Kids' Pedal Tractor Pull. This unidentified little girl is pedaling with all her might in one of the most popular additions to the Kid's Zone, the kids' pedal tractor pull competition. Boys and girls from ages 4 to 12 pedal down a 25-foot path pulling a weight transfer sled filled with between 25 and 250 pounds (depending on the child's age). Every child is cheered to the finish line. (Courtesy of NTFR.)

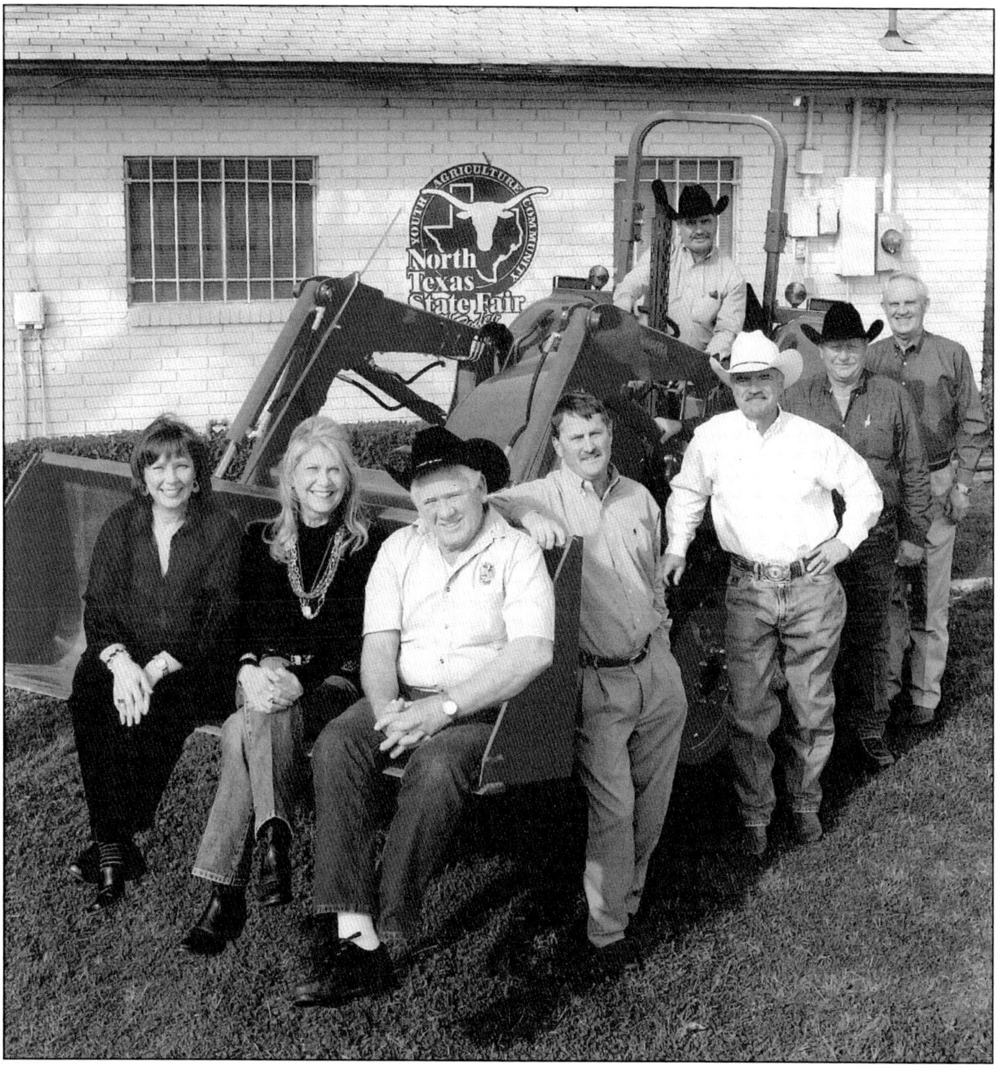

Denton Benefit League (DBL) Tractor. The motto of the Denton Benefit League, founded in 1973, is "enhancing the quality of life in Denton." The women of DBL serve Denton by raising funds for nonprofit organizations, volunteering in the community, and building leadership skills in women. The DBL, one of the hardest-working and most generous organizations in the community, partially funded a tractor to help maintain the fairgrounds. In past years, DBL has provided partial funding for two telephone systems and a color copier, all of which eased the day-to-day tasks of fair employees and volunteers. From left to right, fair executive board and staff Mickie Blagg, Nanci Kimmey, R.D. Martin, Lane Brewer, Carl Anderson, Mark Foster, Harry Hall, and Glenn Carlton (seated in the tractor) are displaying a bucket of appreciation to DBL. (Courtesy of NTFR.)

"It's Gatherin' Time." The 2011 fair theme was "It's Gatherin' Time," reflecting the idea that the NTSFR is an annual reunion for many participants and fairgoers. Crowds were treated to entertainment by the Randy Rogers Band, Tracy Lawrence, the music of two-time bull riding champion Justin McBride, and singing cowboy Colby Yates. (Courtesy of NTFR.)

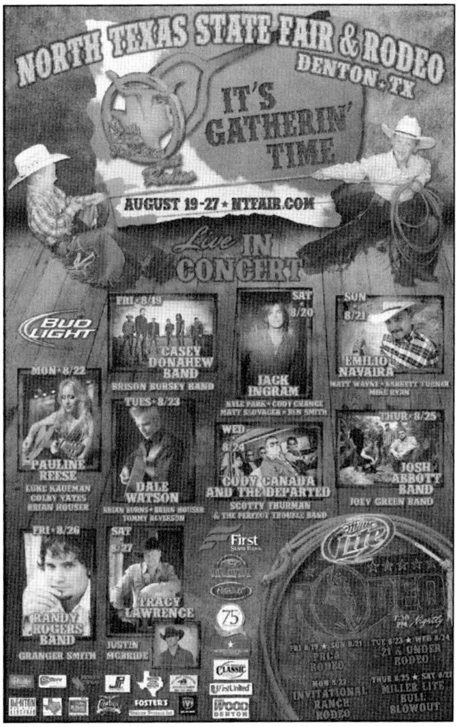

Rodeo Committee. It is impossible to conduct the annual fair without a faithful, hardworking crew of volunteers who serve on the NTSFR committee. Members are responsible for setting up the rodeo arena, working with the stock and the stock contractor, maintaining the equipment and arena for the duration of the event, and working with sponsors and special guests. Tamra Stephens (at center in the first row) sets up cowboy camp and feeds all the volunteers and stock contractors during the fair. (Courtesy of NTFR.)

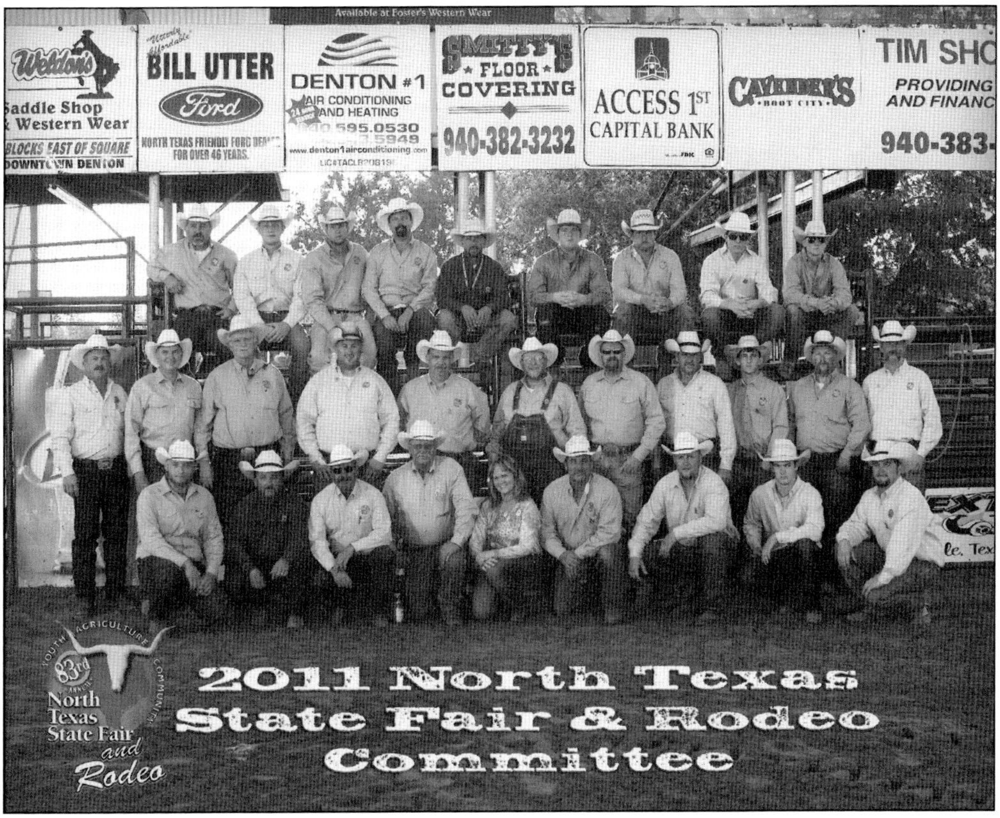

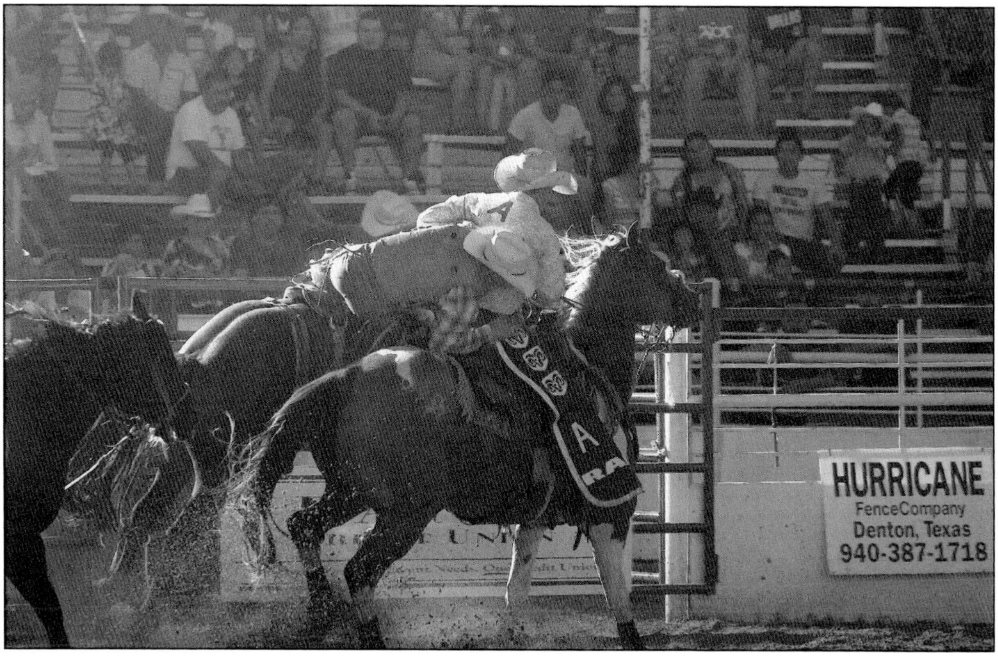

Pickup Artists. Pickup men work in tandem to help bronc riders dismount safely and to guide bulls that might be looking to hook a rider or bullfighter. The Andrews Rodeo pickup cowboys help the bronc rider to safety and are always there in the nick of time. These men are crucial in keeping both two- and four-legged athletes safe. (Courtesy of NTFR.)

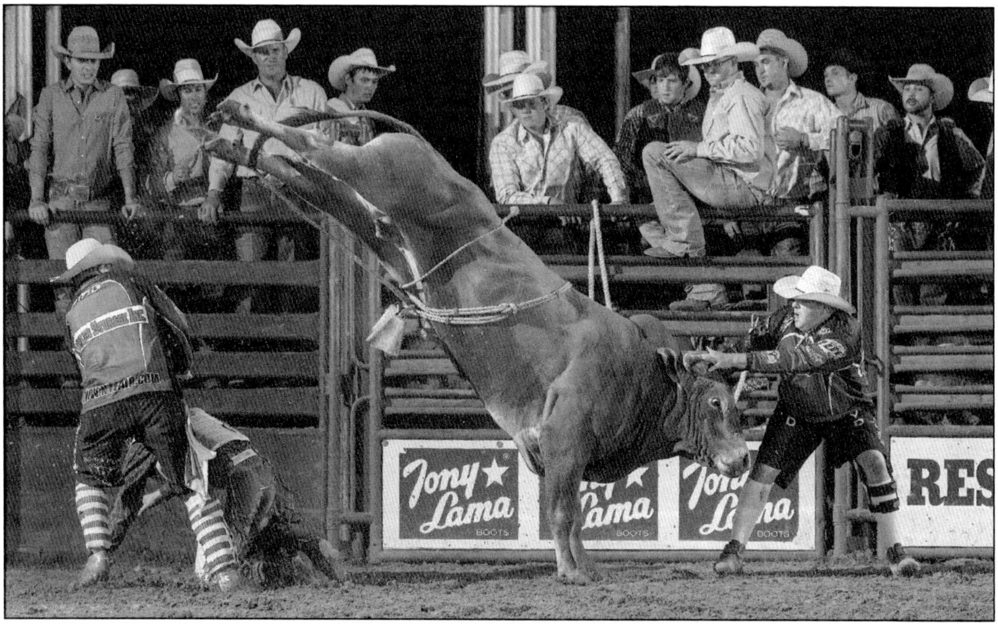

Cowboy Protection Teams. Sixteen of the top bullfighters divide into eight cowboy protection teams to compete for a trophy buckle and prize money. The team's job is to protect fallen riders from rampaging bulls. These teams consist of nationally renowned bullfighters. Each team has a community business sponsor and wears custom jerseys. In this photograph, the men of Team Trailer Storage guard a cowboy while showing off their bullfighting skills. (Courtesy of NTFR.)

Photography Exhibit. A popular competition in the Fair Hall exhibit area is the display of photographs by amateur shutterbugs. Vada Schneider, wearing her white cowboy hat, is carefully studying photography entries, perhaps thinking of someday entering her own snapshots in a future contest. Photographs are judged on composition, originality, style, and content. (Photograph by Alex Lieban; courtesy of NTFR.)

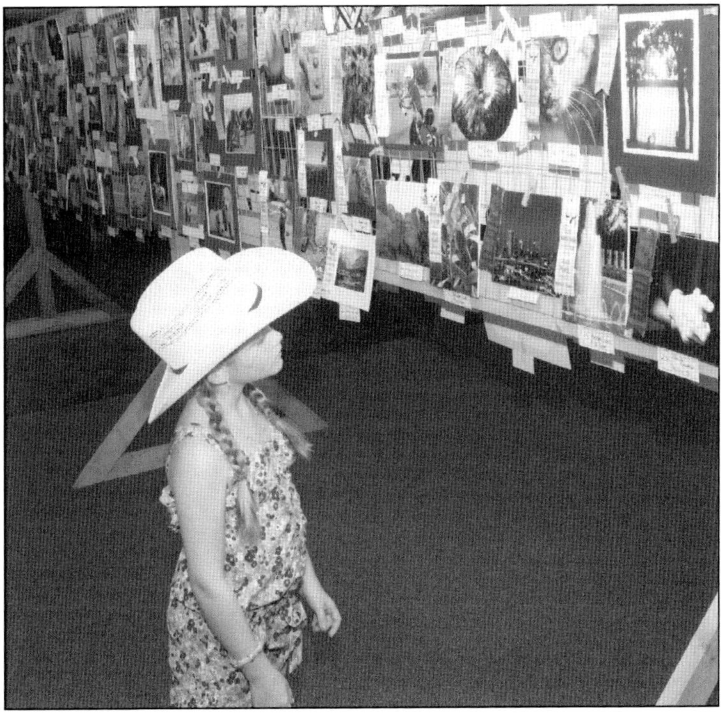

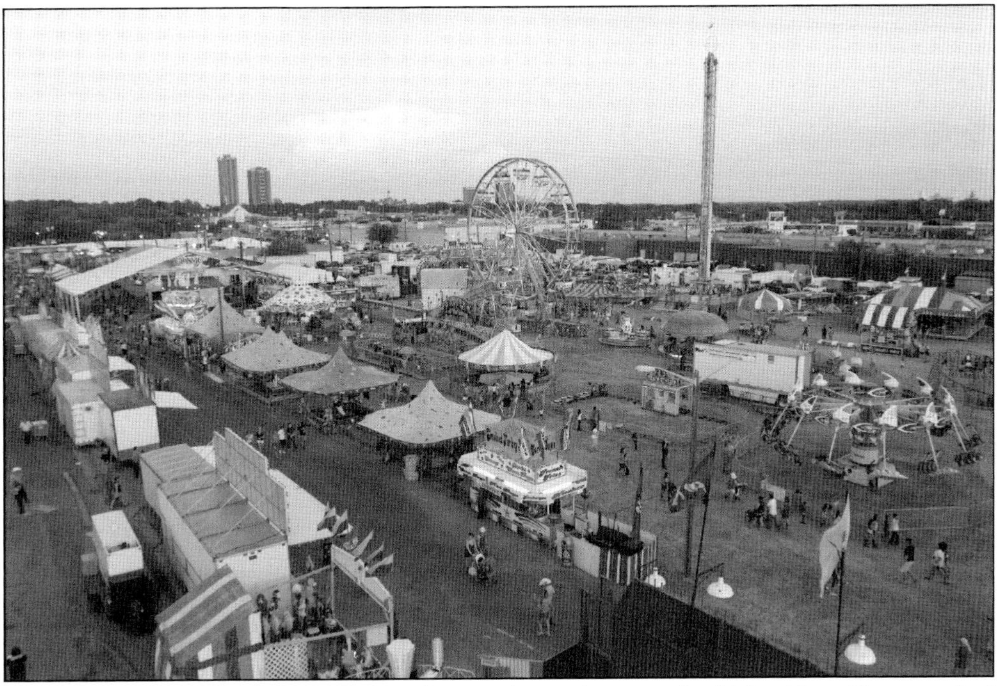

Talley Amusements. There is much to do, see, play, and taste at the fair's midway. From carnival rides and games of chance to corn dogs and the colorful carousel, fairgoers can hardly say they were not thoroughly entertained, did not have enough to eat, or did not enjoy an evening of good family fun during the nine days of the NTSFR. This photograph shows the fair's proximity to Texas Woman's University and to Denton Center Shopping Center. (Courtesy of NTFR.)

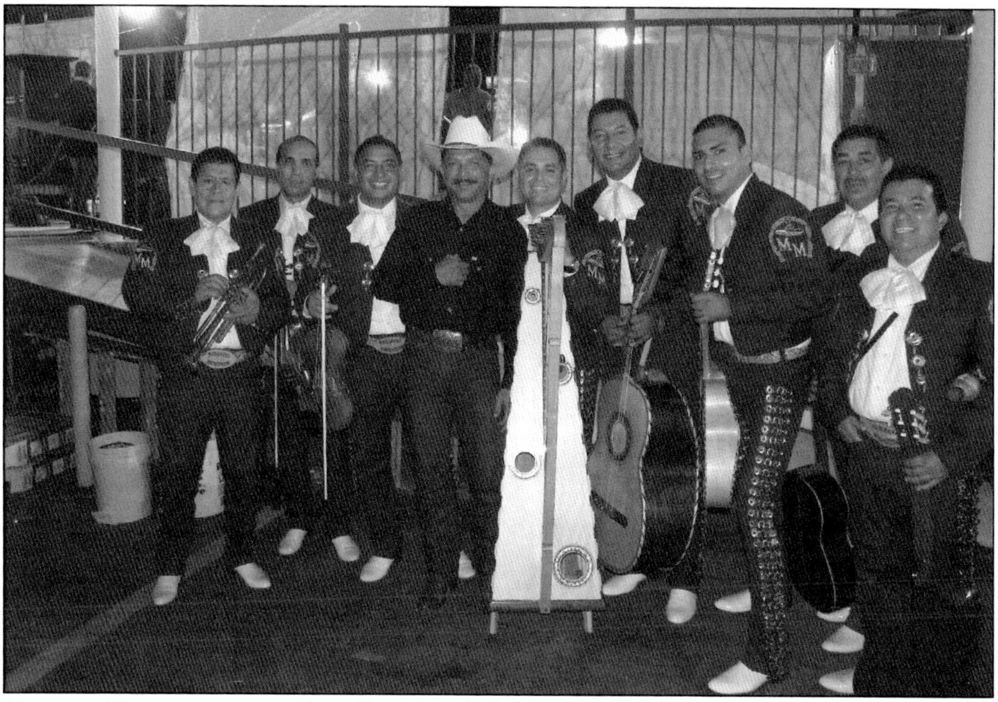

Hispanic Heritage at the Fair. Renowned Tejano and country singer Emilio Navaira (in the white hat) is standing with Mario Fernandez Jr. and his band, Mariachi Michoacan, who performed during Hispanic Heritage Day at the fair. Navaira's successful career in both the United States and Mexico has earned him the title of the "Garth Brooks of Tejano." (Courtesy of NTFR.)

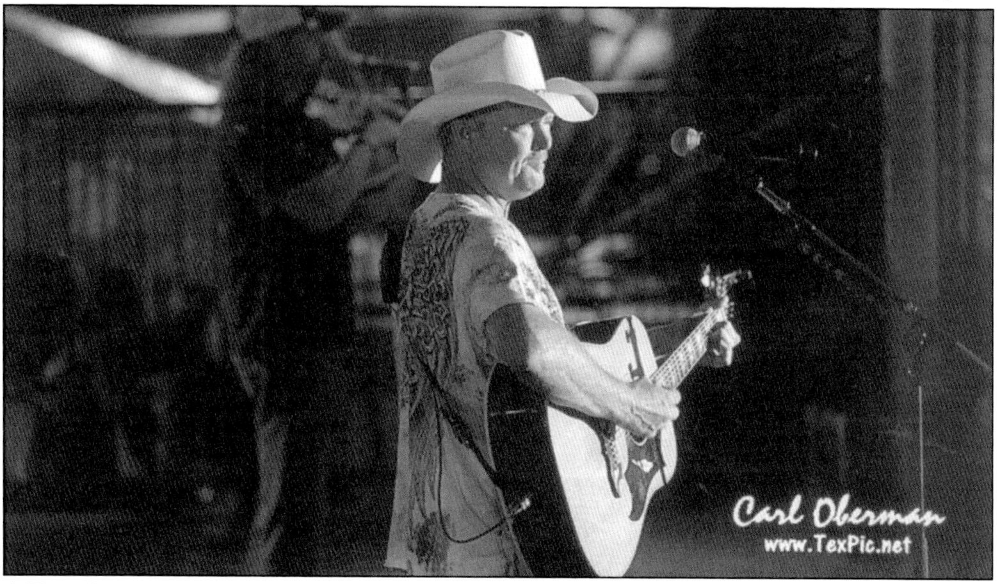

A Fair Friend. Tracy Lawrence is a very recognizable voice in country music, with songs such as "Paint Me a Birmingham," "Time Marches On," and "Find Out Who Your Friends Are." With 22 *Billboard* chart-topping hits and 18 No. 1 singles, Lawrence has sold more than 13 million albums. This multiplatinum, award-winning recording artist has helped shape the sound of country music for two decades. (Photograph by and courtesy of Carl Oberman.)

"The Rodeo is On . . . Turn it Up!" "The Rodeo is On . . . Turn it Up!" was the fair's 2012 theme. This play on words takes its idea from the phrase "the radio is on, turn it up." Fair managers wanted to encourage participants, vendors, and fairgoers to go all out to have a great time. Featured attractions that year included Robert Duck's Great American Duck Race, Trout Fishing, Trackless Train, and Kids' Pedal Tractor Pull. (Courtesy of NTFR.)

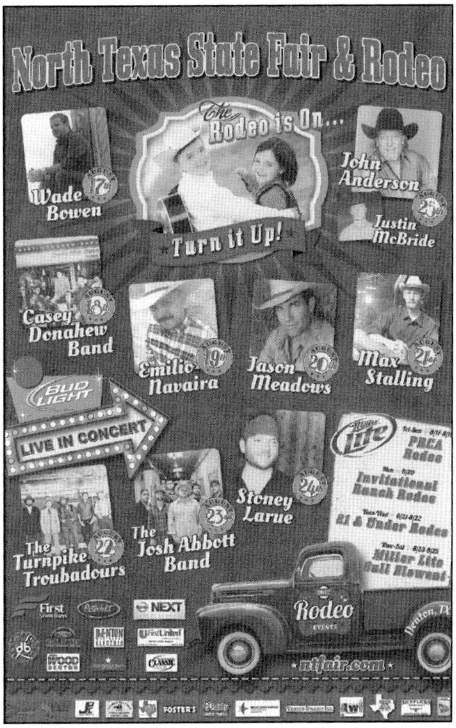

Digital Billboards. The expansion of eight billboards, plus two digital billboards, to the Dallas/Fort Worth metroplex and to Oklahoma increased the advertising potential to a broader audience. The billboard message rotated every eight seconds, allowing moving traffic to view the daily musical lineup. The three rotating images for the last three days of the 2012 fair—featuring Nashville recording artist and main stage performer John Anderson—are reflected in this photograph. (Courtesy of NTFR.)

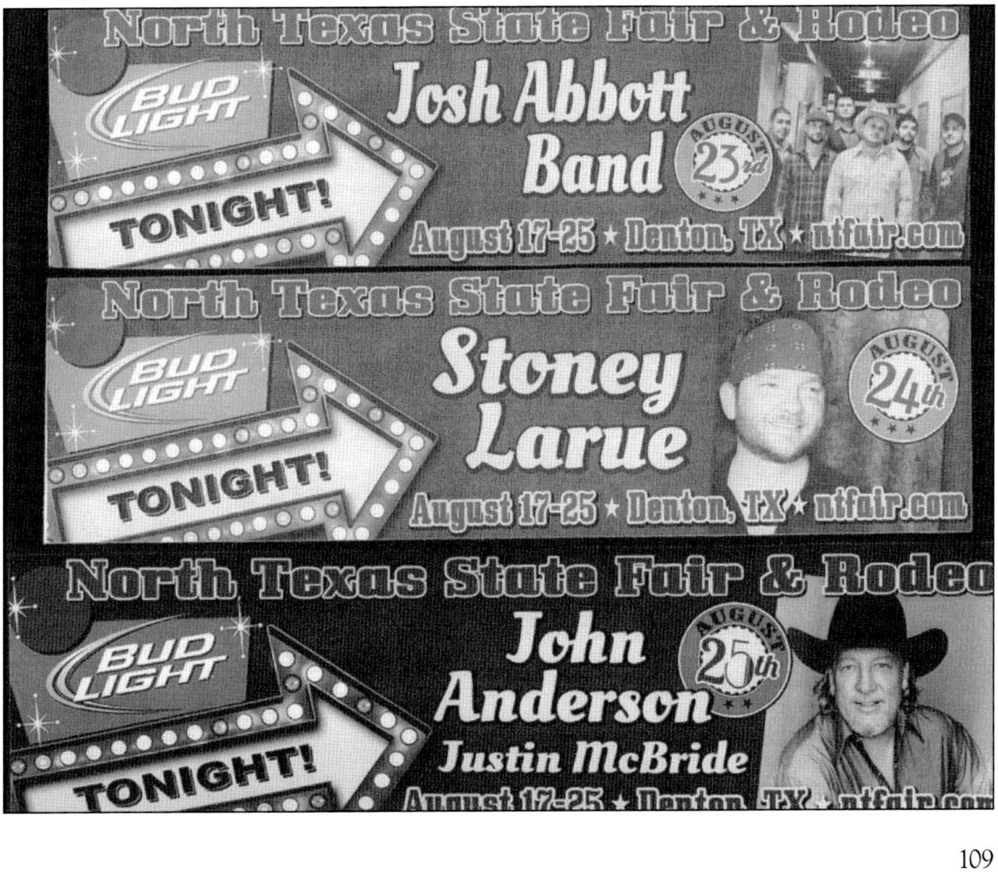

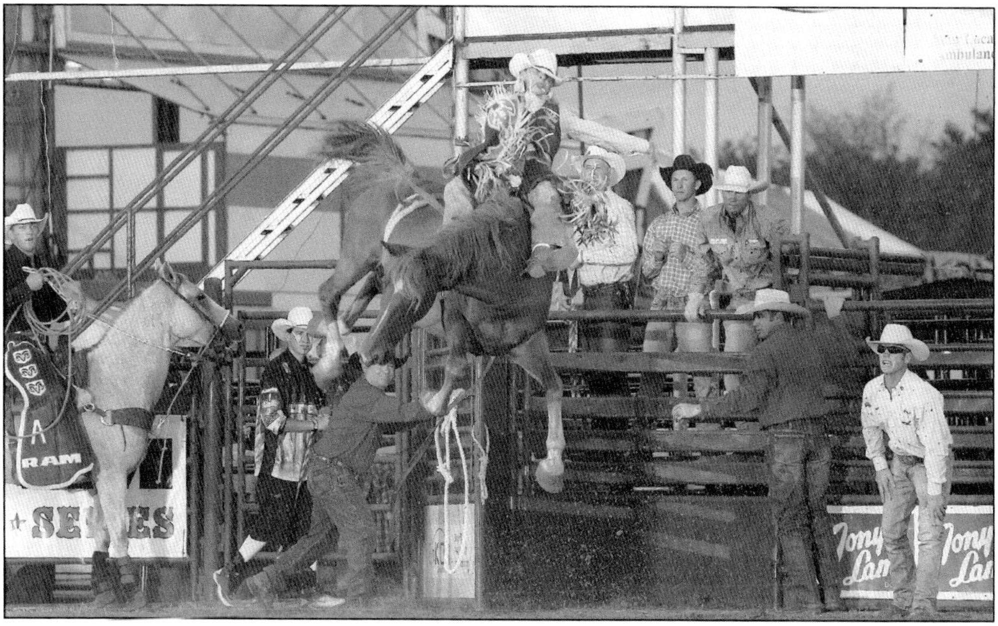

A FRENCH COWBOY IN TEXAS. French-born Eyan Jayne was introduced to the rodeo by his parents, who performed as trick riders at rodeo shows in France and Italy. Jayne moved to Texas at age 16 and earned a rodeo scholarship to Sam Houston State University. After earning his degree, he juggled a full-time teaching job with his NFR quest. Jayne was the first cowboy to represent France at the NTSFR and is the first European-born cowboy to qualify for the 2015 NFR. (Courtesy of NTFR.)

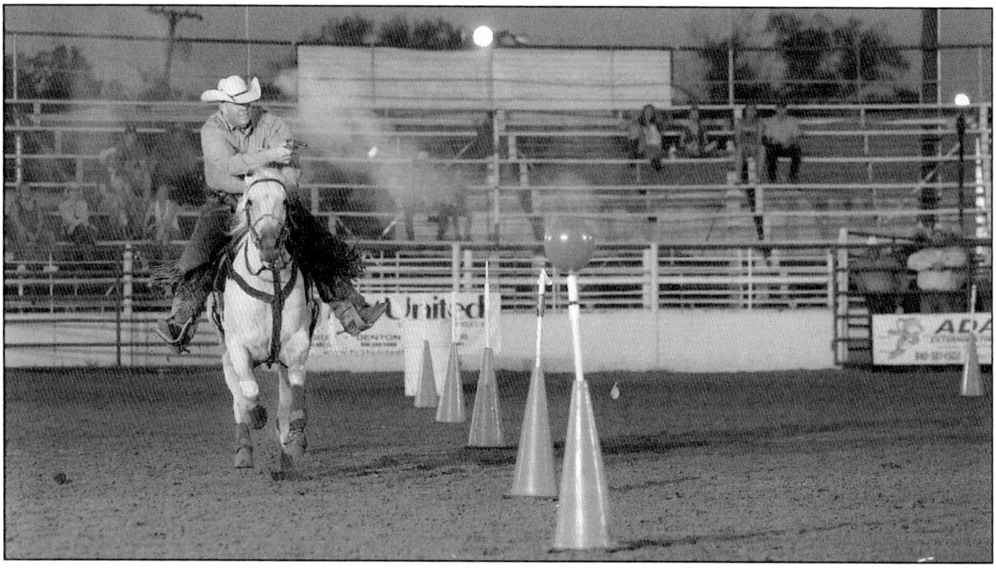

COWBOY MOUNTED SHOOTING. Cowboy mounted shooting requires skill in both horsemanship and shooting. It involves riding a horse while negotiating a challenging course of 10 balloon targets. Blank black powder cartridges are fired from single-action revolvers to break the balloons. This is a high-speed, timed spectator sport in which the competitor who rides the fastest with the least amount of missed targets wins. In this photograph, Allan Watt is about to score a clean run after shooting one last target. (Courtesy of NTFR.)

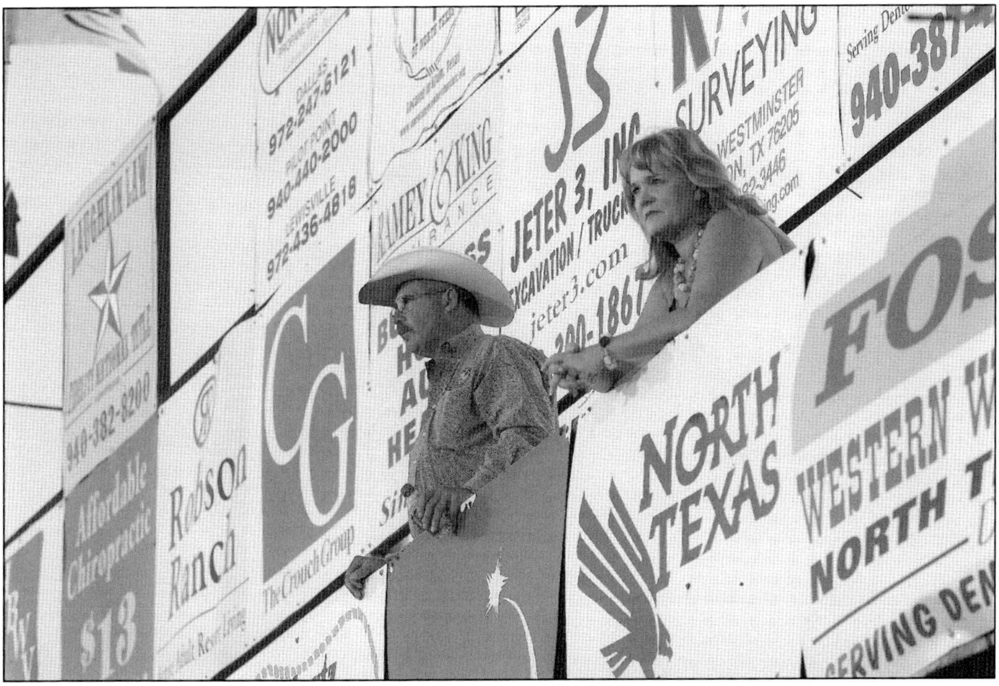

Sizing up the Crowd. By 2012, sponsorships had increased an additional 30 percent, attendance continued to increase exponentially, and bigger names appeared nightly on the stages and in the rodeo arena. Glenn Carlton and Tamra Stephens are on pictured here on the catwalk overlooking a rodeo performance and sizing up the crowd. The inclusion of more free events provided added value and drew larger crowds. (Courtesy of NTFR.)

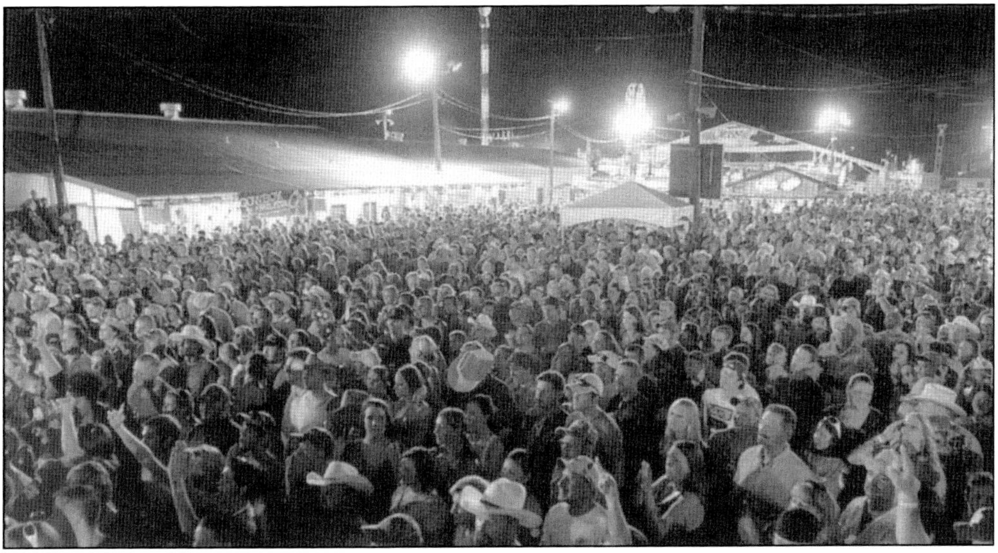

Typical Large Weekend Crowd. This large crowd is typical of the fair's Friday and Saturday night concert crowds. Between 2005 and 2012, fair attendance increased from 90,000 to 150,000. More than $100,000 in capital improvements has made the grounds more accommodating, and additional ticket booths have allowed for quicker entrance into the fairgrounds. (Courtesy of NTFR.)

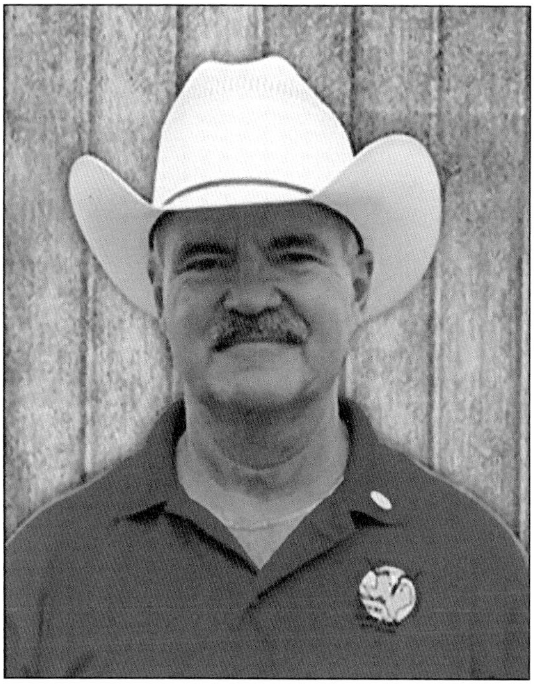

Carl Anderson. Carl Anderson was named president of the North Texas State Fair and Rodeo Association board in 2012. His 19 years on the association board and his community and business leadership in Denton offer the right combination of skills to lead the fair into a new era of excellence. The association's purchase of 111 acres of land north of Denton was negotiated during Anderson's tenure. (Courtesy of NTFR.)

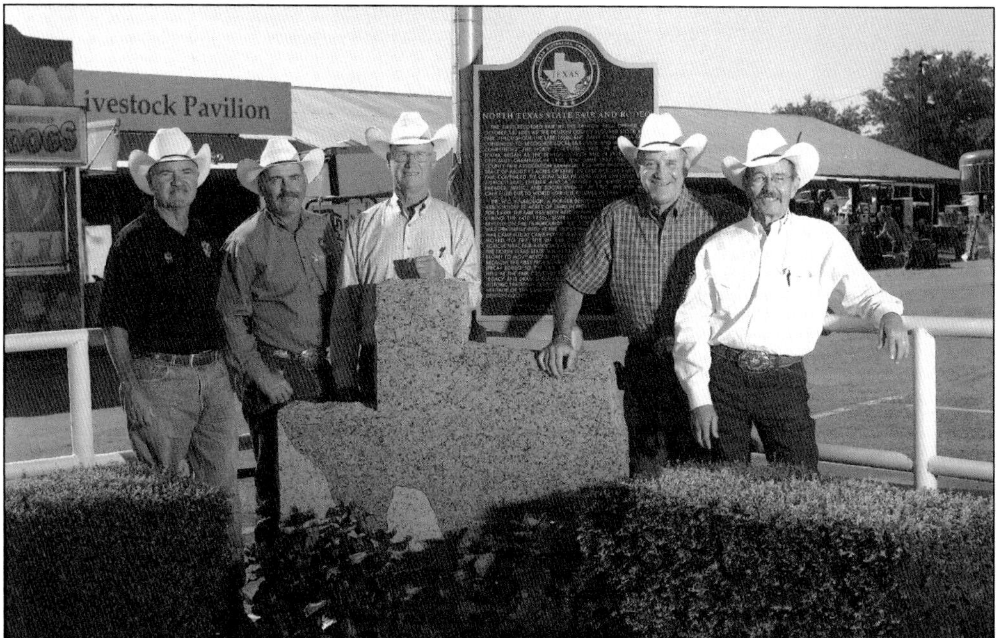

Texas State Historical Marker. From left to right, North Texas State Fair and Rodeo Association (NTSFR) board president Carl Anderson, NTSFR executive director Glenn Carlton, stock contractor Sammy Andrews, former Dallas Cowboy and fair board member Walt Garrison, and rodeo announcer Terry Starnes pose with a State of Texas granite sculpture that marks the overnight campsite of the 1986 Texas Sesquicentennial Wagon Train. The fair was awarded a Texas State Historical Commission Marker—the first subject marker to be awarded to a fair in the state of Texas—in 2012. (Courtesy of NTFR.)

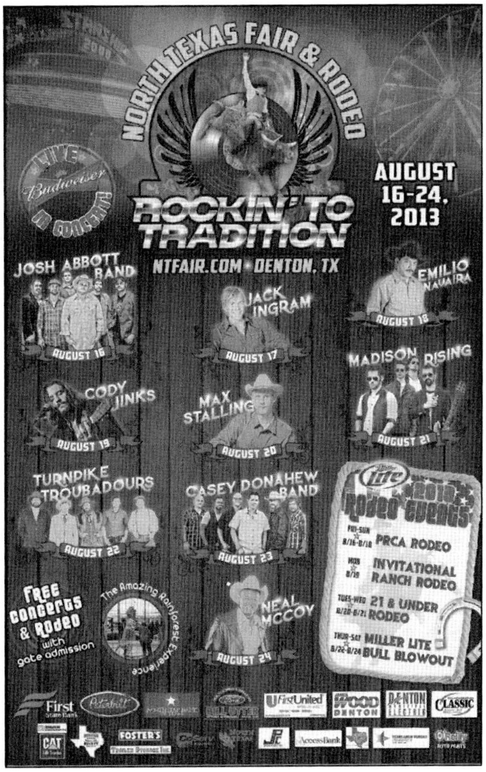

"ROCKIN' TO TRADITION." In 2012, in a change from the typical, the fair broke away from its customary presentation of country music and hired the rock-and-roll band Madison Rising. A video of the band performing "The Star-Spangled Banner" captured the attention of fair management, who hired the group to perform at the fair. This band pays tribute to America's men and women in uniform through a brilliant classic rock sound. It is clear they are on a mission not only to make great music but to send a message that American culture is alive and well. Denton's own patriotic personality, Frenchy Rheault (center), is shown below with Madison Rising. The band members are, from left to right, Tom DiPietro, Dave Bray, Sam Fishman, and A.J. Larsen. The fair offers military service personnel a discounted admission price every year. (Both, courtesy of NTFR.)

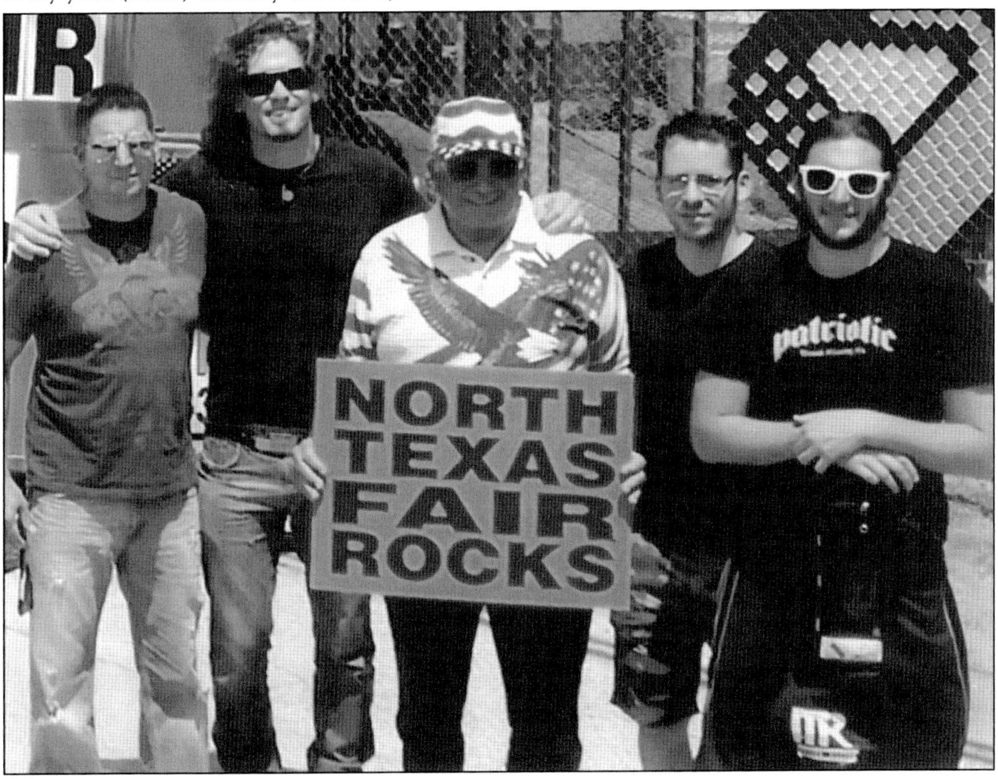

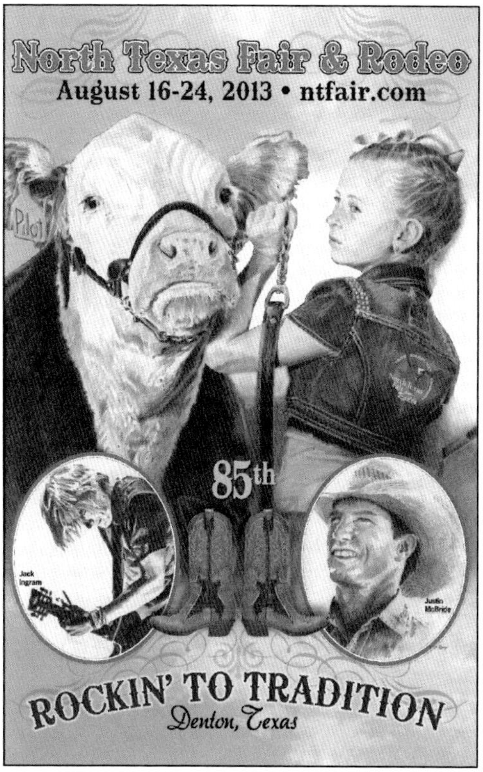

Steers to Studs. This Ron Bonge poster carries on the 2012 theme of "Rockin' to Tradition" by featuring nine-year-old Gracie Clark and her grand champion mini-Hereford steer, Pilot. Texas-born songwriter and performer Jack Ingram and bull riding champion, singer, and rodeo commentator Justin McBride round out the rock-and-roll facet of the 2012 marketing campaign. (Courtesy of NTFR.)

A Cowboy by Another Name. Jesse "Shorty" Wilkins served in the Army National Guard before devoting the last 32 years to working at the fair. Wayne Johnson talked Wilkins into volunteering on the rodeo committee 20 years ago, and he never looked back. In 1995, Johnson and Wilkins went to Hope, Arkansas, to watch rodeo clown Rudy Burns work. They came back with rave reviews, and Burns was hired the next year. (Courtesy of NTFR.)

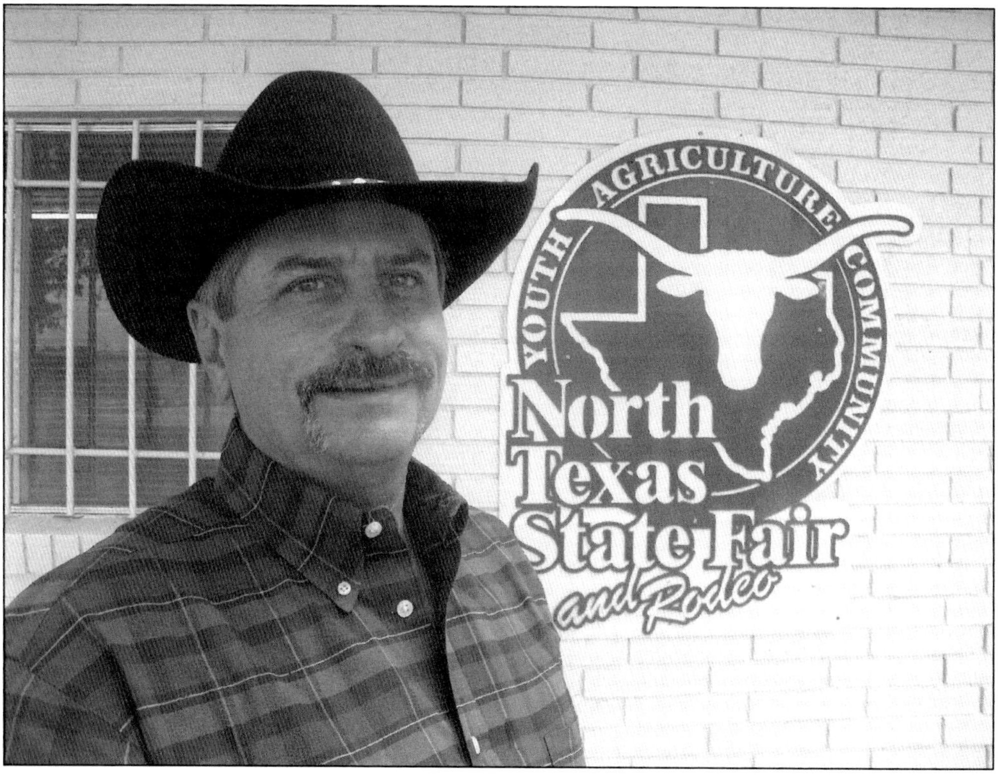

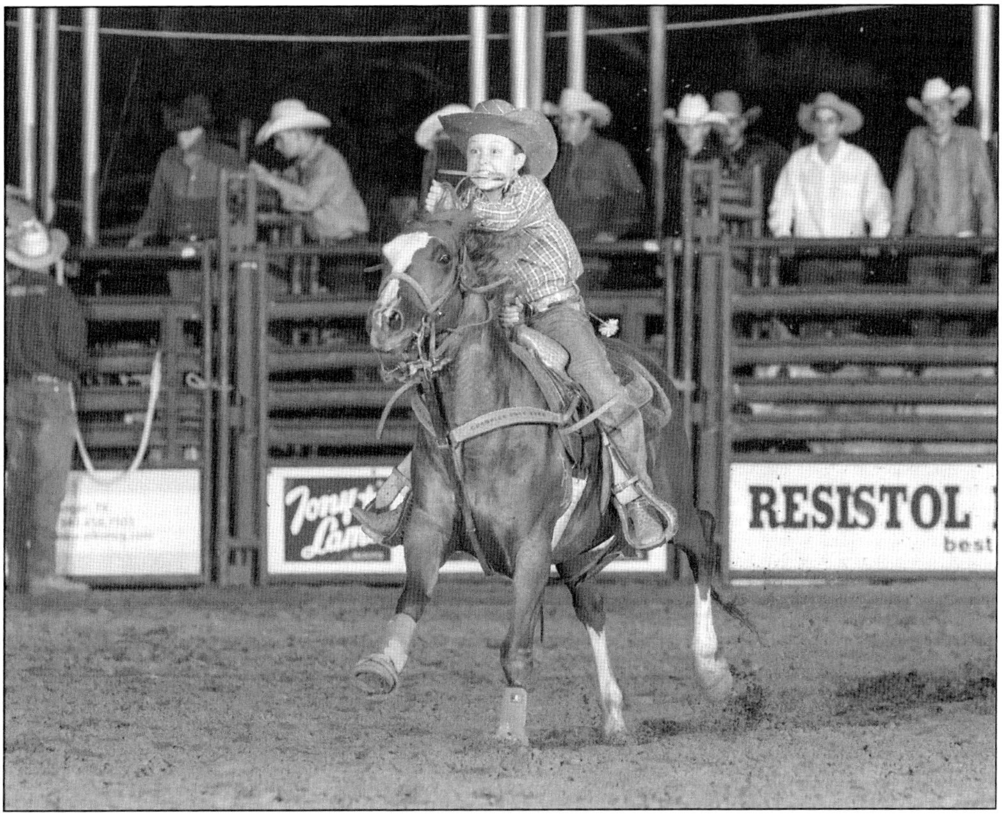

Caught in the "Webb" of Rodeo. A mainstay at the fair, Riley Webb has been mutton bustin' since he was three years old. After learning to rope and mastering rope tricks, he earned his way to the National Finals Rodeo, where he performed for thousands of people. Now, he competes in the 21 and Under Rodeo in goat tying. In this photograph, Webb, clenching his "piggin' string" between his teeth, runs for another win. (Courtesy of NTFR.)

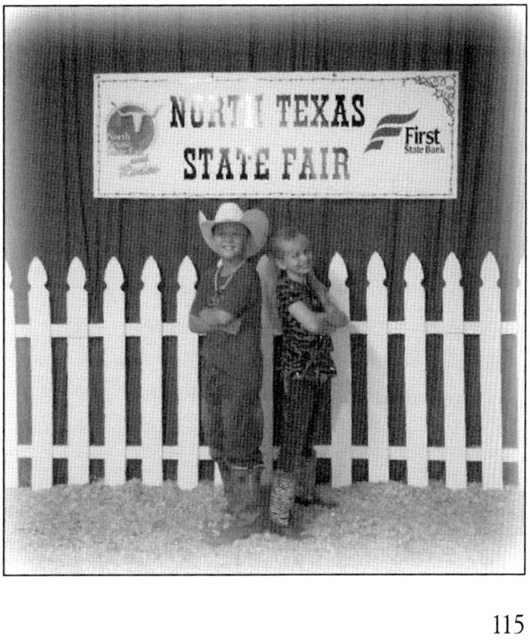

Knowledgeable Young Judges. Dillon Hodge (left) and Carson Esker served as judges for the livestock competition for the Valley View Future Farmers of America at the fair. Livestock judging requires a knowledge of the ideal characteristics of particular animals and teaches skills like effective communication, analytical thinking, decision-making, and the ability to defend choices while working as a team. (Courtesy of NTFR.)

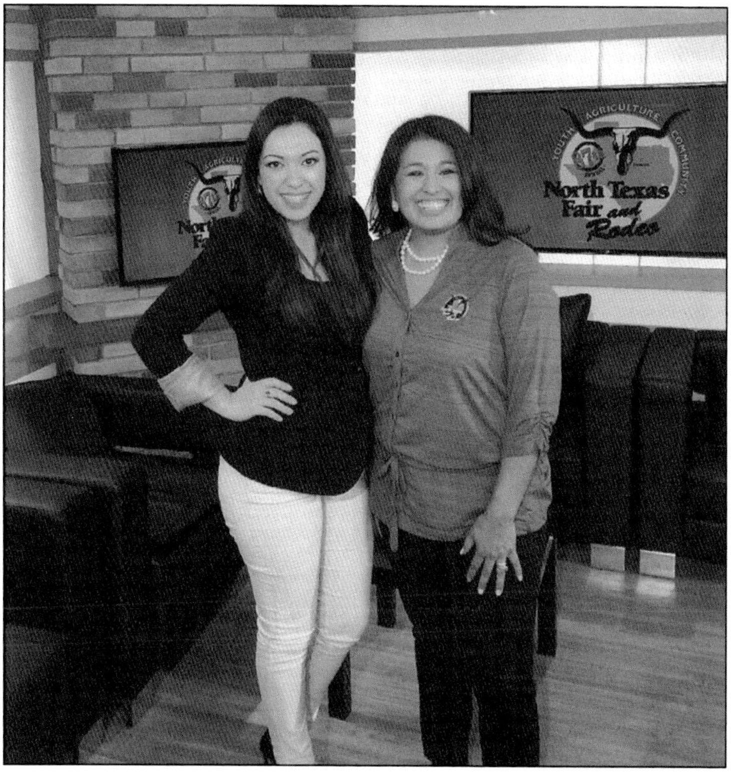

A Partnership with the CVB. Veronica Maldonado (right) assists the North Texas Fair and Rodeo with marketing through a Denton Convention and Visitors Bureau advertising cooperative program. Sonia Salas, television personality from *Despierta Dallas* (*Wake Up Dallas*), interviewed Maldonado on the network program. Maldonado has put her bilingual skills and vivacious personality to good use in promoting the fair. (Courtesy of Veronica Maldonado.)

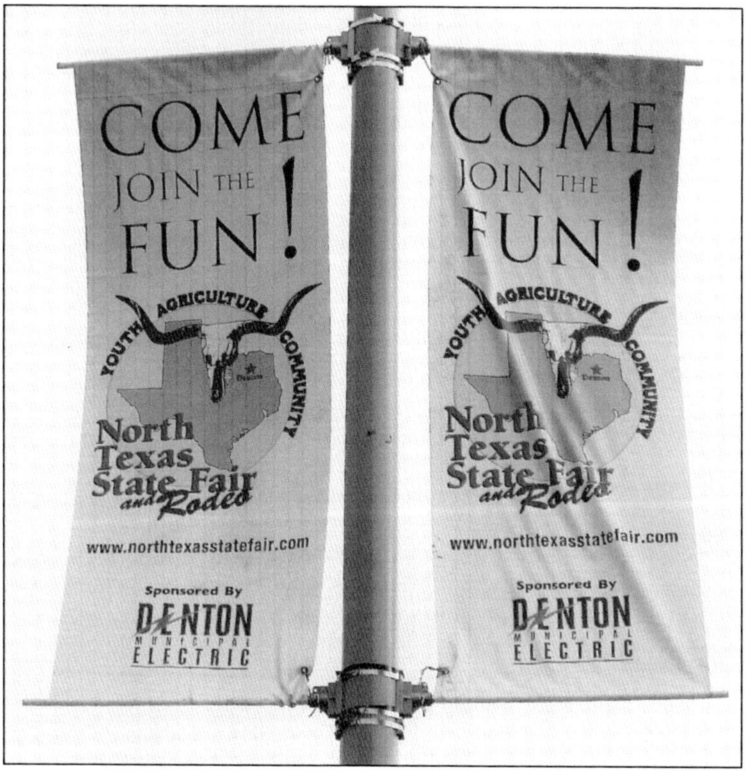

Boulevard Banners. These boulevard banners, produced with sponsorship by Denton Municipal Electric, lead the way down Carroll Boulevard toward the fairgrounds. Whether one is traveling in an automobile along the interstate highway or driving through the heart of town, these banners, along with digital billboards, make it hard for folks to miss that there is an exciting and entertaining event being held in Denton. (Courtesy of NTFR.)

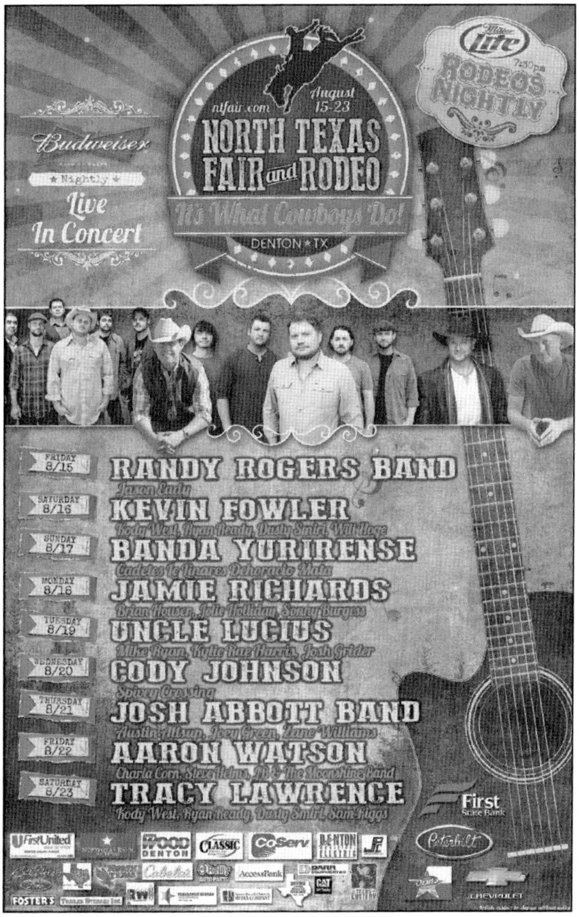

Can-Do Spirit. "It's What Cowboys Do" was the theme for the 2014 fair, reflecting the can-do spirit, courage, authenticity, strength of character, humbleness, chivalry, and heart of the cowboy. The logo features a bucking bronc and cowboy based on World All-Around Rodeo Champion Casey Tibbs. This entertainment poster features the upcoming musical lineup on both Budweiser stages. (Courtesy of NTFR.)

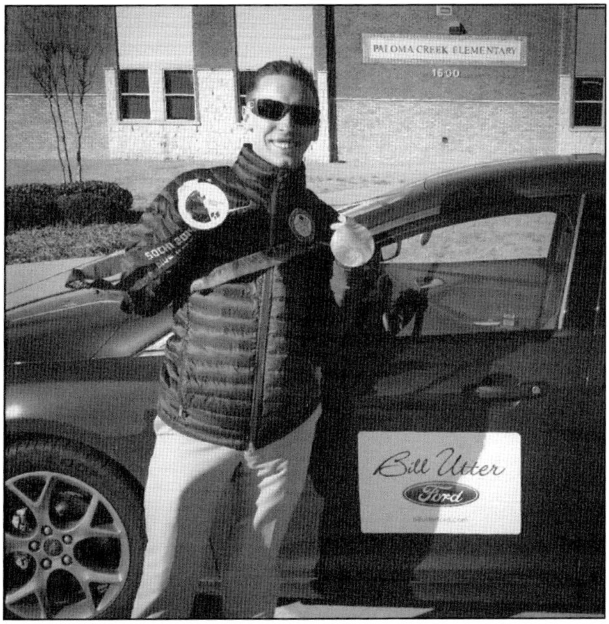

Jordan Malone, Olympian. Jordan Malone, of Denton, was the 2014 fair grand marshal. Malone achieved greatness by winning bronze at the 2010 Winter Olympics in Vancouver and silver at the 2014 Winter Olympics in Sochi in short track speed skating. Accomplished in short track and in-line speed skating, Malone has won numerous world championships while competing all over the world. He currently attends the University of North Texas School of Engineering. (Courtesy of NTFR.)

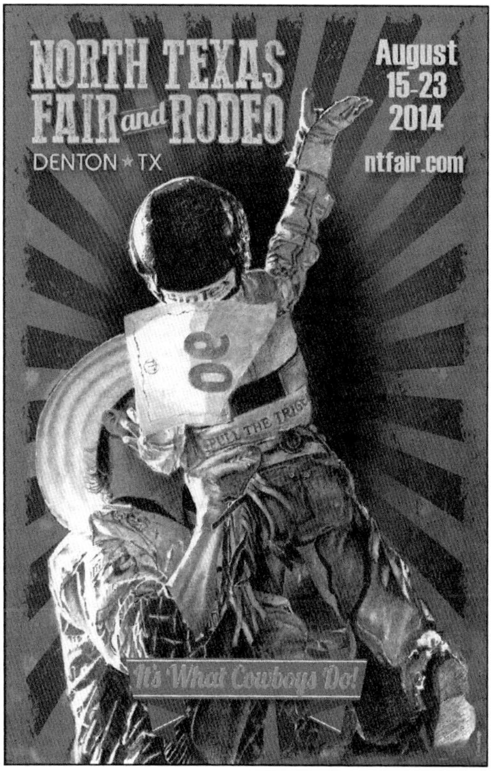

Heroes Have Always Been Cowboys. This heartwarming image of a tough bullfighter lifting up a mutton buster offers an iconic view of what the toughness and tenderness of the rodeo is all about: love of family, love of God, and love of country. This award-winning image was so popular that it has been used by other fairs in their promotional materials. (Courtesy of NTFR.)

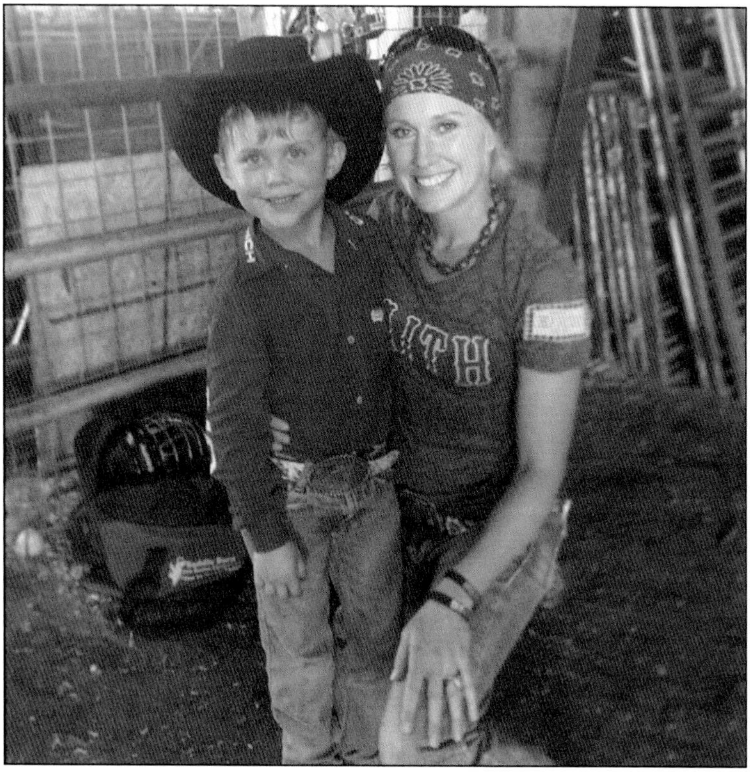

A Chip off the Old Block. Five-year-old Drake Armes, shown here with his mother, Neelley Riley Armes, smiles with excitement as he is about to ride his sheep in the Mutton Bustin' competition. Drake is no stranger to the rodeo. His mother is a professional barrel racer, and his father, Bray Armes, is a professional steer wrestler. (Courtesy of the Armes family.)

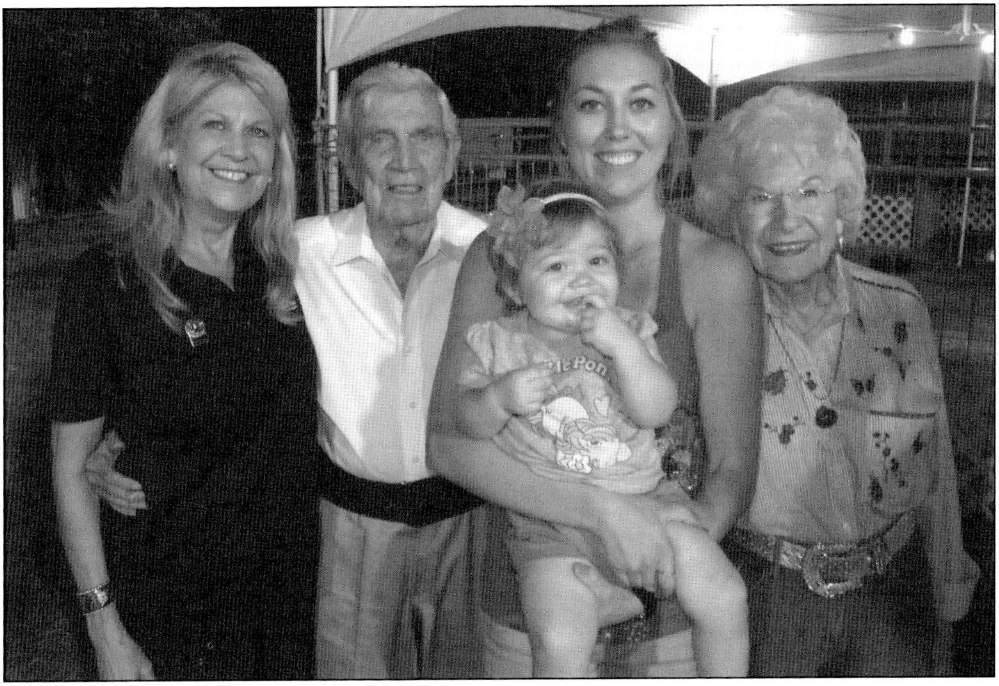

Four Generations of Fairgoers. The fair "bug" catches hold at a very early age and continues throughout a lifetime. Four generations—ranging in age from 2 years old to 88 years old—are shown in this photograph. From left to right are Nanci Kimmey; Nanci's father, the late Bill Monroe; Nanci's daughter Ryan L. Purcell; Nanci's granddaughter Keeli Purcell; and Nanci's mother, Dorcas Monroe. (Courtesy of NTFR.)

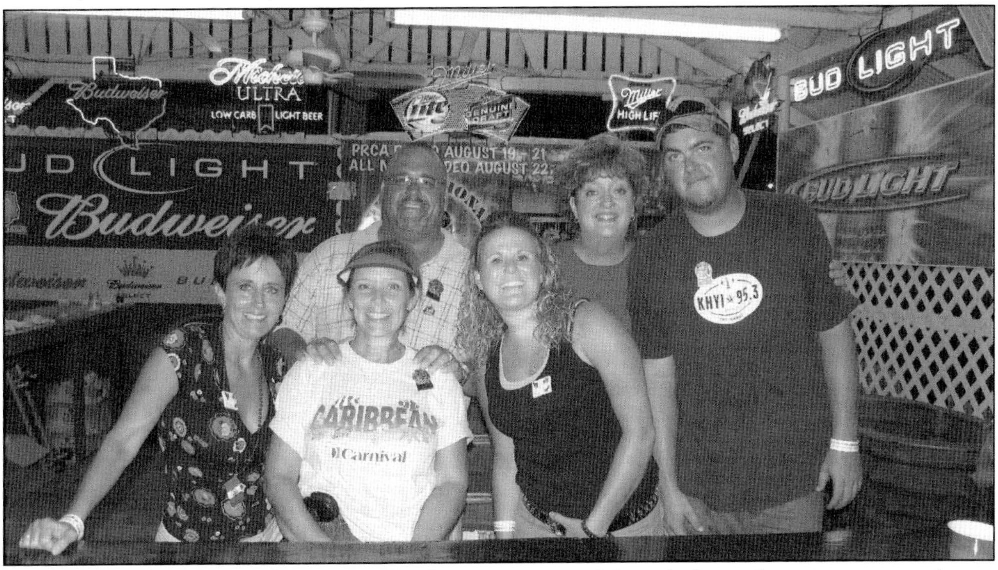

Two Generations of Volunteers. Producing a successful, multifaceted, major event such as a fair requires hundreds of reliable and responsible volunteers who have the same work ethic and enthusiasm as the participants and vendors. From left to right are (first row) Tracy Ford, Mickie Blagg, and Blagg's granddaughter Amanda Kish; (second row) Eddie and Susan Schoenthal and their son Josh. (Courtesy of NTFR.)

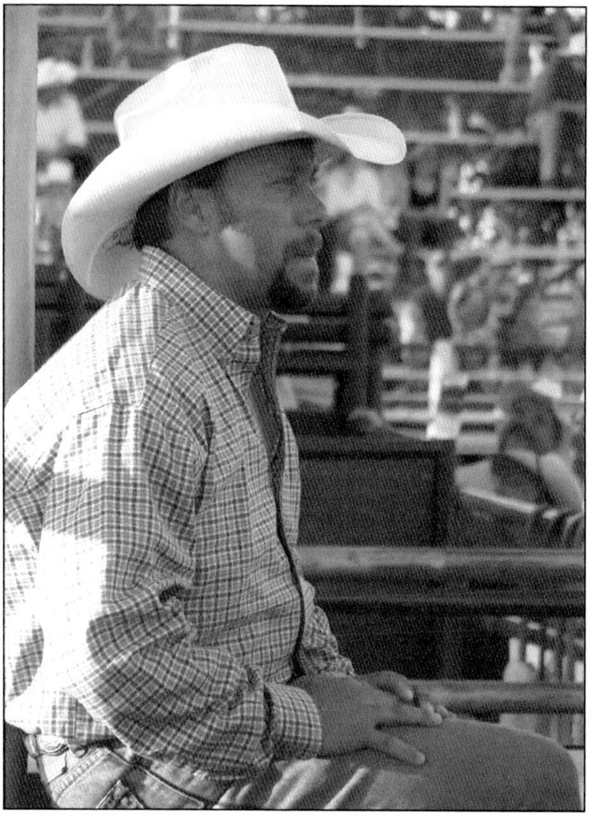

Jon Stratton, Volunteer of the Decade. Jon Stratton can be seen all over the fairgrounds applying his indispensable skills to various projects. This willingness to do anything for the fair earned Stratton the "Volunteer of the Decade" buckle, which was created just for him! Volunteer of the Year award spurs are given out annually, but only Stratton owns this buckle. (Courtesy of NTFR.)

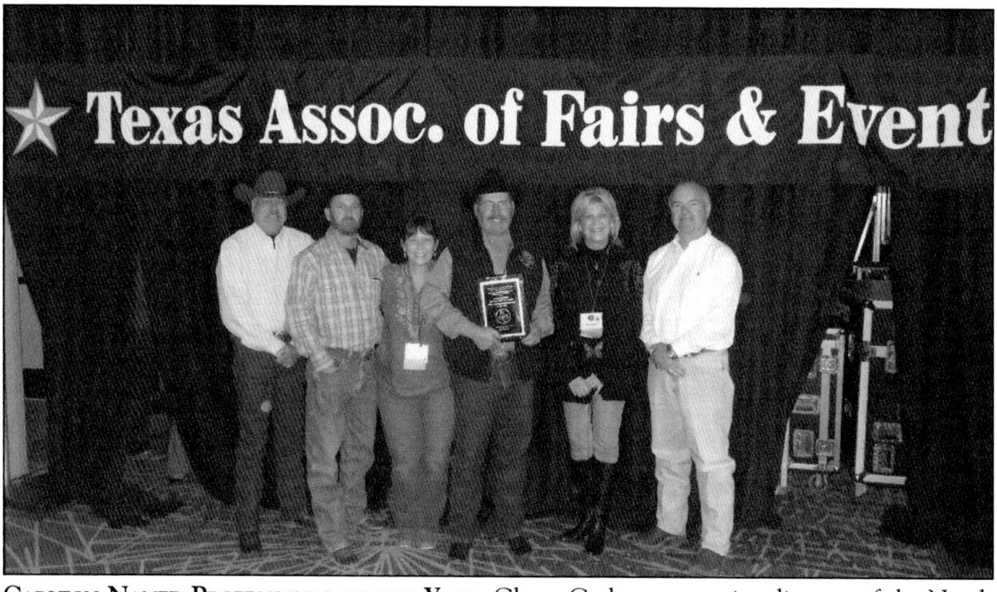

Carlton Named Professional of the Year. Glenn Carlton, executive director of the North Texas Fair and Rodeo, won the coveted Professional of the Year award at the Texas Association of Fairs and Events (TAF&E) annual meeting in 2014. Pictured when he accepted the award are, from left to right, executive board members Jim Fykes, Layne Brewer, and Mickie Blagg; Carlton; Nanci Kimmey; and Carl Anderson, board president. (Courtesy of TAF&E.)

"It's What Cowboys Do!" In 2014 and 2015, fair officials settled on one brand that would carry the fair through the upcoming years. "It's What Cowboys Do!" encompasses all aspects of the fair as a venue for promoting educational, spiritual, and patriotic values, as well as building memories. In honor of his 27 years with the fair, Sammy Andrews—featured on horseback in the center of the poster—was presented with this Ron Bonge print. (Courtesy of NTFR.)

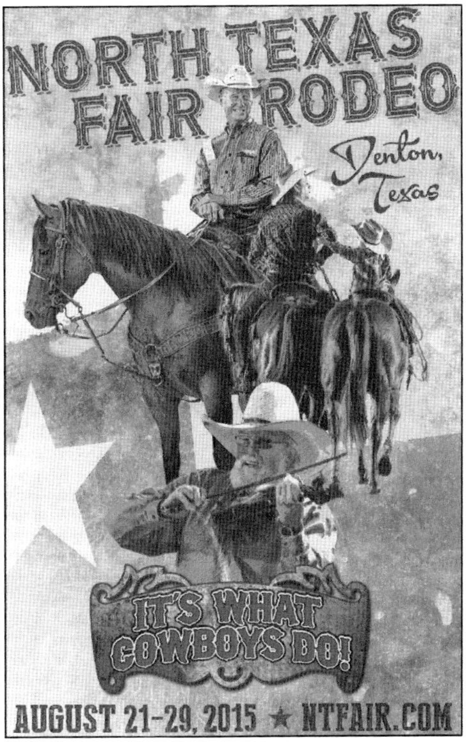

Horse Show. The 2015 North Texas Fair and Rodeo Open Horse Show was held at the Will Rogers Complex in Fort Worth, Texas. Pictured is the grand champion gelding, Hot Roddin in Winter, shown by Dominique Gauthier of Pilot Point, Texas. Horse show superintendent Kim Wendt Collinsworth (left) and Jennifer Hulcher, owner of Equine Salt Water Therapy (center), are presenting Gauthier with her prize. (Courtesy of NTFR.)

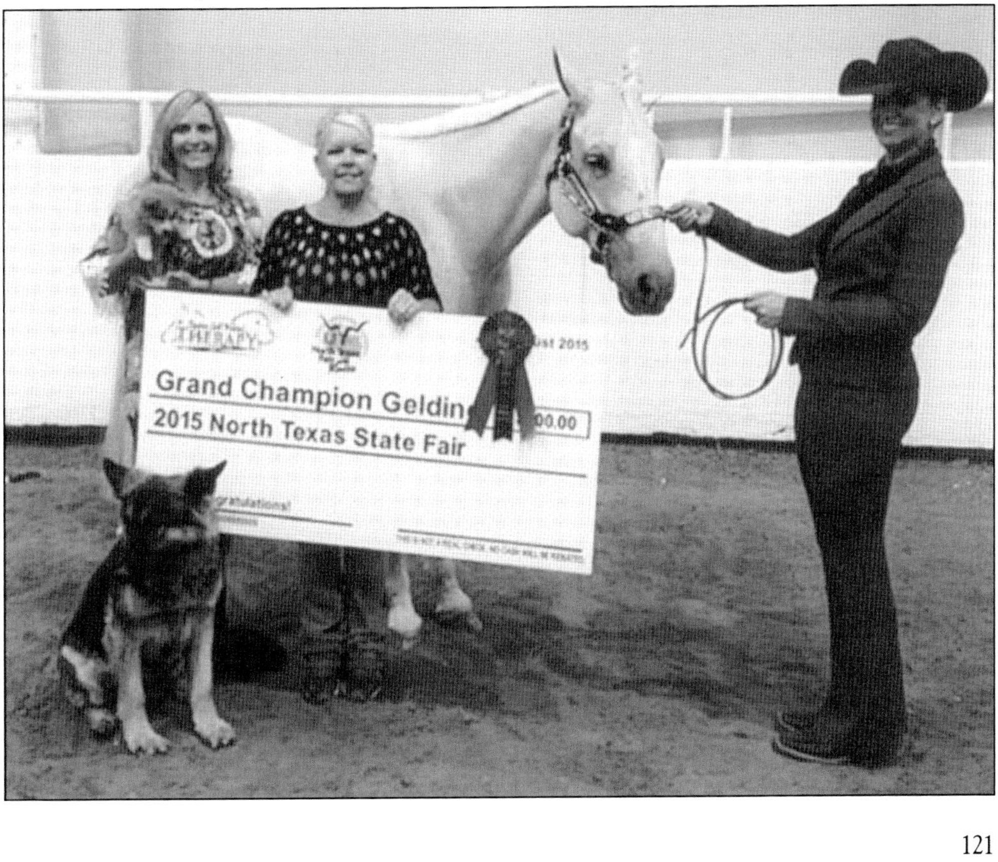

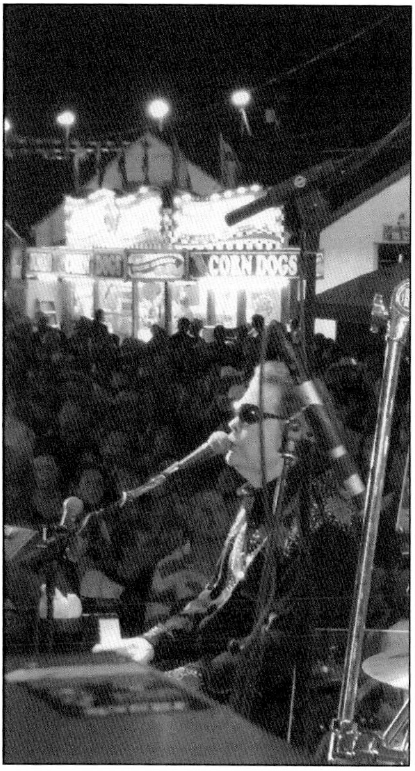

Ronnie Milsap. Ronnie Milsap has not let his blindness deter him. Milsap has earned 40 No. 1 country hits, six Grammy awards, eight Country Music Association (CMA) awards, and four Academy of Country Music (ACM) trophies, including the ACM lifetime honor known as the Pioneer Award. He used pop, rock, and R&B elements to push the borders of traditional country music. Milsap's show, held on August 22, 2015, broke all previous attendance records for fair entertainment. (Courtesy of NTFR.)

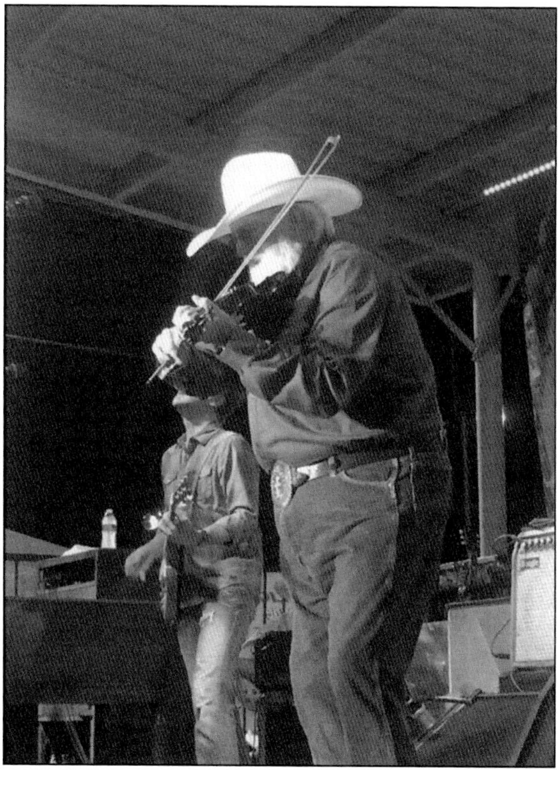

Charlie Daniels Band. Charlie Daniels, a talented and showy fiddler, has become a symbol of conservative country values. Although he is best known for the 1979 song "The Devil Went Down to Georgia," Daniels' career has spanned more than 50 years, and he and his band have sold more than 20 million records. His success has supported cancer research, severely handicapped children, and veterans' organizations. The Charlie Daniels Band's appearance at the fair on August 29, 2015, produced an all-time record-breaking crowd, eclipsing Milsap's record set just seven days earlier. (Courtesy of NTFR.)

Terry Starnes, Rodeo Announcer. Terry Starnes (right) began announcing for the fair on a recommendation from Sammy Andrews. Andrews called Glenn Carlton and said, "I found the guy who is the perfect fit for your rodeo." Shelley Starnes travels with her husband, producing the music that accompanies the fast-paced action. Often described as "the real deal," Terry Starnes personifies the true values and ethics of the cowboy way. (Courtesy of NTFR.)

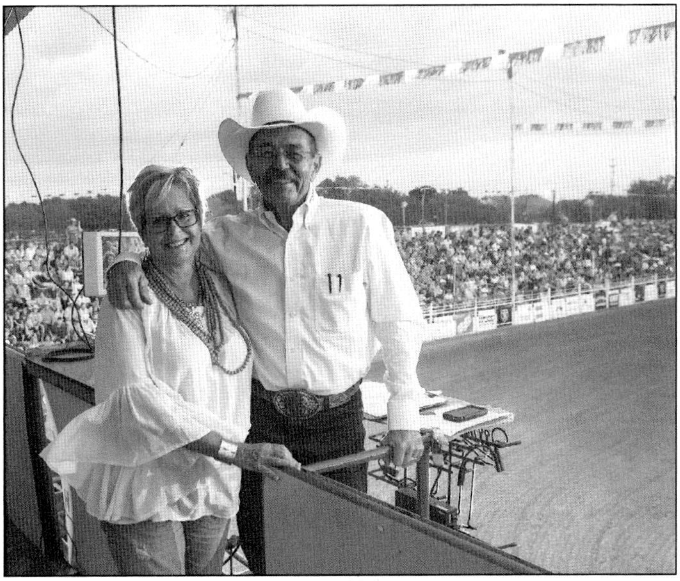

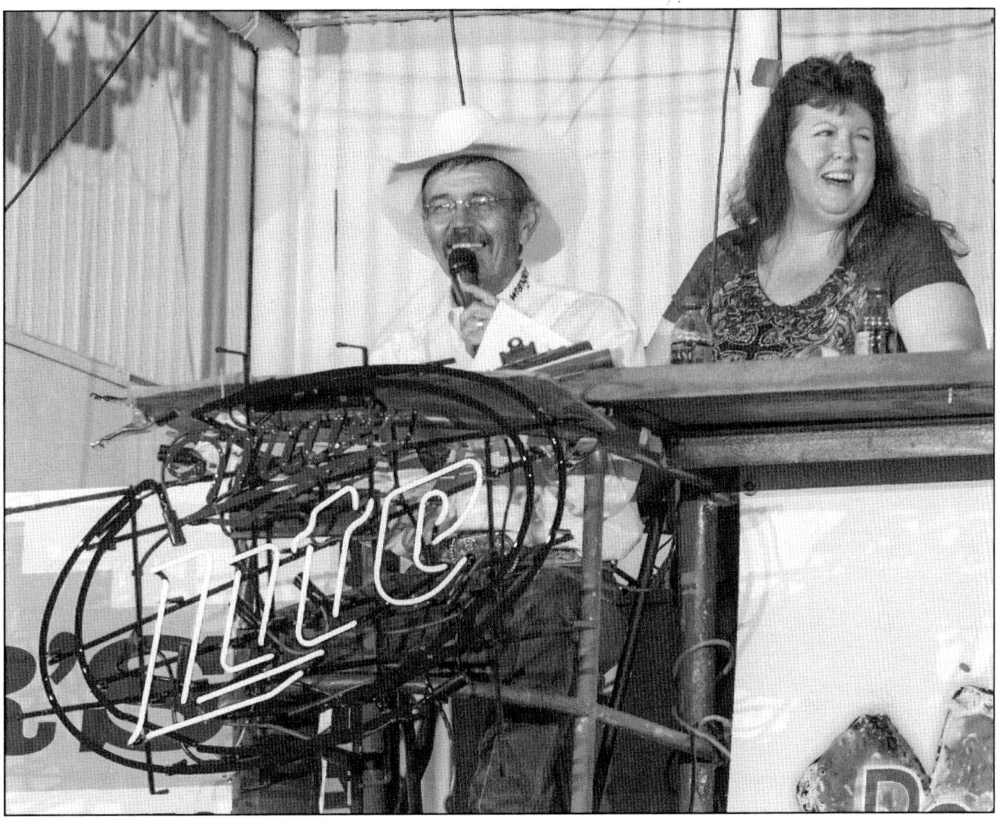

Michele Conn, Rodeo Secretary. Terry Starnes (left) shares a joke with the crowd and Michele Conn, rodeo secretary since 2002. Conn has the daunting tasks of recording contestants' fees; providing contestant information on a day sheet for announcers, judges, stock contractors, and media; timing events; recording results of each event; posting the results; and providing payment information to the Professional Rodeo Cowboys Association (PRCA). (Courtesy of NTFR.)

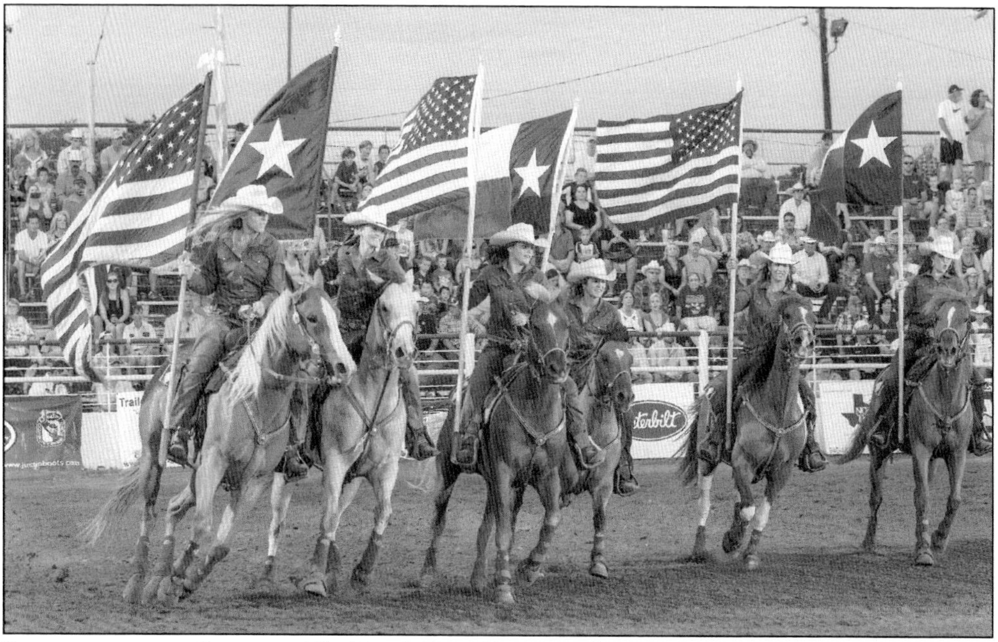

Precision on the Grounds. The North Texas Fairgrounders are an all-female precision-mounted riding team that represents the spirit of the fair. These hardworking ladies are well respected as the heart of the NTFR. They set the tone of the rodeo as they open every performance with a lively routine, as well as presenting the United States, Texas, and sponsor flags. (Courtesy of NTFR.)

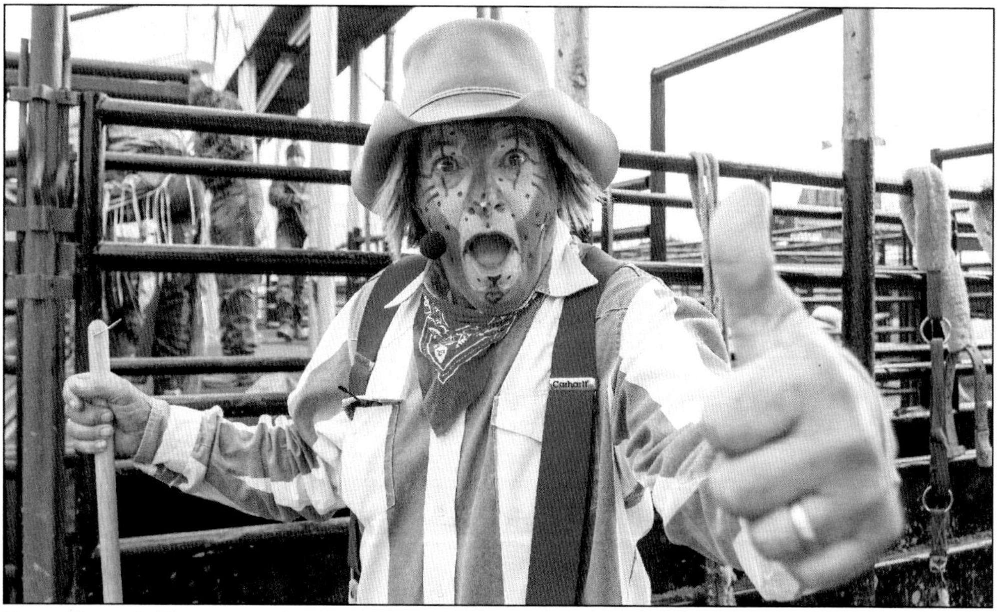

Rudy Burns's Thumbs up Symbolizes the Future Direction of the North Texas State Fair & Rodeo. Since 2005, fair attendance has doubled—to 175,000. Between 2005 and 2015, gross revenues have increased from $750,000 annually to more than $1.75 million. The nightly charity bingo fundraiser boosts this number to more than $3.7 million. The NTSFA has invested $681,000 in capital improvements, acquired the 109-acre site for the future fairgrounds, and continues to contribute about $400,000 into the community each year. (Courtesy of NTFR.)

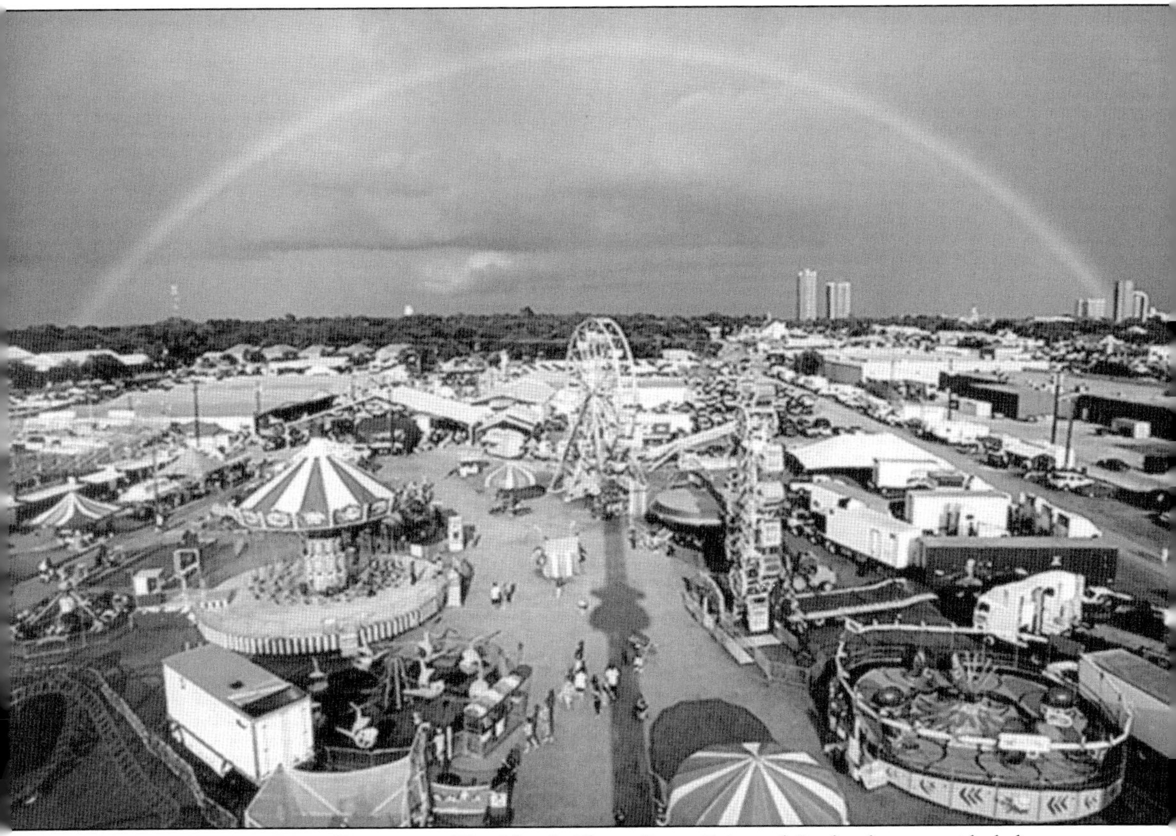

Somewhere over the Rainbow. The North Texas State Fair and Rodeo has provided the area with more than 130 years of cowboy entertainment. The fair began in 1885 as a horse race and fair and was held intermittently until World War II interrupted its run. It has been a continuous staple in Denton since 1949, making it the longest-running annual event in the city. This photograph captures the thrills and spills, the dreams of the cowboys and cowgirls, and the essence of the fair; somewhere "over the rainbow," "dreams that you dare to dream really do come true" from a view at the top of the Ferris wheel, where "skies are blue and troubles melt like lemon drops away above the chimney tops." (Courtesy of NTFR.)

INDEX